THE IRISH BOOK
OF LISTS

In memory of
Jared

THE IRISH BOOK OF LISTS

Julian Ashe

The Collins Press

First published 2007 by
The Collins Press,
West Link Park,
Doughcloyne,
Wilton,
Cork

© Julian Ashe 2007

Julian Ashe has asserted his right to be identified as author of this book

British Library Cataloguing in Publication data.

Ashe, Julian
    The Irish book of lists : a unique compendium
    of things Irish
    1. Ireland - History - Miscellanea
    I. Title
    941.5'002

ISBN-13: 9781905172528

Typesetting: The Collins Press
Font: RotisSansSerif
Printed by CPI in the UK

CONTENTS

FOREWORD

People have being writing lists for centuries and one of the first recorded books of lists goes as far back as 1678 when the Reverend Nathaniel Wanley wrote the *Wonders of the Little World*. The idea of writing lists has not ceased since then. The world today contains huge volumes of information, which we often struggle to absorb. The lists that some of us make on a daily basis are hugely important. They make things easier for us. List making puts things in order; it prioritises, it helps us understand, it helps us function.

Much time and effort has gone into the research for this book and I hope it will provide you with as much enjoyment as I received when I discovered new and intriguing information about Ireland. What I have tried to do is put together the most interesting and informative book of Irish lists imaginable. It is unique as it is the only book of lists about Ireland. This is the ultimate Irish trivia guide and I hope you enjoy it.

I spent a lot of time trying to ensure that all the information within *The Irish Book of Lists* is accurate. But in a book with so many facts, figures and stories, I would be foolish to think that there was not some information that was incorrect or inaccurate. If you identify any errors or omissions, please contact the publisher.

Few books are written without the active support and opinion of others. I'd like to take this opportunity to thank the following people; Alan and Rosemarie Ashe, Jennifer Ashe and Colin Clear, Rachael Ashe and Fintan Palmer, Frank Grennan, John Fairleigh and last but certainly not least, Maria O'Donovan for the support.

HISTORY
AND
GEOGRAPHY

Thirteen Important Years

1. **1791** – Opening of Dublin's Custom House

2. **1848** – The first presentation of the green, white and orange tri-colour at a meeting of the Irish confederation

3. **1879** – Foundation of the Land League

4. **1916** – Easter Rising

5. **1919** – first meeting of Dáil Éireann

6. **1921** – Anglo-Irish treaty signed in London

7. **1922** – Irish Free State established

8. **1946** – Formation of the Irish Naval Service

9. **1949** – Formal declaration of the Republic of Ireland

10. **1971** – Decimal Day. Old coinage changed for decimal currency

11. **1972** – Republic of Ireland votes 5 to 1 to join the European Economic Community (EEC)

12. **1973** – Ireland joins the EEC

13. **1979** – Ireland joins the European Monetary Union, breaking its fixed currency link with Sterling and introducing an exchange rate.

Seventeen Physical Extremities

1. Most northerly point
The most northerly point is Inishtrahull Island, situated in the Atlantic Ocean 7km north of Inishowen Peninsula, county Donegal. It lies at latitude 55.43°N. Of mainland Ireland, the most northerly point is a headland 2km northeast of Malin Head, Inishowen Peninsula, County Donegal. It lies at latitude 55.38°N.

2. Most easterly point
The most easterly point is Big Bow Meel Island, which is a rock situated 900m off the Ards Peninsula, County Down, at longitude 5.42°W. Of mainland Ireland, the most easterly point is Burr Point, Ards Peninsula, County Down, at longitude 5.43°W. It is situated 2km southeast of the village of Ballyhalbert.

3. Most southerly point
The most southerly point is Fastnet Rock, which lies in the Atlantic Ocean 11.3km south of mainland County Cork. It lies at latitude 51.37°N. Of mainland Ireland, the most southerly point is Brow Head, County Cork, which lies 3.8km east of the marginally more northerly Mizen Head. It lies at latitude 51.43°N.

4. Most westerly point
The most westerly point is Tearaght Island, which lies in the Atlantic Ocean 12.5km west of Dingle Peninsula, County Kerry. It lies at longitude 10.70°W. Of mainland Ireland, the most westerly point is Garraun Point, Dingle Peninsula, County Kerry, which is 2.5km northwest of Slea Head. It lies at longitude 10.51°W.

5. Geographical Centre
The geographical centre of Ireland is to be found in eastern County

Roscommon, at a point 3km (2 miles) south of Athlone town.

6. Highest Altitude
The summit of Carrauntoohill, County Kerry, rises to 1,041 metres (3,414 feet) above sea level.

7. Most Populated
The most populated county is County Dublin with more than 1 million people

8. Least Populated
The least populated county is County Leitrim with approximately 30,000 people.

9. Largest County
In terms of area, the largest county is County Cork at 7,457 square kilometres.

10. Longest River
The longest river is the Shannon whose source is Shannon Pot, County Cavan, and which enters the sea between Counties Clare and Limerick after a journey of 386km (240 miles). It is, in fact, the longest river in the British Isles.

11. Largest Lake
The largest lake is lough Neagh, Northern Ireland, which is 396km (153 miles) in area. It forms part of Counties Tyrone, Derry, Antrim, Down and Armagh. It is, in fact, the largest lake in the British Isles.

12. Largest Island
Besides Ireland itself with a surface area of 82,463 square kilometres, the largest offshore island in Irish waters is Achill island, County Mayo, with a surface area of 148 square kilometres.

13. Tallest Waterfall
Ireland's tallest waterfall is Powerscourt Falls, County Wicklow, where the water drops 106m (350 feet).

14. Sunniest Town
The town in Ireland which enjoys the most sunshine is Rosslare, County Wexford, which has over 1,600 hours of sunshine per year (4 hours, 20 minutes per day).

15. Cloudiest Town
The town in Ireland which receives the least sunshine is Omagh, County Tyrone, which has less than 1,200 hours of sunshine per year (3 hours, 20 minutes per day).

16. Wettest Place
The wettest place in Ireland is the Maumturk and Partry Mountains of Counties Mayo and Galway, which receive annually over 2,400mm of rain.

17. Driest Place
The driest place in Ireland is Dublin city which receives less than 800mm of rain per year.

32 Counties and their Meanings

Counties were first introduced to Ireland following the Anglo-Norman invasion in the twelfth century. At that time twelve counties were defined in Leinster and Munster. During the reign of Elizabeth I Counties Longford, Clare, Galway, Sligo, Mayo, Roscommon, Leitrim, Armagh, Monaghan, Tyrone, Derry, Donegal, Fermanagh and Cavan were formed. Improvements in mapping gradually resulted in the counties as we know them today.

1. **County Antrim** – *Aontroim / Countae Aontroma* – meaning 'one holding'

2. **County Armagh** – *Ard Mhacha / Countae Ard Mhacha* – meaning 'Macha's Hill'

3. **County Carlow** – *Ceatharlach / Countae Cheatharlaich* – meaning 'Four Lakes'

4. **County Cavan** – *Cabhán / Countae an Chabháin* – meaning 'The Hollow'

5. **County Clare** – *Clár / Countae an Chláir* - meaning 'Level Land'

6. **County Cork** – *Corcaigh / Countae Chorcaí* – meaning 'Marsh'

7. **County Derry** – *Doire / Countae Dhoire* – meaning 'Oak Wood'

8. **County Donegal** – *Dún na nGall / Countae Dhún na nGall* – meaning 'Fort of the Foreigners'

9. **County Down** – *Dún / Countae Dúin* – meaning 'fort or castle'

10. **County Dublin** – *Áth Cliath / Countae Bhaile Átha Cliath* – meaning 'Town by the Hurdle Ford'

11. **County Fermanagh** – *Fear Manach / Countae Fhear Manach* – meaning 'Men of Manach'

12. **County Galway** – *Gaillimh / Countae na Gaillimhe* – meaning 'Gailleamh's place'

13. **County Kerry** – *Ciarraí / Countae Chiarraí* – meaning 'Sescendants of Ciar'

14. **County Kildare** – *Cill Dara / Countae Chill Dara* – meaning 'Church by the Oak'

15. **County Kilkenny** – *Cill Chainnigh / Countae Chill Chainnigh* – meaning 'Canice's Church'

16. **County Laois** – *Laois / Countae Laoise* – meaning 'Descendants of Laois'

17. **County Leitrim** – *Liatroim / Countae Liatroma* – meaning 'Grey Ridge'

18. **County Limerick** – *Luimneach / Countae Luimnigh* – meaning 'Barren Land'

19. **County Longford** – *Longfort / Countae An Longfoirt* – meaning 'Fortress'

20. **County Louth** – *Lú / Countae Lú* – from the Celtic god Lugh

21. **County Mayo** – *Maigh Eo / Countae Mhaigh Eo* – meaning 'Plain of the Yews'

22. **County Meath** – *Mí / Countaena Mí* – meaning 'Middle'

23. **County Monaghan** – *Muineachán / Countae Mhuineacháin* – meaning 'Place of Thickets'

24. **County Offaly** – *Uibh Fhailí / Countae Uibh Fhailí* – meaning 'Descendants of Fáilghe'

25. **County Roscommon** – *Ros Comáin / Countae Ros Comáin* – meaning 'Coman's Wood'

26. **County Sligo** – *Sligeach / Countae Shligigh* – meaning 'Shelly River'

27. **County Tipperary** – Tiobraid Árainn / Countae Thiobraid Árainn – meaning 'Well of Ara'

28. **County Tyrone** – *Tír Eoghain / Countae Thír Eoghain* – meaning 'Land of Eoghan'

29. **County Waterford** – *Port Láirge / Countae Phort Láirge* – from the Viking '*vadre fjord*': Láirge's harbour

30. **County Westmeath** – *Iarmhí / Countae na hIarmhí* – meaning 'Western Meath'

31. **County Wexford** – *Loch Garman / Countae Loch Garman* – 'Wexford' comes from the Viking '*weiss fjord*' meaning 'white fjord': Garman's Lake

32. **County Wicklow** - *Cill Mhantáin / Countae Chill Mhantáin* – meaning 'Mantan's Church'

FIVE HISTORICAL PROVINCES OF IRELAND

The four provinces (*cúige* – singlar: *cúigí* – plural) are known as:

1. **Connacht** – *Connacht(a)* / *Cúige Chonnacht* – meaning 'Conn's land'

2. **Munster** – *An Mhumhain* / *Cúige Mumhan* – meaning 'Land of Mumha's men'

3. **Leinster** – *Laighin* / *Cúige Laighean* – meaning 'place of broad spears'

4. **Ulster** – *Ulaidh* / *Cúige Uladh* – meaning 'Land of Ulaid's men'

5. The word *cúige* originally meant 'a fifth', as in one-fifth of Ireland, and comes from the fact that Meath, as seat of the High King of Ireland, was once a province in its own right, incorporating modern Counties Meath, Westmeath and parts of surrounding counties. Meath was later absorbed into Leinster.

Ten Place-names and their Meanings

1. Athlone
From the ancient word for a ford (*áth*). The ford of Luan (a man's name).

2. Ballymoney
Bally, from *baile*, a town, and money from *muine*, meaning scrub. The town of the shrubbery.

3. Carrickfergus
From the Irish *carraig*, meaning a rock, and the male name Fergus, i.e., Fergus' rock.

4. Cashel
From the Irish *caiseal*, meaning circular stone fort.

5. Dundrum
From the Irish *dún*, meaning fort or palace, and the Irish *droma*, meaning ridge or hill.

6. Glendalough
From the Irish *gleann*, meaning glen or valley, *dá* meaning two and *loch* meaning lake.

7. Loughrea
From the Irish *loch*, meaning lake, and the Irish *riabhach* meaning grey. Grey lake.

8. Mallow
Mallow was known in the Annals as Mágh-Ealla, the plain of the river Allo, which was how that part of the Blackwater River used to be known.

9. Naas
From the Irish *nás*, a fair or a meeting place.

10. Tramore
From the Irish *trá*, meaning strand or beach, and *mór* the Irish for big. The big beach.

23 Facts about the Book of Kells

1. The **Book of Kells** (less widely known as The Book of Columba) is an ornately illustrated manuscript, produced by Celtic monks around AD 800. It is one of the most lavish illuminated manuscripts to survive the medieval period. Because of its technical brilliance and great beauty, it is considered by many scholars to be one of the most important works in the history of medieval art.

2. It contains the four Gospels of the Bible in Latin, along with prefatory and explanatory matter, all decorated with numerous colourful illustrations and illuminations.

3. Today the **Book of Kells** is on permanent display at the Trinity College Library in Dublin where it is catalogued as MS 58.

4. The **Book of Kells** represents the high point of a group of manuscripts produced from the late sixth-century through the early ninth-century monasteries in Ireland, Scotland and northern England, and in continental monasteries associated with Irish or English foundations.

5. The fully developed style of the ornamentation of the **Book of Kells** places it late in this series, either from the late eighth or early ninth century.

6. The name '**Book of Kells**' is derived from the Abbey of Kells in Kells, County Meath, where it was kept for much of the medieval period.

7. The Abbey of Kells was founded in the early ninth century, at the

time of the Viking invasions, by monks from the monastery at Iona (off the western coast of Scotland).

8. The date and place of the production of the manuscript has been the subject of considerable debate. Traditionally, the book was thought to have been created in the time of St Columba (also known as St Columcille), possibly even the work of his hands. It is generally accepted that this tradition is false based on palaeographic grounds (that is to say, the style of script in which the book is written did not develop until well after the life of Columba).

9. There are at least five competing theories about the place of origin for the manuscript. Firstly, the book may have been written in Iona and brought to Kells, in its current, incomplete state and never finished. Secondly, the book may have been started at Iona and brought to Kells where it was brought to its current, incomplete state. Thirdly, the manuscript may have been produced in the scriptorium at Kells. Fourth, it may have been produced in the north of England, perhaps at Lindisfarne, and brought to Iona and from there to Kells. Finally, it may have been the product of an unknown monastery in Scotland. (The second theory, that it was begun at Iona and finished at Kells, is currently the most widely accepted. Regardless of which theory is true, it is certain that Kells was produced by Columban monks closely associated with the community at Iona.) Wherever it was written, the **Book of Kells** was definitely to be found at Kells by the twelfth century and almost certainly by the early eleventh century.

10. An entry in the Annals of Ulster for 1006 records that 'the great Gospel of Columkille, the chief relic of the Western World, was wickedly stolen during the night from the western sacristy of the great stone church at Cenannas on account of its wrought shrine'. (Cenannas was the medieval Irish name for Kells.) The manuscript

was recovered a few months later – minus its golden and bejewelled cover 'under a sod' (an informal British term for a youth or man). If one assumes, as is generally assumed, that this manuscript is the **Book of Kells**, then the early eleventh century is the earliest date for the location of the manuscript. The force of ripping the manuscript free from its cover may account for the large sheets of paper folded in the middle to make two leaves (or four pages) missing from the beginning and end of the **Book of Kells**.

11. In the twelfth century, land (a document incorporating an institution and specifying its rights; including the articles of incorporation and the certificate of incorporation) pertaining to the Abbey of Kells were copied into some of the book's blank pages, giving the earliest confirmed date for the manuscript's presence at Kells. (The copying of charters into important books such as the **Book of Kells** was a widespread medieval practice.)

12. The twelfth-century writer, Gerald of Wales, in his *Topographia Hibernica*, described, in a famous passage, seeing a great *gospel book* in Kildare which many have since assumed was the **Book of Kells**. The description certainly matches Kells: since Gerald claims to have seen his book in Kildare, he may have seen another, now lost, book equal in quality to the **Book of Kells**, or he may have been confused as to his location when seeing Kells.

13. The Abbey of Kells was dissolved due to the ecclesiastical reforms of the twelfth century. The abbey church was converted to a parish church in which the **Book of Kells** remained.

14. The **Book of Kells** remained in Kells until 1654. In that year Cromwell's cavalry was quartered in the church at Kells and the governor of the town sent the book to Dublin for safekeeping. The book was presented to Trinity College in Dublin in 1661 by Henry

Jones, who was to become bishop of Meath after the Restoration. Except for short periods of time, when the book has been exhibited elsewhere, the book has remained at Trinity College since the seventeenth century. It has been displayed to the public in the Old Library at Trinity since the nineteenth century.

15. In 2000, the volume containing the Gospel of Mark was sent to Canberra, Australia, for an exhibition of illuminated manuscripts. This was only the fourth time the **Book of Kells** had been sent abroad for exhibition. Unfortunately, the volume suffered what has been called 'minor pigment damage' while on its way to Canberra. It is thought that the vibrations from the aeroplane's engines during the long flight may have caused the damage.

16. The **Book of Kells** contains the four gospels of the Christian scriptures written in black, red, purple and yellow ink in an insular medieval script known as a majuscule script, preceded by prefaces, summaries and concordances of gospel passages.

17. Today it consists of 340 (fine parchment prepared from the skin of a young animal, e.g. a calf or lamb) vellum leaves, called folios.

18. It is believed that some 30 folios have been lost.

19. The book, as it exists now, contains preliminary matter, the complete text of the Gospels of Matthew, Mark and Luke, and the Gospel of John through John 17:13. The remainder of John and an unknown amount of the preliminary matter is missing and was perhaps lost when the book was stolen in the early eleventh century.

20. The extant preliminary matter consists of two fragments of lists of Hebrew names contained in the gospels, the *Breves causae* (summaries of the old Latin transcripts of the gospels) and the

Argumenta (collections of legends about the evangelists) of the four gospels, and the Eusebian canon tables.

21. Francoise Henry has identified at least three scribes in this manuscript, whom she has named Hand A, Hand B and Hand C.

22. Surprisingly, given the lavish nature of the work, there was no use of gold or silver leaf in the manuscript. The pigments used for the illustrations had to be imported from all over Europe; the immensely expensive blue lapis lazuli (an azure blue semi-precious stone) came from Afghanistan.

23. The book had a sacramental, rather than educational purpose. A large, lavish Gospel Book, such as the **Book of Kells** would have been left on the high altar of the church, and taken off only for the reading of the Gospel during Mass. However, it is probable that the reader would not actually read the text from the book but rather recite from memory.

SEVENTEEN FACTS ABOUT NEWGRANGE

1. **Newgrange** is one of the finest examples in Western Europe, of a passage-grave or passage-tomb.

It was constructed around 3200 BC, according to the most reliable Carbon 14 dates available from archaeologists. This makes it more than 600 years older than the Giza Pyramids in Egypt, and 1,000 years older than Stonehenge.

2. In 1993, **Newgrange** and its sister sites Knowth and Dowth were designated as a World Heritage Site by United Nations Educational Scientific and Cultural Organisation (UNESCO) due to their outstanding cultural legacy.

3. **Newgrange** was 'rediscovered' in 1699. The landowner at the time, Charles Campbell, needed some stones and had instructed his labourers to carry some from the cairn. It was at this time that the entrance to the tomb was discovered.

4. **Newgrange** sits on the top of an elongated ridge within a large bend in the Boyne River about five miles west of Drogheda. This area is of great importance to Irish history – legend tells us the foundations of Christianity were laid here.

5. The name **'Newgrange'**, or New Grange, is relatively modern. The area around **Newgrange** was once part of the lands owned and farmed by the monks of Mellifont Abbey, and would have been known as a 'grange'.

6. The Tuatha Dé Danann, who ruled Ireland in ancient mythology, were said to have erected **Newgrange** as a burial place for their chief, Dagda Mór, and his three sons. One of his sons, Aonghus, is

often referred to as Aonghus of the Brugh (a passage tomb), and it was traditionally believed that he, in fact, was owner of the Brugh, and that a smaller mound between **Newgrange** and the Boyne was owned by the Dagda.

7. In some texts, **Newgrange** was said to have been the burial place of Lugh Lámhfada (Lugh of the Long Arm) who was the spiritual father of the great mythical hero Cúchulainn.

8. **Newgrange** was said to have been the place where the great mythical hero Cúchulainn was conceived by his mother Dechtine. His spiritual father, Lugh, visited Dechtine in a dream while she stayed at the Brugh.

9. The romantic tale of Aonghus and Caer, who both flew to **Newgrange** and lived there in the form of swans, could be linked to the stars. Interestingly, **Newgrange** is a wintering ground for the Whooper Swan which migrates from Iceland every October and returns in March.
.

10. The mound contains an estimated 200,000 tonnes of material, and it has been estimated that construction would have taken about 30 years using a workforce of about 300.

11. At one time, there was what was described as a 'pyramidal-shaped' stone in the centre of the chamber. Some time after it was recorded by Thomas Molyneaux, it disappeared and has not been seen since.

12. There is some debate as to whether the so-called 'Great Circle' was ever a complete circle at all. There are twelve surviving standing stones around the mound of **Newgrange** out of a possible original 35 to 38 orthostats (standing stones).

13. Studies have produced data which shows that the 'Great Circle' stones in **Newgrange** were astronomical and calendrical in function.

14. Gold objects have been found at **Newgrange**, including two ancient gold torques (torcs), a golden chain and two rings, which were discovered by a labourer digging near the entrance in the 1800s.

15. One find of particular interest to archaeologists is Roman coins, many of which were reported to have been found at **Newgrange**. The first recorded find of a Roman coin was in 1699, and coins were still being found as late as the 1960s when **Newgrange** was being excavated. These included some gold coins and pendants, and some were found to be in mint condition. A total of 21 Roman coins have been found. A number of pendants and beads were found, something which is common to Irish passage graves in general.

16. On the summer/winter Solstice, the light of the rising sun enters the roofbox at **Newgrange** and penetrates the passage, shining onto the floor of the inner chamber. The sunbeam illuminates the chamber of **Newgrange** for just seventeen minutes.

17. It is an astronomical fact that at certain times during its nineteen-year cycle, the moon shares the same declination, and therefore the same rising horizontal direction, as the midwinter sunrise. Therefore, there are times during the moon's cycle when it too would be visible inside **Newgrange**.

Eleven Facts about Blarney

1. The village of **Blarney** lies 5 miles north west of Cork city and its name being derived from the Irish *An blarna* meaning 'the plain'. Near the village, standing almost 90 feet in height, is the solidly built castle of Blarney.

2. Cormac MacCarthy erected the present castle, the third constructed at the site, in 1446. Built on a rock, above several caves, the tower originally had three storeys. On the top storey, just below the battlements on the parapet, is the world famous **Blarney Stone.**

3. Said to give the gift of eloquence to all who kiss it, kissing the stone is for some people a difficult physical feat. In past times, to kiss the Stone people were hung by their heels over the edge of the parapet. Nowadays, you first sit with your back towards the stone and then someone sits upon your legs or firmly holds your feet. Next, leaning far back and downward into the abyss while grasping the iron rails, you lower yourself until your head is even with the stone to be kissed.

4. One local legend claims that an old women, saved from drowning by a king of Munster, rewarded him with a spell that if he would kiss a stone on the castle's top, he would gain a speech that would win all to him.

5. It is known, however, when and how the word **Blarney** entered the English language and the dictionary. During the time of Queen Elizabeth I, Dermot McCarthy, the ruler of the castle, was required to surrender his fortress to the queen as proof of his loyalty. He said he would be delighted to do so, but something always happened at the last moment to prevent his surrender. His excuses became so frequent and indeed so plausible that the official who had been

demanding the castle in the name of the queen became a joke at the Court. Once, when the eloquent excuses of McCarthy were repeated to the Queen, she said 'Odds bodikins, more **Blarney** talk!' The term Blarney has thus come to mean 'the ability to influence and coax with fair words and soft speech without giving offence'.

6. **Blarney** Castle was originally a timber hunting lodge built in the tenth century, which was replaced by a stone castle in 1210. The present-day castle was completed by Dermot McCarthy, King of Munster, in 1446.

7. Following the Battle of the Boyne in 1690, all Irish chiefs were stripped of their powers and the McCarthys were again forced to leave **Blarney** Castle. The castle was sold to Sir James Jefferyes, Governor of Cork, in 1703.

8. The castle is now owned and managed by the Trustees of the **Blarney** Castle Estate.

9. The walls of the castle are 18 feet thick.

10. The stone is believed to be half of the Stone of Scone which was originally owned by Scotland. Scottish kings were crowned over the stone, because it was believed to have special powers.

11. The stone was given to Cormac McCarthy by Robert the Bruce in 1314 in return for his support in a battle.

Eleven Dates in the History of the 'Modern' Irish Republican Army since Independence (up to 2000)

1. **1968** – First civil rights marches in Northern Ireland. These were hugely successful civil rights marches by the Catholic minority in Northern Ireland, brought on by years of political and economic discrimination. They were trying to put pressure on the government in Northern Ireland. They were attempting to achieve basic freedom, individual rights, freedom of speech and assembly.

2. **1969** – Riots throughout Northern Ireland, particularly Derry and Belfast, between Catholics, Protestants and the RUC (Royal Ulster Constabulary). The situation got so bad that the British army was sent into Belfast. Much of west and north Belfast resembled a war zone. Houses were torched and there were forced evictions. The Irish Republican Army (IRA) split between those who favoured military action and those who favoured political means.

3. **1972** – Bloody Sunday in Derry involved a Catholic civil rights march that was to be policed by Britain's First Batallion of the Parachute regiment. They lost control and shot dead thirteen civilians and injured seventeen others. The events outraged nationalist Ireland.

4. **1976** – Prison protests by IRA inmates in the new H-Block prison begin. Nationalist prisoners were frustrated at not being treated as political prisoners or prisoners of war. They initially refused to wear prison uniforms, wearing their blankets instead. They then refused to slop out their cells, instead smearing their excrement on their cell walls. This became known as the dirty protest.

5. **1980** – The first hunger strike begins. The prisoners finally decided to embark on hunger strikes in a bid to win recognition that their imprisonment was politically motivated.

6. **1981** – Hunger strikes end with ten deaths.

7. **1993** – The Irish Taoiseach, Albert Reynolds, negotiates the Downing Street Declaration with the British government. This was an agreement to resolve the Northern Ireland situation by diplomatic and political means.

8. **1994** – The IRA council votes five to one with one abstention for a four-month ceasefire.

9. **1995** – First British troop withdrawals from Northern Ireland.

10. **1998** – The Good Friday Agreement was reached between the political parties involved.

11. **2000** – The IRA army council agrees in principle to put weapons 'beyond use'.

Seven Irish Sea Loughs

1. Belfast Lough

Belfast Lough (Irish: *Loch Laoigh*) is a large intertidal sea lough situated at the mouth of the River Lagan on the east coast of Northern Ireland. The inner part of the lough comprises a series of mudflats and lagoons. The outer lough is restricted to mainly rocky shores with some small sandy bays. Belfast Lough is the gateway for the city of Belfast to the Irish Sea.

Belfast Lough is a wide expanse of water, virtually free of strong tides, lying between Orlock Point and Blackhead, extending westwards to the port of Belfast. It's ideal as a stopping off point on Irish Sea passages.

Coastal towns include Holywood, Bangor, Carrickfergus. Holywood and Bangor are situated on the southern side of the lough in County Down whilst Carrickfergus is on the northern side in County Antrim. Popular for sailing the lough has two marinas one at Bangor, the other located in Carrickfergus.

The lough hosts two Royal Yacht Clubs.: one at Cultra just outside Holywood, 'The Royal North of Ireland Yacht Club', and the 'Royal Ulster' based in Bangor.

2. Carlingford Lough

Carlingford Lough (Irish: *Loch Cairlinn*) or 'Fjord of Carlinn' as it is believed it was called following the Vikings invasion of this area in the eight-century, mainly as it resembled their homeland and now remains one of the most picturesque inlets on the east coast. Around 8 miles long, it is bordered by the magical Cooley Mountains to the south and the famous Mourne Mountains to the north, which do sweep down to the sea. The entrance is guarded by the Block House, on which island also sits the Haulbowline Light House and on the north shore Green Castle. At the other end of the lough is the first ship canal in Europe, again guarded by round towers and the Narrow Water Keep and Castle.

As you move up the lough you pass Greenore Point and Harbour, further along the southern shore lies Carlingford, a town steeped in history, which is watched over by St John's Castle. Across the lough lies Killowen and the town of Rostrever.

3. Lough Foyle
Lough Foyle (Irish: *Loch Feabhail*) is the name given to the estuary of the River Foyle. It starts where the Foyle leaves Derry. It separates the Inishowen peninsula from Northern Ireland.

In the summer, a ferry service operates between County Donegal and County Derry over Lough Foyle.

There is a saying that when one is on a boat on Lough Foyle, one is at the only place in the world where north is south, and south is north.

4. Larne Lough
Larne Lough (Irish: *Inbhear Latharna*) is a lough or inlet in County Antrim, near the town of Larne, along Ireland's northeast coast. The lough is situated between Island Magee (a peninsula) and the mainland.

Larne Lough is designated as an Area of Special Scientific Interest, Special Protection Area, and Ramsar Site in order to protect the wetland environment, particularly due to the presence of certain bird species and shellfish.

5. Lough Swilly
Lough Swilly (Irish: *Loch Súili*) in Ireland is a fjord-like body of water lying between the eastern side of the Inishowen Peninsula in County Donegal and the rest of northern Donegal.

At the northern extremeties of the lough are Fanad Head and Dunaff Head. Towns situated on the lough include Buncrana on Inishowen and Rathmullan on the western side. At the southern end of the lough lies Letterkenny.

The Lough was used as an anchorage by the Royal Navy during the First World War. The British also built a number of forts to protect the Lough and the remains of these can be seen at Lenan Head, Dunree (now a museum) and at Buncrana. The lough was also one of the Treaty Ports specified in the Anglo-Irish Treaty.

6. Strangford Lough

Strangford Lough (Irish: *Loch Cuan*) is a lough in County Down, separated from the Irish Sea by the Ards peninsula. It is a popular tourist attraction noted for its fishing and the picturesque villages and townships which border its waters. The most notable of these is Portaferry, a small village of around 3,000 people with a reputation for hospitality and a lively atmosphere in the pubs and restaurants. Some consider the region to be home to some of the most beautiful scenery in Ireland.

This stunning island-studded sea lough is the largest inlet in the British Isles covering 150 square kilometres. Almost totally landlocked, the lough is approached from the Irish Sea through the 8km-long fast running tidal Narrows, which open out into more gentle waters The lough is a conservation area and its abundant wildlife is recognised internationally for its importance.

7. Galway Lough (also known as Galway Bay)

Galway Lough (Irish: *Loch Lurgain* or *Cuan na Gaillimhe*) is a large bay/sea lough on the west coast of Ireland, between County Galway in the province of Connacht to the north and the district of the Burren in County Clare in the province of Munster to the south. Galway is located on the north-east side of the bay. It is about 30 miles long and from 7 miles to 20 miles in breadth. The Aran Islands are to the west across the entrance and there are numerous small islands within the bay. Galway Bay is famous for its unique traditional sailing craft, the Galway Hooker.

Nine Irish Inland Loughs

1. Lough Allen
Lough Allen (Irish: *Loch Aillionn*) is situated on the River Shannon, in the north-central part of Ireland, near the border. Most of the lake is in County Leitrim, with a smaller portion in County Roscommon. The lake lies to the south of the river's source, near the Iron Mountains.

2. Lough Conn
Lough Conn (Irish: *Loch Conn*) is in County Mayo in the province of Connaught and covers about 14,000 acres (57km). With its immediate neighbour to the south, Lough Cullin, it is connected to the sea by the River Moy. Lough Conn is noted for its trout and salmon fishing.

3. Lough Corrib
Lough Corrib (Irish: *Loch Coirib*) is a lake in the west of Ireland. The River Corrib/Galway river connects the lake to the sea at Galway. It is the largest loch in the Republic of Ireland and second largest in Ireland after Lough Neagh; it covers some 200 sq km. Loch Coirib is a corruption of Loch nOirbsean which, according to placename lore, is named after the Danann navigator Orbsen Mac Alloid (commonly called Manannán Mac Lir, 'The Son of the Sea', for whom the Isle of Man is named). In Irish the loch is also called *An Choirib* ('the Corrib').

4. & 5. Lough Derg
There are two loughs (lakes) in Ireland of the name Lough Derg (Irish: *Loch Deirgeirt*) : Lough Derg in Munster is the second largest lake in Ireland and borders Counties Tipperary, Galway, County Clare and others. Lough Derg is a small lake in County Donegal and is famous for Christian pilgrimages.

6. Lough Erne

Lough Erne (Irish: *Loch Éirne*) refers to two lakes in Ireland, situated along the River Erne. This waterway is found in the northwest, with the lakes located in Counties Fermanagh and Cavan. The river flows in a north-westerly direction, beginning by flowing north, and then curving west into the Atlantic. The southernmost lake is further up the river and so is named Upper Lough Erne. The northern lake is Lower Lough Erne.

Lough Erne is a particularly scenic waterway in Ireland, it is renowned for its beautiful setting. The area is also popular for fishing. The town of Enniskillen in Northern Ireland is situated between the lakes.

7. Lough Gur

Lough Gur (Irish: *Loch Gur*) is in County Limerick, near the town of Bruff. The lake forms a horseshoe shape at the base of Knockadoon Hill. It is one of Ireland's most important archaeological sites. Man has been present in Lough Gur since about 3,000 BC and there are numerous megalithic remains here.

The largest stone circle in Ireland at Grange is located near the lake. The remains of at least three *crannógs* are present, and remains of Stone Age houses have been unearthed (the house outlines are known as 'The Spectacles'). A number of ring forts are found in the area, with one (a hillfort) sitting atop the hill that overlooks the lake. Some are Irish national monuments.

8. Lough Neagh

Lough Neagh (Irish: *Loch nEathach*) in Northern Ireland is the largest lough, or body of fresh water by surface area, in the British Isles, with an area of 388 square kilometres. Approximately 30km (20 miles) long and 15km (9 miles) wide, the lake is situated some 30km to the west of Belfast. The lough is very shallow round the margins and has an average depth in the main body of the lake of about 9m

(30 feet); although at its deepest the lough is about 25m (80 feet) deep.

Five of the six counties of Northern Ireland have shores on the Lough: Antrim, Armagh, Londonderry, Down and Tyrone.

9. Lough Ree

Lough Ree (Irish: *Loch Rí*) is a lake in the midlands of Ireland, the second of the three major lakes on the River Shannon. Lough Ree is the second largest lake on the Shannon after Lough Derg. The lake serves as a border between Counties Longford and Westmeath (both in the province of Leinster) on the eastern side and County Roscommon in the province of Connacht on the eastern side. The lake is popular for fishing and boating. The town of Athlone is situated at the southern end of the lake, and has a harbour for boats going out on the lake. The small town of Lanesboro is at the northern end of the lake.

The island of Inchcleraun (Irish: *Inis Cloithreann*) in the northern part of the lake is the site of a monastery founded in the early Christian era and contains the remains of several ancient churches. In Irish legend, Queen Maeve was killed on this island.

Fourteen Islands

1. Ireland's Eye

Ireland's Eye is a small island off the coast of County Dublin, situated directly north of Howth Harbour. The island is easily reached by regular tourist boats.

The ruins of a Martello Tower and an eighth-century church are the only signs of previous habitation. In Celtic times the island was called Eria's Island. Eria was a woman's name and this became confused with Erin, the Irish name for Ireland. The Vikings substituted the word Island with Ey, their Norse equivalent, and so it became known as Erin's Ey and ultimately Ireland's Eye. Its most spectacular feature is the huge freestanding rock called the Stack. It has a surface area of 90 hectares (53 acres)

2. Bull Island or North Bull Island

Bull Island or North Bull Island is an island located in Dublin Bay, about 5km long and 800m wide, lying roughly parallel to the shore. It is less than two centuries old, having been formed by sand building up after the North Bull Wall was built in the nineteenth century to shelter Dublin Port. The island is connected to the mainland by a wooden road bridge at the southern (city) end, and by a causeway approximately halfway along.

Bird life on the island has been protected by legislation since the 1930s, and it was designated a national nature reserve in 1988. As well as two golf courses (the Royal Dublin and St Anne's), the island also has an interpretive centre. Dollymount Strand on the island is a popular walking and recreational area for Dubliners.

3. Dalkey Island

Dalkey Island is situated about 10 miles south of Dublin just south of Dun Laoghaire harbour. The island is now uninhabited but there are the remains of houses, a church and a Martello Tower. Located less than 300m offshore, the island comprises of 9 hectares (22 acres).

Dalkey Island, only five minutes by local boat from Coliemore Harbour, is an important site of ancient and historic remains. Artefacts from the Island, now housed in the National Museum in Dublin, are evidence that the original occupants were from the Mesolithic or Middle Stone Age. Settlers continued to use the site through the Iron Age and Early Christian period.

There is evidence that it was inhabited in the fourth millennium BC (6000 years ago) and was also used as a Viking base. There are the ruins of another church, dating from the seventh century, named after St Begnet. This was altered on the east side when builders used it as living quarters while building the nearby Martello Tower and gun battery in 1804. An older wooden church was probably here before the present stone one was built.

A promontory fort was located at the northern end of the island, its presence is still visible today in the form of a ditch. A herd of goats, originally put there in the early 1800s, remains there today but they are replacements of the original goats which were removed.

The ruined stone church was built in the ninth/tenth century and was probably abandoned when the Vikings used the island as a base to form part of the busiest port in the country at that time. In the early nineteenth century, the British Admiralty erected the Martello Tower, one of eight dotted along the Dun Laoghaire coastline as an early warning defensive device against the one-time threat of invasion during the Napoleonic era. Today, a haven of peace and tranquility, the only surviving inhabitants are goats and rabbits.

4. Saltee Islands

The Saltee Islands are a pair of small islands lying 5km off the southern coast of County Wexford known as *Oileán an tSalainn* in Irish. The two islands are Great Saltee (89 hectares) and Little Saltee (40 hectares). They have been uninhabited since the early twentieth century and privately owned by the Neale family since 1943. Boat trips are available, leaving from the village of Kilmore Quay on the mainland.

5. Skellig Islands
The Skellig Islands are two small, uninhabited steep and rocky islands lying about 16km west of Bolus Head on the Ivereagh Peninsula in County Kerry known as *Na Scealga* in Irish.

The smaller island is Little Skellig, the larger Great Skellig or Skellig Michael. Both are known for their birdlife, and both are statutory nature reserves. Great Skellig is known for its ruined monastery which has been a UNESCO world heritage site since 1996.

6. Valentia Island
Valentia Island, Europe's westernmost inhabited location, lies in the southwest of County Kerry in the Republic of Ireland. It is linked to the mainland by a bridge at Portmagee, as well as by a ferry which sails from Reenard Point to Knightstown, the island's main settlement. The permanent population of the island is 650, and the island is approximately 11km long by 3km wide.

Valentia was the eastern terminal of the first transatlantic telegraph cable, laid in 1857 and operated until 1966.

7. Blasket Islands
The Blasket Islands are a group of islands off the west coast of Ireland, forming part of County Kerry. They were inhabited until 1953 by an Irish-speaking population. Many of the descendants currently live in Springfield, Massachusetts, and some former residents still live on the Dingle Peninsula, within sight of their former home.

The islanders were the subject of much anthropological and linguistic study at the end of the nineteenth and beginning of the twentieth centuries and, thanks partly to outside encouragement, a number of books were written by islanders that record much of the islands' traditions and way of life. They are known as Na Blascaodaí in Irish. The largest Blasket is 6.4km long and 1.6km wide.

8. Aran Islands

The Aran Islands (or Árainn in Irish) are a group of three islands located at the mouth of Galway Bay, on the west coast of Ireland.

The largest island is Inishmore, the second largest is Inishmaan and the smallest and most eastern is Inisheer. Irish is the spoken language on all three islands, and is the language used for the names of the islands and many of the islands' villages and place-names. Together the islands comprise 18 square miles or 47 square kilometres.

9. Inishbofin

Inishbofin (Irish: *Inis Bo Finne*, meaning White Cow Island) is an island about 8km off the coast of Connemara, County Galway, Ireland. It's about 5.5km long and 3km wide, and has around 200 inhabitants. It is popular with artists. Inishbofin can be reached by ferry from the pier in Cleggan.

10. Clare Island

Clare Island is a mountainous island guarding the entrance to Clew Bay in County Mayo. It is famous as the home of the pirate queen, Grace O'Malley (Granuaile). Between 120 and 130 people live there today. It has a surface area of 4,000 acres or 16 square kilometres, and is 8km long by 4.8km wide

Clare Island was, throughout the Middle Ages, part of the lands of the O'Malley family. The ruins of an O'Malley tower house, known as Grace O' Malley's castle because of its most famous resident, are close to the pier at the eastern edge of the island. The small Cistercian Abbey near the south coast of the island was founded by the O'Malleys and contains the O'Malley tomb, the possible burial site of Grace O'Malley. The Abbey is known for its rare medieval ceiling paintings.

11. Clew Bay

Clew Bay, in County Mayo, is a natural ocean bay. It is known as *Cuan Mó* in Irish. It contains Ireland's best example of sunken drumlins. According to tradition, there is an island in the bay for every day of the year. The bay is overlooked by Croagh Patrick, Ireland's holy mountain, and the mountains of north Mayo. Clare Island guards the entrance of the bay. The bay was the focus of the O'Malley family possessions in the Middle Ages, and is associated with Grace O'Malley. Clew Bay, along with Clare Island, was another territory associated with Grace O'Malley. Her family charged people to fish this area.

12. Achill Island

Achill Island in County Mayo is the largest island off Ireland, and is situated off the west coast. It has a population of 2,700 and is approximately 57 square miles. It is known as *Oileán Acla* in Irish, and is 15 miles long by 4 miles wide or 20km long by 9km wide. Achill is attached to the mainland at Achill Sound by Michael Davitt Bridge. Early settlements are believed to have been established on Achill around 3000 BC. A paddle dating from this period was found at the *crannóg* near Dookinella. The island is made up of 87 per cent peat bog.

13. Tory Island

Tory Island (Irish: *Toraigh*) is an island 12km off the north-west coast of County Donegal. It is approximately 5km (3 miles) long and 1km (0.75 miles) wide. It has a population of 170, divided among four towns – East Town, West Town, Middletown and Newtown. It is part of the Donegal gaeltacht and Irish is widely spoken on the island.

Since the 1950s, the island has been home to a small community of artists, and has its own art gallery. One of the artists is Patsy Dan Rodgers, who holds the position of King of Tory. This king has no formal power but is chosen by consensus by the islanders to represent the community.

14. Rathlin Island
Rathlin Island (Irish: *Reachlainn*) is an island off the coast of County Antrim in Northern Ireland, and is the northernmost point of the region. Ten km from the mainland, Rathlin is the only inhabited offshore island in Northern Ireland, and is the most northerly inhabited island off Ireland. The L-shaped island is 7km from east to west, and 4km from north to south. Rathlin is located only 25km from the Mull of Kintyre, the southern tip of Scotland's Kintyre peninsula. It is part of the Moyle District Council area.

The island formerly boasted a population of around 1,000, but its current winter population is around 75. This is swelled by visitors in the summer, who mostly come to view the cliffs and their huge seabird populations. Rathlin Island's dialect of Irish is now extinct but was in many respects closer to Scottish Gaelic in some of its features than Irish, particularly the southern dialects.

Nine Mountain Ranges

1. Wicklow Mountains

The Wicklow Mountains are a range of mountains in the south-east of Ireland. They run in a north-south direction from immediately south of Dublin across County Wicklow and into County Wexford. None of the Irish mountains is particularly high: in this range Lugnaquilla is the highest peak at 926m (3039 ft). Mullaghcleevaun at 847m is the second highest. The River Slaney has its source south west of Lugnaquilla and then flows south along the western slopes of the mountains for some 45 miles before entering the St George's Channel at Wexford. The Turlough Hill power station is the only pumped storage hydroelectricity scheme in Ireland: it is located on the Wicklow Gap midway between Hollywood and Glendalough. In the midst lies Glendalough.

2. MacGillycuddy's Reeks

MacGillycuddy's Reeks (*Na Cruacha Dubha*, meaning 'The Black Tops') are a mountain range in County Kerry, Ireland. Stretching slightly over 19km (12 miles), they include Carrauntoohill, which at 1,041.3m (3,409 ft) is the highest mountain in Ireland, two other 1,000 m peaks – Beenkeragh (1,010m) and Caher (1,001m) – and over 100 other Hewitts (peaks of over 2,000 ft). The mountains, part of the Armorican Highlands, are of glacial-carved sandstone and are situated on the Iveragh peninsula near the Lakes of Killarney.

The name of the range dates to the eighteenth century, from the Irish clan MacGillycuddy (or McGillycuddy) which owned land in this part of County Kerry for a long time prior, and continued to do so until the latter part of the twentieth century.

3. Mountains of Mourne

The granite Mountains of Mourne are located in the first proposed national park of Northern Ireland, an Area of Outstanding Beauty.

The mountains are located in County Down, near the town of Newcastle. The highest peak in the Mournes (and Northern Ireland) is Slieve Donard at 2,796 feet (852m). The famous Silent Valley Reservoir is located in the centre of the region. It lies in the valley between Slievenalogh and Slieve Binnian. The Mountains of Mourne are visited by many tourists, hillwalkers, cyclists and rock climbers. The Mourne Wall is a 22 mile (35km) dry-stone wall crossing fifteen summits, built by the Belfast Water Commissioners between 1910 and 1922 to enclose the water catchment area in the Mournes.

4. Sperrins or Sperrin Mountains

The Sperrins, or Sperrin Mountains, are a range of hills in Ulster and one of the largest upland areas in Ireland.

The Sperrins Region is located in the centre of Northern Ireland, stretching from the western shoreline of Lough Neagh in County Tyrone to the southern portions of County Derry. The region has a population of some 150,000 and is a designated area of outstanding natural beauty.

5. Bluestack Mountains

The Bluestack Mountains are the major mountain range in the south of County Donegal in western Ulster. They provide an almost impass-able barrier between the south of the county, such as Donegal town and Ballyshannon, and the towns to the north and west such as Dungloe and Letterkenny. The road between the two parts of the county goes through the Barnesmore Gap.

6. Twelve Bens or Twelve Pins

The Twelve Bens or Twelve Pins is a picturesque mountain range in Connemara in the west of Ireland. They are modest in height (max-imum 730m) but a pleasant climb in fine weather, with superb views. Topographically, this range is partnered with the Maumturks range on the other side of the lonely Inagh Valley (and the route of the Western Way long-distance path).

7. Maumturks/Maamturks

The Maumturks/Maamturk (also known as the Turks) are a picturesque mountain range in Connemara in the west of Ireland. They are less well known than their more famous neighbours, the Twelve Bens, on the other side of the Inagh Valley (and of the Western Way long-distance path). They are not very high (maximum 667m) but a pleasant climb in fine weather, with superb views and no congestion.

8. Galtee Mountains

The Galtee Mountains (Irish: *Na Gaibhlte*) are a mountain range in Munster, located in Ireland's Golden Vale, across parts of Counties Limerick, Tipperary and Cork. The Galtees are Ireland's highest inland mountain range, taking the form of a high ridge which rises up almost sheer from the surrounding plain. The highest peak in the Galtees is Galteemore which rises to 919m (3,018 feet).

The area has a tradition of dairy farming, and the name 'Galtee' is synonymous with one of Ireland's largest food companies that began in the area. Mitchelstown, nestled on the Cork side of the mountains, is the main market town and centre of commerce for the region.

9. Silvermines

Silvermines are a mountain range, a town in that mountain range, and a defunct mining site in County Tipperary. Towards the south of this range is the highest peak in the mountains, Keeper Hill (Irish: *Sliabh Cimeálta*) which rises to 695m, dominating the area.

Recently, the area has come to media attention because the town of Silvermines has had the integrity of its water supply threatened by pollution from the tailings left behind at the mine.

NINE MUSEUMS

1. Hunt Museum

The Hunt Museum on Rutland Street in Limerick. Holding a personal collection donated by the Hunt family, it was originally situated in the University of Limerick before being moved to its present location. It can now be visited in the old custom house, an historic eighteen-thth century building by the River Shannon. Limerick's bustling quays began at this area of the river, recently made home to a marina.

The Hunt Museum holds about 2,000 different artifacts, both from Ireland and abroad. The oldest pieces are from Stone Age Ireland and ancient Egypt. The collection includes the Antrim Cross (a ninth-century bronze and enamel cross), a small sketch by Picasso and a bronze horse from a design by Leonardo da Vinci for a large monument.

2. National Museum of Ireland (NMI)

The National Museum of Ireland (NMI) is the main museum in Ireland. It has three centres in Dublin and Mayo, with a strong emphasis on Irish art, culture and natural history.

The archaeology and history section on Kildare Street includes the Ardagh Chalice and the Tara Brooch, both especially famous examples of early medieval metalwork in Ireland, as well as prehistoric ornaments from the Bronze Age. Many of these pieces were found in the nineteenth century by peasants or agricultural labourers, when population expansion led to cultivation of land which had not been touched since the Middle Ages. The museums of The Royal Irish Academy and the Royal Society of Antiquaries of Ireland formed the basis for the Archaeology and History section of the museum at Kildare Street. This is the original site opened in 1890 as the Dublin Museum of Science and Art. This site also included Leinster House until 1922, now the home of the Oireachtas.

Decorative arts and history, including the great seal of the Irish Free State, is kept at the Collins Barracks site on Dublin's Benburb Street. This is a former military barracks named after Michael Collins in 1922 and was opened in 1997. It is the administrative centre.

The natural history centre is on Merrion Street in Dublin and has fossil and taxidermied specimens of animals from around the world.

3. Pearse Museum

The Pearse Museum is dedicated to the memory of Patrick Pearse, educationalist and nationalist who was executed for his part in the 1916 Rising.

The museum is situated on the southside of Dublin, in the suburb of Rathfarnham. It was formerly the home of Pearse's experimental school, St Enda's, and now contains an exhibition on his life and ideas.

The museum is an eighteenth century house situated in scenic parkland and is open seven days a week from 10am.

4. Tower Museum

The award-winning Tower Museum in Union Hall Place, Derry opened in 1992, tells the tangled story of Derry from its origins in the sixth century right up to the present day using high technology and modern audio-visual presentation methods. Just inside the city walls, a sixteenth-century tower house, built originally for the local Gaelic chieftains, the O'Donnells, was reconstructed to house the museum. The many facets of the city's troubled history are impartially told and include the Siege of Derry in 1688-89, events in Ireland leading to partition in the early 1920s and the more recent troubles in Derry, including the 1969 battle of the Bogside.

5. National Library of Ireland

The National Library of Ireland is based in Kildare Street, Dublin, and is a cultural institution under the aegis of the Department of Arts,

Sport and Tourism. Its mission is to collect, preserve and make available books, manuscripts and illustrative material of Irish interest.

The library does not lend books and reading takes place in the various reading rooms. There is also a copying service and it is possible to get photocopies, photographs, slides, or microfilm of most items in the collections. The library has an ongoing programme of exhibitions.

6. The Ulster Folk and Transport Museum

Established by an Act of Parliament in 1958, the Ulster Folk Museum was set up to illustrate the way of life and the traditions of the people of the North of Ireland. This was primarily in response to the speed at which the countryside and people's way of life was changing and the need to preserve and record a heritage in danger of disappearing.

The Cultra site at Cultra, Holywood, County Down, formerly the estate of Sir Robert Kennedy, was acquired in 1961 and the museum first opened to visitors in 1964. With the opening in 1993 and 1996 of the award-winning Rail and Road Galleries, the Ulster Folk and Transport Museum became firmly established as a museum of international importance.

The museum, part of National Museums and Galleries of Northern Ireland (MAGNI), has won many awards and ranks among Ireland's most important cultural, educational and tourist facilities.

7. Ulster American Folk Park

The Ulster American Folk Park, an open-air museum in Castletown, Omagh, County Tyrone, tells the story of emigration from Ulster to America in the eighteenth and nineteenth centuries and provides visitors with a 'living history' experience on its outdoor site. Costumed demonstrators go about their everyday tasks in the traditional manner in authentically furnished Old and New World buildings.

The Ship and Dockside Gallery features a full-size reconstruction of an early nineteenth-century sailing ship of the type that carried thousands of emigrants across the Atlantic and a major indoor exhibition, 'Emigrants', complements the outdoor site. The Centre for Migration Studies can assist those who wish to find out more about emigration and the way of life of emigrants and settlers.

8. Famine Museum

The Famine Museum in Strokestown, County Roscommon has Mary Robinson, former president of Ireland, as its patron.

The Famine Museum commemorates the Great Irish Famine of the 1840s, the single greatest social disaster of nineteenth-century Europe. Between 1845 and 1850, when blight devastated the potato crop, in excess of 2 million persons – approximately one-quarter of the entire population – either died or emigrated. The Famine is a central event in recent Irish history and consiousness for both Irish people and emigrant populations throughout the world.

9. Irish Museum of Modern Art (IMMA)

The Irish Museum of Modern Art, which was established in Dublin in May 1991, is the country's leading national institution for the collection and exhibition of contemporary art. The collection of artworks owned by or on long-term loan to the museum consists of works by twentieth-century Irish and non-Irish artists. The collection has been developed by purchase, loans and donations, as well as by the commissioning of new works.

The museum, which is housed in the Royal Hospital in Kilmainham presents retrospectives, solo exhibitions, group exhibitions and projects. The museum also shows its collection in rotating temporary displays, as well as exhibitions and projects organised by the museum's Education and Community Department.

EIGHT RIVERS

1. River Boyne

The River Boyne in Leinster courses for about 112km (70 miles). It rises at Trinity Well, Newbury Hall, near Carbury, County Kildare, and flows towards the Northeast through County Meath to reach the Irish Sea at Drogheda. Salmon and trout can be caught in the river, which is surrounded by the Boyne Valley. It is crossed just west of Drogheda by the Boyne River Bridge.

Despite its short course, the Boyne has historical, archaeological and mythical connotations. It passes near the ancient city of Trim, Trim Castle, the Hill of Tara (the ancient capital of the High Kings of Ireland), Navan, the Hill of Slane, Brú na Bóinne (an archaeological site), Mellifont Abbey, and the medieval city of Drogheda. In the Boyne Valley can also be found other historical and archaeological monuments, like Loughcrew, Kells, Celtic crosses, castles and more. The Battle of the Boyne took place near the banks of the Boyne in 1690 during the Williamite war in Ireland.

Referring to legendary stories, it was in this river where Fionn mac Cumhail captured Fiontán, the Salmon of Knowledge. It was also said that the river was named after the goddess Boann ('queen' or 'goddess'), according to Francis Dinneen, a lexicographer of the Irish Gaelic language, and Boyne is an anglicised form of the name.

2. River Liffey

The Liffey (Irish: *An Life*) flows through Dublin.

The Liffey rises in the Sally Gap, near to Kippure, a mountain in Wicklow, and flows for around 125km (75 miles) through Counties Wicklow, Kildare and Dublin before entering the Irish sea in Dublin Bay. There are three hydro-electric power stations along the river, at Poulaphouca, Golden Falls and Leixlip. Towns along the river include Ballymore Eustace, Newbridge, Leixlip and Lucan before the river reaches the city of Dublin at its mouth. The River Liffey has been used for many centuries in trade, from the Viking beginnings of the city up to recent times.

3. River Avoca,

The Avoca, or historically Ovoca, is a river in County Wicklow. It is contained completely within the county. The Avoca starts life as two rivers, the Avonmore and the Avonbeg. These join at The Meeting of the Waters (the Vale of Avoca), a local beauty spot celebrated by Thomas Moore in his song of the same name.

The Avoca flows into the Irish Sea at Arklow where it widens into a large estuary, giving Arklow its Irish language name an t-Inbhear Mór (the big inlet). The village of Avoca is situated on the river.

4. River Barrow

The River Barrow is one of The Three Sisters, the other two 'sisters' are the River Suir and the River Nore. The Barrow is the longest and the biggest of the three rivers. The Barrow is the second longest river in Ireland, after the River Shannon.

5. River Lee

The Lee (*An Laoi* in Irish) is a river in the Republic of Ireland, flowing through County Cork and Cork city to Cork Harbour on Ireland's south coast. A hydro-electric scheme was built on the river, upstream from Cork city, and this part of the river now contains Carrigadrohid and Inniscarra reservoirs.

6. River Corrib

The River Corrib in the west of Ireland flows from Loch Coirib / Lough Corrib through Galway to Galway Bay. The river has only a length of four miles from the lough to the sea, and is said to be the shortest in Europe. It is also among the most powerful, especially after a few days rain, and is popular with local whitewater kayakers.

The correct name for the river in English is the Galway River. In Irish it is sometimes called *An Ghaillimh* ('the Galway') and also incorrectly called the *Abhainn na Coiribe*. The legend concerning its naming states that it was called after Gailleamh the daughter of a Fir Bolg chieftain, who drowned in the river.

The word *Gaillimh* is believed to mean 'stony' as in 'stony river'. The commonly held myth that the city takes its name from the Irish word Gallaibh, 'foreigners' i.e., 'the town of the foreigners' (from Gall, a foreigner) is incorrect as the name *Gaillimh* was applied to the river first and then later onto the town. Indeed, the earliest settlement at Galway was called *Dún Bhun na Gaillimhe*, or 'the town at the end of the Galway (river)'.

The river gave its name to the town, which grew to a city, and from c. 1570 onwards, the city gave its name to the county.

7. River Moy

The River Moy (Irish: *Abhainn na Muaidhe*) rises in the Ox Mountains in County Sligo in the northwest of Ireland. For the greater part of its length the Moy flows southwestward, entering County Mayo and passing not far from Swinford before turning north near the village of Kilmore and heading for the historic town of Ballina, where it empties into Killala Bay and the Atlantic Ocean. The river is noted as one of the best salmon fisheries in Europe, and the beautiful Moy valley, with its ancient churches and abbeys, is a prominent tourist destination.

8. River Shannon

The River Shannon (Irish: *Sionainn*), Ireland's longest river, divides the west of Ireland (mostly the province of Connaught) from the east and south (Leinster and most of Munster). The river has been an important waterway since antiquity. First mapped by Ptolemy, the 259km (161 miles) long river flows generally south from the Shannon Pot in County Cavan before turning west and emptying into the Atlantic Ocean through the 113km (70 miles) long Shannon Estuary. Limerick city stands watch at the point where the river water meets the sea water of the estuary.

The river rises in the Cuilcagh Mountains in south County Fermanagh, and flows through eleven of Ireland's 32 counties. Lakes on the Shannon include Lough Allen, Lough Ree and Lough Derg. Tributaries include the River Suck and the River Brosna.

The Shannon is the longest river in the British Isles. Despite being more than 300km (200 miles) long, it rises only 76m (250 feet) above sea level, so the river is easily navigable, with only a few locks along its length. There is a hydro-electric generation plant on it at Ardnacrusha, belonging to the ESB.

LOCAL
HISTORY

Eighteen Place-names in Dublin and their Meanings

1. College Green
It was renamed College Green after Trinity College was founded there by Queen Elizabeth I in the 1600s. Originally it was known as Hoggen Green (which comes from the Scandinavian word for mound). It was near the Thingmote, the Viking assembly place.

2. Constitution Hill
Originally called Glasmunogue, it is renamed due to its proximity to the King's Inns Law Society.

3. Cornmarket
This was the site of the corn and grain market during medieval times.

4. Crampton Quay
Crampton Quay and Court are named after Philip Crampton, a wealthy bookseller, and Lord Mayor of Dublin in 1758.

5. Crane Lane
Crane Lane is named after a public crane located near the old Custom House.

6. Crown Alley
Crown Alley derived its name from a tavern sporting the sign of the crown.

7. Earlsfort Terrace
It was named after John Scott, Baron Earlsfort, later earl of Clonmel.

8. Essex Gate

This is named after the Earl of Essex who was a member of the Capel family and was Viceroy for a period. It was also a gate into the medieval city.

9. Fitzwilliam Square

The Fitzwilliam family developed this land as part of their great estate on the southside of the Liffey, hence the name.

10. Harold's Cross

Harold's Cross was so called because a tribe called the Harolds lived in the Wickow Mountains and the Archbiship of Dublin would not allow them nearer to the city than that point.

11. James' Gate

This is now best known as the home of the Guinness Brewery. In the past there was a city gate here and it is also close to St James' Church, combined to give it its name.

12. Meeting House Lane

So named because of the many religious establishments that were based here in the seventeenth century.

13. St Stephen's Green

Originally the four malls have different names – north was Beaux Walk, south was Leeson's Walk, east was Monk's Walk, and west was French Walk. It was named after St Stephen's church and leper hospital which was sited in the vicinity of Mercer Street.

14. Stoneybatter

An ancient royal highway ran from the Hill of Tara to Glenadalough. It was paved with stones, much like Roman roads had been. The Irish for it was *Bóthar na Gloch* or Stoney Road. From this we got Stoney

Bóthar which later became Stoneybatter.

15. Temple Bar
Temple Bar was named after the Temple family, specifically after Sir William Temple, whose house and gardens were located there in the early seventeenth century. The official *Temple Bar Guide* adds that 'a bar was the name for a walkway by a river, so the path used by the Temple family became known as the Temple Bar'. An alternative view is that the Temple Bar area is so called because it housed the first Jewish temple built in Ireland. The word 'bar' refers to the refusal of Catholics to allow the Jewish community to enter any of the adjoining commercial premises.

16. Usher's Island
This location got its name from an island formed by a branch of the River Camac which divided at the north end of Watling Street. John Usher had leased this former island from the corporation in 1597.

17. Westland Row
It was originally known as Westlands after William Westland who owned the property in the area.

18. Wood Quay
Originally the street was built on wooden piles, driven into the river bed from which its derives its name. It is also the site of a former Viking city.

52 STREET NAMES IN DUBLIN
AND THEIR MEANINGS

1. Abbey Street
This street was named Abbey Street because it lay beside the medieval St Mary's Abbey.

2. Adelaide Road
This road is named after Queen Adelaide – wife of William IV.

3. Andrew's Lane
This lane gets its name from St Andrew's Church, which was the chapel for the Irish parliament.

4. Amiens Street
It was originally known as The Strand and subsequently named after Viscount Amiens, First Earl of Aldborough, whose family home was nearby.

5. Anglesea Street
Anglesea Street commemorates another prominent resident of the area, Arthur Annesley, created Earl of Anglesea in 1661.

6. Arnott Street
This street is named after Sir John Arnott who developed the area with James Lombard after whom a street is also named.

7. Aungier Street
Aungier Street was built on an area of land that traditionally had not been built on. In old maps before the street was built you can see the other streets curving around the area. The Aungier family acquired this land which had belonged to a Carmelite monastery.

8. Aughrim Street

Was originally part of Blackhorse Lane. It was renamed to celebrate the centenary of the Battle of Aughrim which took place in 1691.

9. Baggot Street

Baggot Rath Castle stood at what is now the junction of Waterloo Road and Baggot Street. Baggot Street is named after Lord Robert Bagod, who was given the Manor of Rath in the thirteenth century.

10. Bolton Street

This street was named in 1724 after Lord Lieutenant Charles Powlett, who was the Earl of Bolton.

11. Bride Street

This is named after St Bride's Church (which was a pre-Viking foundation). The church was demolished as part of the Iveagh Trust Scheme in the late 1800s. The Iveagh Trust Scheme was a project of urban renewal in Edwardian Dublin, commissioned by the Earl of Iveagh to clean up Dublin's slums.

12. Capel Street

Lord Arthur Capel and Earl of Essex was Lord Lieutenant from 1672-77. This is named after his family.

13. Castle Street

Before the construction of Lord Edward Street this was the main street to Dublin Castle.

14. Cathal Brugha Street

Originally called Gregg Lane, the stret name was later changed to that of a signatory of the 1916 Rising.

15. Chancery Street
Chancery Courts was traditionally one of the four courts – and the street lies behind what is now called the Four Courts.

16. Clare Street
This street is named after the Earl of Clare, Denzille Holles.

17. Clarence Street
Clarence Street was named after the Duke of Clarence.

18. Clarendon Street
Clarendon Street was named after another Wide Streets Commissioner, the Earl of Clarendon.

19. College Street
College Street was so called due to its proximity to Trinity College.

20. Cope Street
The Fownes family owned land in this area, and Cope was one of member of the family.

21. Crane Lane
Crane Lane is named after a public crane located near the old Custom House.

22. Crowe Street
Crowe Street is named after William Crow, owner of the site of the suppressed monastery of St Augustine in the late sixteenth century. The Dublin Philosophical Society, the Irish counterpart of the Royal Society of London, with which Sir William Petty, William Molyneux and other illustrious figures were associated, met in 1684 at a building in Crowe Street known as the 'Crow's Nest'.

23. Dame Street
Dame Street derives its name from Dame's Gate, the eastern gate of the city, adjoining the Church of St Mary del Dame.

24. Dawson Street
This was named after Harry Dawson who designed Dawson, Grafton, Anne and Harry Streets in the area.

25. D'Olier Street
This was amed after city Sheriff in 1788, Jeremiah D'Olier.

26. Earl Street
This street was developed by Henry Moore, Earl of Drogheda, who named many of the streets in the locality after himself, Henry Street, Moore Street, Earl Street, Of Lane (now Off lane) and Drogheda Street.

27. Eden Quay
William Eden, a former Chief Secretary to Ireland, had helped John Beresford to plan and improve Dublin. He had requested that if their plans succeeded, for a street or square to be named after him.

28. Ely Place
The first house built in this area was developed by Gustavus Hume and was leased to Henry Loftus, Viscount of Ely, later Earl of Ely and hence the name.

29. Essex Street
It was originally called Orange Street and earlier again Smock Alley, but was later named after the Viceroy Earl of Essex, Arthur Capel, who was Irish Lord Lieutenant from 1672-7.

30. Exchequer Street
The Royal Exchequer was based here in the middle ages.

31. Fishamble Street
This was the main area for fish processing in medieval Dublin hence the name.

32. Fleet Street
Fleet Street in London was named after the river Fleet, and as there is no such river in Dublin, the naming of Fleet Street here was just plain imitation or it may refer to fleets of ships coming up the river to moor here. Originally this marked the edge of the south bank of the Liffey along with Temple Bar.

33. Gardiner Street
At one time the Gardiners owned 25 percent of the city within the canals. Luke Gardiner, as head of the Gardiner Estate, was responsible for laying out much of this part of Dublin. The Street is named after him.

34. Grafton Street
Grafton Street was named after the Earls of Grafton who owned land in this area.

35. Harcourt Street
Named after Lord Harcourt, a former Lord Lieutenant of Ireland.

36. Jervis Street
Sir Humphrey Jervis, Dublin Lord Mayor and business man bought much of the estate and laid out the area around St Mary's Abbey.

37. Kildare Street
Named after the Fitzgeralds, Earls of Kildare and Leinster, who built Leinster House.

38. Leeson Street
It was renamed in 1728 after the Leesons, Earls of Milltown, who were a brewing family. Originally it was known as Suesey Street.

39. Leinster Street
Named due to its proximity to the Leinster House of the Fitzgerald family, Earls of Kildare and Leinster. Leinster House in Dublin was originally built as a private home for the Duke of Leinster. At that time, the most fashionable part of Dublin was the North Side and he was asked why he was building on the South Side. He said 'Where I go, fashion follows me' ... and to this day the most fashionable part of Dublin is the south side.

40. Marlborough Street
Named after the Duke of Marlborough for his famous victories.

41. Molesworth Street
This was originally known as Molesworth Fields and named after Viscount Molesworth who laid it out removing several houses on Dawson Street so they would intersect.

42. Montgomery Street
Named after Elizabeth Montgomery, wife of Luke Gardiner. Montgomery Street was once the biggest red-light district in Europe with an estimated 1,600 prostitutes. It was known locally as the 'Monto' and this is the origin of the song 'Take me up to Monto'.

43. Moore Street
Now known for its fruit and vegetable market. Developed by Henry Moore, Earl of Drogheda who named a lot of the Streets in the area after himself ; Henry Street, Moore Street, Earl Street, Of Lane (now Off lane), and Drogheda Street.

44. Nassau Street

Renamed in the 1700s after the Royal House of Nassau. Originally it was known as St Patrick's Well Lane.

45. O'Connell Street

In the nineteenth century this was known as Sackville Street after a lord lieutenant. After Independence, it was renamed O'Connell Street after the Liberator Daniel O'Connell. Originally developed by the earls of Drogheda and known as Drogheda Street. At one time it was the widest street in Europe.

46. Parliament Street

Parliament Street owes its name to the fact that it was built with the aid of a grant from, the Irish Parliament in 1757. This was the first development of the board of Wide Streets Commissioners which was created by an Act of Parliament specifically to develop this thoroughfare. The street completes the north-south axis of Capel Street, with the vista being terminated by City Hall.

47. Parnell Street

Parnell Street was renamed after the Irish statesman – Charles Stewart Parnell. It had originally be known as Great Britain Street.

48. Parkgate Street

Parkgate Street was so named because of the main city side entrance to the Phoenix Park, hence Parkgate.

49. Patrick Street

Patrick Street was named after St Patrick's Cathedral, construction of which started in 1191. The cathedral was built on the site of an earlier site that was believed to have been started by St Patrick.

50. Pearse Street

Pearse Street was originally known as Moss Lane, then Great Brunswick Street, and later Pearse Street after Padraig Pearse, leader of the 1916 Easter Rising.

51. Sean McDermott Street

Sean McDermott Street was named after one of the signatories of the Proclamation of Independence of 1916. Previously known as Gloucester Street, it was earlier called Great Martin's Lane.

52. Townsend Street

This was originally known as Lazers Hill but was renamed after the Lord Lieutenant and General Governor of Ireland, Viscount George Townsend, in the eighteenth century.

Seven Castles

1. Rock of Cashel

The town of Cashel (meaning castle or fortress) in County Tipperary is home to one of Ireland's great historical sites – the Rock of Cashel. Towering over the town from its perch on a 200-foot-high outcrop of limestone, the Rock was once the seat of the Kings of Munster. It was visited by St Patrick in 450 and Brian Boru was crowned King of Ireland here in the tenth century. Granted to the church in the twelfth century by the O'Brien clan king, the Rock became the seat of the archbishop and it was at this time that Cormac's Chapel was built there. In 1647 the Rock was ransacked by Cromwellian forces under the leadership of Lord Inchiquin. Today the impressive stone walls enclose a round tower, the cathedral, a twelfth-century romanesque chapel, high crosses and other structures. The gothic cathedral dates back to the thirteenth century and includes a central square tower and living quarters. The steps of the tower lead to the summit roof walk. The smaller structure of Cormac's Chapel displays some typical romanesque features while the Hall of the Vicar's Choral at the entrance to the Rock is a fifteenth-century house which has recently been restored. This museum, offering guided tours and housing interesting exhibits, includes silverware and a St Patrick's Cross.

2. Trim Castle

Trim Castle, County Meath, is the largest and one of the most important Norman military constructions in Ireland. Its well-deserved reputation as the king of Irish castles rests upon its imposing curtain walls enclosing over three acres, its fine gatehouses, and its enormous isolated keep – all of which project a visually striking image of foreboding might and great power.

The first fortification on this site above the banks of the Boyne was a motte erected by Hugh de Lacy in 1172. After this was destroyed by Roderick of Connaught in 1174, de Lacy embarked on building another castle, the nature of which has not yet been established.

The design of the keep is most unusual, comprising a massive square block with towers projecting from the middle of each face (only three out of the original four remain). On plans it looks like a combination of a square and a Greek cross.

3. Blarney Castle

Blarney Castle, County Cork, is probably Ireland's best-known castle, and it receives thousands of visitors every year. The castle today was actually the third one built, and features ruins of a stone keep and towers dating to the 1400s.

Legends hold that 4,000 Munster men aided Robert the Bruce during the battle of Bannockburn, and in return he presented half of the Stone of Scone to the men in gratitude for their help.

This is the foundation for the legend of the famous 'Blarney Stone'. When visiting, tourists grasp an iron rail while bending over backwards to kiss the Blarney Stone and receive the 'Gift of the Gab'. This well-known phrase reportedly was said by Queen Elizabeth I, who became exasperated with Lord Blarney's talent for endless debate without ever acquiescing to her point of view.

4. Bunratty Castle

The fashion for renovating castles and using them to host 'medieval banquets' may have begun at Bunratty, County Clare, which was restored in the 1950s under the brilliant guidance of Percy le Clerc and filled with Lord Gort's magnificent collection of medieval furniture and tapestries. It is now one of Ireland's main tourist attractions and justifiably so – for no other castle gives a more lasting impression of later medieval life.

The castle once stood on an island in a tidal creek with a view of the water-traffic entering and leaving the port of Limerick. The present building was erected between 1450–67 by the MacNamara or MacConmara family and passed through marriage to the O'Briens *c.* 1500. It was remodelled by Donough O'Brien, the 'Great', (fourth) Earl of Thomond, who succeeded in 1581.

5. Cahir Castle

Superbly set on a rocky island in the River Suir, this impressive fifteenth-century castle in County Tipperary – the largest of its period in Ireland – was considered impregnable until the advent of heavy cannon. Described by one Elizabethan commentator as 'the bulwark for Munster and a safe retreat for all the agents of Spain and Rome', it fell to Devereux, Earl of Essex, in 1599 after it had been battered for two days with artillery. It surrendered without a fight to Inchiquin in 1647 and again to Cromwell in 1650.

The present castle appears to be largely the work of Seamus Gallda (James the Foreigner), ancestor of the Butlers, Barons of Cahir. After the death of his father, the third Earl of Ormonde, in 1405, James Butler made Cahir his principal seat and embarked on a building programme. This work was continued by his successors during the fifteenth and sixteenth centuries. By 1599 the castle had reached its present appearance when illustrated in *Pacata Hibernia*. The only subsequent alterations took place in the 1840s when Richard Butler, the thirteenth Baron Cahir, restored the castle and replaced the picturesque Irish battlements with more solid English ones. The great hall on the east side of the inner ward was also rebuilt at this time, though its original form extended further south, and the main fireplace now lies outside in the open.

6. Dublin Castle

Dublin Castle was the seat of British rule in Ireland until 1922. The building itself mainly dates from eighteenth century, though a castle has stood on the site since the days of King John, the first Lord of Ireland. The castle served as the seat of British government of

Ireland under the Lordship of Ireland (1171–1541), Kingdom of Ireland (1541–1800) and United Kingdom of Great Britain and Ireland (1800–1922).

The castle ceased to be used for government purposes when the Irish Free State came into being in 1922. It served for some years as temporary Courts of Justice (the Four Courts, the home of the Irish courts system had been destroyed in 1922). Once the courts moved out, Dublin Castle was used for state ceremonial.

After major refurbishment, the castle is now used as a conference centre. It is also a major tourist venue. During Ireland's presidencies of the European Community/Union, European Council meetings have taken place there.

7. Ross Castle

There are few castles anywhere in Ireland that can boast such an enchanted setting as this ruined tower house on the shore of Killarney's Lower Lake. Built in the late fifteenth century, this County Kerry castle is fairly typical of its type, with square bartizans on diagonally opposite corners and a thick end wall containing a tier of chambers and a winding mural stair.

The castle was the chief seat of the O'Donaghue Mors, hereditary rulers of this district and descendants of the ancient kings of Munster. After the Desmond rebellion, their fortified lands were acquired by the MacCarthy Mors from whom they were purchased by Sir Valentine Browne, ancestor of the Earls of Kenmare. In 1652 the castle was held by Lord Muskerry against a Cromwellian force of 1,500 foot and 700 horse soldiers, commanded by Edmond Ludlow.

Eleven Statues in Dublin

1. **The Famine Monument** – Custom House Quay

2. **O'Connell Monument** (Daniel O'Connell) – O'Connell Street

3. **Parnell Monument** (Charles Stewart Parnell) – O'Connell Street

4. **Sir John Gray** – O'Connell Street

5. **Jim Larkin** – O'Connell Street

6. **Thomas Davis** – College Green

7. **Henry Grattan** – College Green

8. **James Joyce** – North Earl Street

9. **Molly Malone** – Grafton Street

10. **Archbishop Coyningham** – Kildare Place

11. **Robert Emmet** – St Stephen's Green

Twelve Archaeological Sites

1. Wedge Tombs

There are about 505 wedge tombs known in Ireland. These mega-lithic tombs are characterised as having a gallery constructed with side-stones which decrease in height from the western to the east-ern end, and are either parallel or give a wedge-shaped appearance. They usually have an outer revetment walling which is close set and emphasises the wedge shape. They are roofed with large stones which sit directly on the walls of the gallery and are usually orient-ed north-east to south-west. The entrance, placed at the east, is often closed by a single stone.

2. Ceremonial Enclosures

Another type of public monument consisted of a circular or oval area defined by either a bank, ditch, standing stones or a combina-tion of these. These sites are described as embanked enclosures, which appear to relate to the henges of Britain, and stone circles. The embanked enclosures of the Boyne Valley region in County Meath can be up to 110m in diameter with a flat-topped earthen bank enclosing a circular to oval domed or hollowed area with a sin-gle entrance.

3. Bronze Age Burials

The Bronze Age period lasted in Ireland from about 2500 BC to about 500 BC and the burials of the period show a wide degree of variety with both pits and stone cists used. The pits can be simple holes or can be stone lined and range from circular to oval. More substantial stone-built rectangular and polygonal cist graves, like at Keenoge, County Meath, were also used. The cists were also buried in holes in the ground. In some instances the cists can assume the proporations of small, underground, megalithic tombs.

4. Barrows

Barrows have been constructed in Ireland since the Middle Neolithic period and were in use until the early centuries AD. They may cover or contain megalithic Linkardstown-type cists of the Neolithic era, all of the burials type of the Bronze Age, or cremations or inhumations of the Iron Age. In the east of Ireland the mounds of these sites have been levelled in large numbers, leaving ring-ditches, or they have been remodelled into ceremonial enclosures, as at Tara, or medieval mottes as at Rathmore, County Kildare. Excavation has revealed that a significant number of barrows belong to the Iron Age (c. 300 BC-100 AD), but many are of Bronze Age date as well. The barrows are often found in groups or cemeteries where a number of types can be found together.

5. Cairns

Barrows have been constructed in Ireland since the Neolithic period, when they covered megalithic tombs and were in use until the fourth or fifth centuries AD. Unlike barrows, cairns are a by-product of agricultural clearance and in upland areas and, on thin soils covering exposed geological formations would have been a readily available building material. Cairns are usually of three types: high cairns, resembling bowl barrows, which often covered passage tombs; much lower cairns of less than 2m in height with flat tops; and ring cairns, which enclosed a central burial. A number of the cairns covering megalithic tombs had Bronze Age cists added to them or had the central chambers re-used for Bronze Age burials.

6. Stone Circles

These monuments consist of a ring of free-standing stones, uneven in number and symmetrically arranged so that one stone, the axial stone, is set directly opposite two stones, usually the tallest, marking the entrance to the circle. Characteristically, the stones reduce in height to the axial stone, which is set consistently in the south-western part of the circle. Though divided into two groups, five-stone and multiple-stone circles, they are essentially one type of monument with a common basic design. The circles appear to have been deliberately orientated so that the main axis of the circle (a line extending from the middle of the gap between the entrance stones across to the centre of the axial stone) is aligned north-east/south-west – those sectors of the horizon in which the sun rises or sets at significant times during the year, an equinox or solstice.

7. *Fulachta Fiadh*
Fulachta fiadh were an integral component of the Bronze Age landscape and provide significant evidence of activity in areas with little evidence of artifact deposition. Usually they consist of horseshoe-shaped heaps of heat-fractured stone mixed with charcoal and dark soil, associated with lined rectangular water troughs and hearths. They are also called burnt mounds.

8. Ringforts
Ringforts are the most common site type in Ireland. They were primarily built and used during the Early Christian period, 500–1200 AD. They are differentiated from cashels in having enclosing banks composed of dumped earth and sometimes a mixture of earth and stone. However, these distinctions are not clear cut and some sites had earthen banks faced with stone, or had sections of the enclosing element composed alternately of earth or stone. In some cases the enclosing element is so eroded or robbed out and sod covered that it can be difficult to determine if it had originally been a wall or bank.

9. Cashels
Cashels were constructed at the same period and fulfilled the same functions as ringforts. They differ in their construction technique, being assembled rather than quarried and piled up, and therefore

usually lack an enclosing fosse. The usual technique was to construct two concentric drystone walls of medium-sized blocks and slabs, limestone was the preferred material, set on a foundation of large boulders. The are between was then infilled with rubble. The construction technique allowed for some elaboration and in some case chambers were built into the walls, sometimes linked to souterrains, and stone steps might lead to broad wall walks. The walls are often, when well preserved, 2m or higher.

10. Souterrains

Souterrains are artificial, subterranean (or semi-subterranean) structures built to allow access and usually associated with habitation. They are common in ringforts and cashels of the Early Christian period c. AD 500-1200 A.D and appear to have been used as an underground bolt-hole if a ringfort was attacked. The simpler examples, without complex chambers and defensive arrangements such as creeps, were probably also a secure place to store valuables and perishable foods such as meat, butter or grain. In a sense the souterrains could represent the most defensive aspect of a ringfort and it has been suggested that their uneven distribution may indicate that they were constructed by tribal groupings engaged in struggles with neighbouring groups.

11. Medieval Moated Sites

These rectangular sites, enclosed by water-filled moats and earthen banks, probably topped by palisades, where constructed by the Anglo-Normans to protect their manor houses. To date the majority of these sites are known from the south-east of the country, especially Tipperary and Wexford, and appear to have been constructed along the marches or border lands of the Anglo-Norman colony and the Gaelic lands. Excavations have indicated that these sites were constructed and used from the late thirteenth to the mid-fourteenth centuries.

12. Mottes

Mottes are flat-topped earthen mounds with a fosse at the base. Some, but not all, sites have a sub-rectangular area enclosed by a bank and fosse, known as a bailey, contiguous to the fosse. They were usually constructed at strategic locations, river crossings or on important routeways. Sometimes the builders used pre-existing ringforts and even burial mounds as the bases of these sites. The sites were constructed by Anglo-Norman lords at an early stage of the Norman conquest, in the thirteenth century.

Seven Famous Bridges

1. O'Connell Bridge, Dublin
At the hub of Dublin city, O'Connell Bridge, formerly Carlisle Bridge, was built in 1790 as one of the links in the Wide Streets Commissioners' plan to connect north and south with a great axial route. The plan was completed when Westmoreland Street was driven through to College Green a few years later. In 1880 the bridge was widened and is now famous for being as broad as it is long.

2. St Mary's Bridge, Drogheda
St Mary's Bridge stands approximately on the site of the earliest construction of hurdles and clay, from which the town takes its title, in Irish, *Droichead átha* or the bridge of the ford.

While it was scarcely possible to ford the river here, it would still have been feasible to span it, even with a primitive bridge, at an early date. The river, entering the town from the west, is almost 600 feet wide, narrowing at this point to only 110 feet, before expanding again to 450 feet in the docks area. The town grew around this crossing, which opened up a transport route north and south, and the harbour below was developed to accommodate seaborne trade.

3. Salmon Weir Bridge, Galway
One of the most impressive sights in Galway is hundreds of salmon lying in season in the clear bed of the Corrib River, waiting to go up river to the spawning grounds. The Salmon Weir is famous in Galway's history. It was originally granted by Henry III to the Earl of Ulster. The Franciscans held the fisheries until the suppression of the monasteries under Henry VIII, when they were given to the Lynch family. Cromwell dispossessed the Lynches, and the Eyres, who gave their name to Eyre Square, acquired them. The Salmon Weir Bridge is now state property.

4. Parliament Bridge, Cork

Parliament Bridge was built in 1806 to commemorate the Act of Union. It is an elegant, single-arched bridge and built mainly from limestone. It was designed by William Hargrave. It replaced an earlier bridge on the same site which was damaged by a flood in 1804 and is one of Cork city's oldest bridges, spanning the south channel of the River Lee.

5. The Craigavon Bridge, Carlisile Square, Derry

The first bridge built across the River Foyle was a wooden structure erected in 1789-91. The structure allowed for a drawbridge as the inhabitants of Strabane had navigational rights to the river. It was built between Bridge Street and Fountain Hill. The second bridge was a steel structure built in 1863 a little further upstream, near the site of today's Craigavon Bridge. This was completed in 1933 and the two-tier structure allows the lower deck to carry goods on rail tracks between the city's railway stations. The lower deck has been converted for road usage now and both decks of the bridge carry a heavy flow of traffic to and from the city.

6. Carrick-a-Rede Rope Bridge

Just outside Ballintoy on the main coast road from Bushmills to Ballycastle is one of the National Trust's most popular properties, Larrybane, which is linked by footpath by the famous Carrick-a-Rede rope bridge to Carrick-a-Rede Island.

Carrick-a-Rede, which means the rock in the road, was given this name because the island and adjacent shallow channel between it and the mainland act as a barrier to migrating salmon. They are deflected north into the nets laid by local fishermen who use the bridge to get to the fishery on the island. A rope bridge has spanned the 60-foot gap between the mainland and Carrick-a-rede Island for at least 200 years. It is put up in April and remains in place until early September.

7. The Ha'penny Bridge, Dublin

The elegant, metal, pedestrian bridge spanning the Liffey between Merchants' Arch and Liffey Street is one of Dublin's best-known landmarks. Erected in 1816, it was among the earliest cast-iron structures of its kind and was named Wellington Bridge.

Although its official title is now Liffey Bridge, it is universally known as the Ha'penny Bridge after the toll levied on its users. No payment is now required to take this delightful route across the river.

Twelve Notable Buildings

1. Newgrange

Newgrange, located in County Meath, is the most famous of all Irish prehistoric sites. It is known as a passage tomb. Originally built c. 3200 BC it lay lost for centuries until the late seventeenth century. It was much restored between 1962 and 1975. It consists of a vast man-made stone and turf mound retained within a circle of huge kerb stones topped by a high, inward-leaning wall of white quartz. A long passage leads to a cruciform chamber under the mound. Every year, at the time of the winter solstice, the sun shines directly along this passage into the chamber for about fifteen minutes as it rises.

2. Dublin Castle

Dublin Castle was the seat of British rule in Ireland until 1922. The building itself mainly dates from the eighteenth century, though a castle has stood on the site since the days of King John, the first Lord of Ireland. The castle served as the seat of British government of Ireland under the Lordship of Ireland (1171-1541), Kingdom of Ireland (1541-1800) and United Kingdom of Gre at Britain and Ireland (1800-1922).

The castle ceased to be used for government purposes when the Irish Free State came into being in 1922. It served for some years as temporary Courts of Justice (the Four Courts, the home of the Irish courts system, had been destroyed in 1922.) Once the courts moved out, Dublin Castle was used for state ceremonial purposes.

After major refurbishment, the castle is now used as a conference centre. It is also a major tourist venue. During Ireland's presidencies of the European Community/Union, European Council meetings have taken place there.

3. Trinity College

Founded in 1592 by Elizabeth I, Trinity College, in Dublin is Ireland's oldest university, and the only constituent college in the University of Dublin. It is located on College Green, opposite the former House of Parliament (now Bank of Ireland). The campus now occupies 47 acres.

During its early life, Trinity was a university exclusively for the Protestant ascendency class. Roman Catholics were first admitted in 1793 (prior to Cambridge and Oxford), though they had to obtain the permission of the Catholic Archbishop of Dublin to take up a place, until well into the twentieth century. In 1873 all religious tests were abolished. Women were admitted to Trinity College for the first time in 1904. The first woman professor was appointed in 1934.

The library in Trinity College is the largest research library in Ireland and contains 4.25 million books. The Book of Kells, the library's most famous asset, can be seen in the Long Room of the old library.

4. Irish Houses of Parliament

The Irish Houses of Parliament (also known as the Irish Parliament House, now called the Bank of Ireland, College Green, due to its modern-day use as a branch of the bank) was the world's first purpose-built, two-chamber parliament house. It served as the seat of both chambers of the Irish parliament of the kingdom of Ireland for most of the eighteenth century until that parliament was abolished in the Irish Act of Union in 1800.

The design of this radical new Irish parliamentary building, the only purpose-built Irish parliamentary building in history, was trusted to a talented young architect, Edward Pearce, who was himself a Member of Parliament. Pearce's design for the new Irish Houses of Parliament was revolutionary. The building was effectively semi-circular in stape, occuping nearly an acre and a half of ground.

The building underwent extensions by renowned architect James Gandon (as Pearce died young).

In 1802 the fledgling Bank of Ireland bought the building from the British government for use as its headquarters. One proviso is stipulated; it must be so adapted that it never could be used as a parliament again. The House of Lords chamber survived almost unscathed. It was used as the board room for the bank until the 1970s, when the Bank of Ireland moved its headquarters elsewhere.

5. Leinster House

Leinster House is the former ducal palace in Dublin that has served since 1922 as the parliament building of the Irish Free State, and the Republic of Ireland.

Ireland's senior peer, the Earl of Kildare, had a seat in the Lords. From the late eighteenth century Leinster House (then called Kildare House) was the Earl's official Dublin residence. When the Earl was made the first Duke of Leinster, the family's Dublin residence was renamed Leinster House.

In 1924, due to financial constraints, plans to turn the Royal Hospital into a parliament house were abandoned; Leinster House instead was bought, pending the provision of a proper parliament house at some stage in the future. A new Senate or Seanad chamber was created in Duke's old ballroom, while wings from the neighbouring Royal College of Science were taken over as used as Government Buildings

6. The Custom House

The Custom House is a Palladian eighteenth-century building in Dublin which houses the Department of the Environment, Heritage and Local Government. It is located on the North Bank of the River Liffey, on Custom House Quay, between Butt Bridge and Talbot Memorial Bridge. It was designed by James Gandon to act as the new custom house for Dublin Port. When it was completed in 1791, it cost IR£200,000 to build – a huge sum at the time.

As the port of Dublin moved further downriver, the building's original use became obsolete, and it was used as the headquarters of local government in Dublin. During the Anglo-Irish war in 1921, the Irish Republican Army burnt the building down, in an attempt to distrupt British rule in Ireland.

When peace returned a few years later, the building was restored by the Irish Free State government. Further restoration and cleaning was done by the Office of Public Works in the 1980s.

7. The Four Courts
The Four Courts in Dublin is the Republic of Ireland's main courts building. It is the location of the Irish Supreme Court, High Court and Central Criminal Court.

The Four Courts was built between 1796 and 1802 by well-known architect James Gandon, who also built Dublin's Custom House. The building originally housed the four courts of Chancery, King's Bench, Exchequer, and Common Place, hence the building's name. A major revision in the legal structures in the late nineteenth century saw these courts replaced but the building retained its historic name.

Unfortunately in 1922 the Four Courts was gutted during the Civil War. For a decade, the old courts system (until 1924), then the new Free State courts system, was based in the old viceregal apartments in Dublin Castle. In 1932, a rebuilt and remodelled Four Courts was opened again.

Though one of Dublin's most spectacularly beautiful buildings, the Four Courts was for many decades poorly maintained, with unattractive additional buildings added at the back. The interior was also poorly maintained and decorated. Its exterior still shows the effects of the events of 1922, with its façade containing bullet holes, which deliberately were not removed, to remind people of its complex history.

8. General Post Office
Built in 1818 halfway along O'Connell Street, Dublin (formerly

Sackville street), the General Post Office (GPO) became a symbol of the 1916 Easter Rising. Members of the Irish Volunteers and Irish Citizen Army seized the building on Easter Monday (24 April) and Pádraig Pearse read out the Proclamation of the Irish republic from its steps. The rebels remained inside for almost a week, but shelling from the British eventually forced them out. Inside the building is a sculpture of the legendary Irish warrior Cúchulainn, dedicated to those who died for their part in the Easter Rising.

9. St Patrick's Cathedral

St Patrick's Cathedral in Dublin, formally known as the National Cathedral and Collegiate Church of Saint Patrick is the larger of Dublin's two Church of Ireland cathedrals.

During the episcopate of John Comyn, Archbishop of Dublin, the original, wooden, Celtic St Patrick's church stood on the site, which was outside the walls of Dublin, c. 1911, and was raised to the status of cathedral. The present building, the largest church in Ireland, was built between 1200 and 1270, though a major rebuilding in the 1870s, necessitated by the belief that the cathedral was in imminent danger of collapse, means that much of the current building and decoration dates from the Victorian era.

10. Christchurch Cathedral

Christchurch Cathedral (Cathedral of the Most Holy Trinity) in Dublin is the older of the city's two medieval cathedrals, having been founded by St Laurence O'Toole. It has been the seat of the archbishop of Dublin (initially Roman Catholic, then Church of Ireland) since medieval times.

The cathedral was built by the Vikings at their original settlement at Wood Quay, along the River Liffey quayside. The cathedral was the location of the coronation of Lambert Simnel as 'King Edward VI', a boy pretender who sought unsuccessfully to depose Henry VII of England.

The cathedral was extensively removated in Victorian times. While the renovation preserved the seriously decayed structure from collapse, it remains difficult as a result to tell which parts of the interior are genuinely medieval and which parts are Victorian pastiche.

The cathedral is famously purported to contain the tomb of Strongbow, a medieval Welsh peer and warlord who came to Ireland at the request of King Diarmuid MacMorrough and whose arrival marked the beginning of English involvement in Ireland.

11. The Royal Hospital

The Royal Hospital Kilmainham in Dublin is the finest seventeenth-century building in Ireland. It was built in 1684 by James Butler, Duke of Ormond and Lord Lieutenant of Ireland to King Charles II, as a home for retired soldiers and continued in that use for over 250 years. The style is based on Les Invalides in Paris, with a formal façade and a large, elegant courtyard. The Royal Hospital was restored by the Irish government in 1984 (its three-hundredth anniversary) and opened as the Irish Museum of Modern Art (IMMA).

12. Kilmainham Jail

Kilmainham Jailor Gaol, in Dublin, has played an important part in Irish history, as many leaders of Irish rebellions were imprisoned and some executed there. The jail has also been used as a set for several films.

Over the 140 years it served as a prison, it held in its cells many of those involved in the campaign for Irish independence. The leaders of the Easter Rising, 1916, were held and executed here. The last prisoner held in Kilmainham was Éamon de Valéra. It was abandoned as a jail in 1924 and, following lengthy restoration, it is now a museum of prison life.

TOURIST INFORMATION

Eighteen Top Attractions in Dublin

1. The General Post Office (GPO)
Built in 1818 on O'Connell Street (formerly Sackville street), the GPO became a symbol of the 1916 Easter Rising. Members of the Irish Volunteers and Irish Citizen Army seized the building on Easter Monday (24 April) and Padraig Pearse read out the Proclamation of the Irish republic from its steps. The rebels remained inside for almost a week, but shelling from the British eventually forced them out. Inside the building is a sculpture of the legendary Irish warrior Cúchulainn, dedicated to those who died for their part in the Easter Rising.

2. Dublin Writers Museum
Dublin Writers Museum is an eighteenth-century restored mansion located at the north end of Parnell Square. The museum celebrates the works of some of Ireland's best writers, including: Behan, Joyce, Shaw, Swift, Wilde and Yeats. It is also home to an impressive collection of paintings, photographs and memorabilia about the various writers.

3. The Hugh Lane Gallery of Modern Art
The Hugh Lane Gallery of Modern Art, so named after the art collector who bequeathed his collection to Dublin, is located at the north end of Parnell Square. Guided tours, recitals, and lectures are offered. It houses one of Ireland's foremost collections of modern and contemporary art and includes works by Manet, Monet, Renoir and Degas.

4. Old Jameson Distillery
Old Jameson Distillery, on Bow Street in Smithfield Village, tells the story of the 'Water of Life'. Guided tours are offered in the original distillery and at the end you get a taste.

5. The National Museum of Ireland

The National Museum of Ireland has centres in four sites: three in Dublin and one in County Mayo.

The Natural History Musuem is the oldest branch and is based in Merrion Square. It houses specimens of wildlife, flora, animals and mammals.

The Archaeology and History Museum is based on Kildare Street and houses artifacts from 2000 BC to the twentieth century. Its exhibits include many archaeological treasures of Celtic and medieval art, such as the Ardagh Chalice and the Tara Brooch.

At Collins Barracks is the Museum of Decorative Arts and History and it includes displays and exhibitions of Ireland's social, economic and military history.

6. Phoenix Park

Phoenix Park is lthe largest enclosed city park in Europe. 'Áras An Uachtaráin', the official residence of the President of Ireland, is located in the park as well as the Dublin Zoological Gardens.

7. Dublin Zoological Gardens

Dublin Zoological Gardens are located at Phoenix Park and it is one of the finest zoos in Europe. It is home to a wide variety of animals, birds and reptiles.

8. Temple Bar

The Temple Bar area is an historical and eclectic area, home to art, theatre, music, pubs, cafés and the highest concentration of restaurants in the city. There is the food market in Meeting House Square (held at the weekends), unique shops, book and music stores. It also plays host to many open-air events.

9. Trinity College

Trinity College is one of the world's oldest centres of learning, dating back to the sixteenth century. The library is home to the world renowned ninth-century Book of Kells, a Latin text of the four gospels, with meticulous artwork. The campanile of 1853 is said to mark the site of the monastery of All Hallow, upon which Trinity College was first built.

10. Grafton Street
Grafton Street is an upscale commercial district, with lots of hip shops, great pubs, restaurants, music and interesting side streets to explore.

11. National Gallery
The National Gallery, located on Merrion Square, houses many important art exhibits and sculptures by Irish and European artists inicluding Jack B. Yeats, Louise le Brocquy, Vermeer, Gainsbourg and Caravaggio.

12. Guinness Brewery and Hop Store
Guinness Brewery and Hop Store provides exhibitions and tells of the Guinness Experience over 250 years of history. You end up in the Gravity Bar, with a pint and a great view of Dublin.

13. Dublin Castle
Dublin Castle was the seat of British rule in Ireland until 1922. Most of the building dates from the eighteenth century, though a castle has stood on the site since the days of King John, the first Lord of Ireland. The Castle served as the seat of British government of Ireland under the Lordship of Ireland (1171-1541), Kingdom of Ireland (1541-1800) and United Kingdom of Great Britain and Ireland (1800-1922). The castle is a tourist attraction and, following major refurbishment, is also used as a conference centre. During Ireland's presidencies of the European Union, including most recently in the first half of 2004, it has been the venue of many meetings of the European Council.

14. James Joyce Museum, Joyce Tower
The James Joyce Tower in Sandycove was one of a series of Martello

towers built to withstand an invasion by Napoleon and now holds a museum devoted to the life and works of James Joyce, who made the tower the setting for the first chapter of his masterpiece, *Ulysses*.

Beautifuly located eight miles south of Dublin on the coast road, this tower is the perfect setting for a museum dedicated to Joyce, a writer of international renown, who remains, worldwide, the writer most associated with Dublin. Joyce's brief stay here inspired the opening of his great novel *Ulysses*. The gun platform with its panoramic view, and the living room inside the tower are still much as he described them in his book. The museum's collection includes letters, photographs, first and rare editions and personal possessions of Joyce, as well as items associated with the Dublin of *Ulysses*. *Ulysses* was set on 16 June 1904.

15. Chester Beatty Library

The museum was voted European Museum of the Year 2002 and Irish Museum of the Year 2000.

Situated in the heart of the city centre, the Chester Beatty Library's exhibitions open a window on the artistic treasures of the great cultures and religions of the world. The library's rich collection of manuscripts, prints, icons, miniature paintings, early printed books and *objets d'art* from countries across the world offers visitors a visual feast. Egyptian papyrus texts, beautifully illuminated copies of the Qur'an, the Bible, European medieval and renaissance manuscripts are among the highlights of the collection.

Turkish and Persian miniatures and striking Buddhist paintings are also on display, as are Chinese dragon robes and Japanese woodblock prints. In its diversity, the collection captures much of the richness of human creative expression from about 2700 BC to the present day.

16. Irish Museum of Modern Art

The Irish Museum of Modern Art (IMMA) is Ireland's leading national institution for the collection and presentation of modern and contemporary art. The museum presents a wide variety of art in a dynamic programme of exhibitions, which regularly includes bodies of work from its own collection and its award-winning Education and Community Department. It also creates more widespread access to art and artists through its National and Artists' Studio programmes.

The museum is housed in the magnificent, seventeenth-century Royal Hospital building, in Kilmainham, whose grounds include a formal garden, meadow and medieval burial grounds.

17. Abbey Theatre

The Abbey Theatre is Ireland's national theatre. It was founded by Nobel Laureate, William Butler Yeats and Lady Augusta Gregory in 1904 and has played a vital and often controversial role in the literary, social and cultural life of Ireland.

Renowned as a writer's theatre, its stage has boasted some of the world's greatest theatrical works from such writers as J.M. Synge and Sean O'Casey through to modern day classics from Brian Friel, Tom Murphy, Frank McGuinness, Hugh Leonard, Tom Mac Intyre and Sebastian Barry.

The Abbey Theatre, along with its smaller studio theatre, The Peacock, continues to nurture new writing as well as presenting international modern classics. As an icon of world theatre, The Abbey Theatre welcomes overseas visitors every year.

18. National Concert Hall

Based in Dublin's city centre, the National Concert Hall is rated by performing artists as one of the finest in Europe.

Since its opening in 1982, the hall has established itself as Ireland's premier centre for the performance of live music. As well as weekly performances by the resident orchestra, the RTÉ National Symphony Orchestra, the National Concert Hall promotes a programme of visiting international soloists and orchestras in addition to concerts of jazz, contemporary and traditional Irish music.

Twenty Top Attractions outside Dublin

1. The Burren

The Burren in County Clare (Irish: *bhoireann*, meaning 'stony place'), is over 500 square miles of karstic limestone. It is in the northwest corner of County Clare. The area is a haven for botanists and ecologists because of the unique flora and rock. The ground surface is a floor of grey rock with long parallel grooves, known as grykes. Rainwater seeps through the porous rocks to the underground caves and lakes that swell with overflow, appearing in full lakes that disappear after the rain. There is an amazing variety of flora with Arctic, Alpine and Mediterranean plants growing in spring and summer. It is possible to walk your way to the discovery of ancient civilisation on a 26-mile, sign-posted 'Burren Way' from Ballyvaghan to Liscannor. There are stone dolmens, ring forts, churches, *crannógs,* monasteries, and holy wells. The Burren has over 60 Stone Age burial monuments and 400 Iron Age ring forts.

2. Cliffs of Moher

The Cliffs of Moher just south of Doolin, in County Clare, are one of the most spectacular sights of The Burren. These majestic cliffs rise more than 700 feet above the wind swept Atlantic Ocean. They stretch five miles along the west coast of Clare from the Hag's Head to just beyond O'Brien's Tower. Composed of shale and sandstone, the cliff's ledges make ideal roosting homes for birds. One of the best views can be enjoyed from O'Brien's Tower, built in the early 1800s. On a clear day you can see as far as the mountains of Kerry, Connemara and the Aran Islands. There are marked paths along the cliffs to explore. Visitors are advised to dress tightly, as it is perpetually windy in the area and weather conditions change rapidly. Caution is also recommended around the edges of the cliffs. A visitor's centre with a café is located near the parking lot.

3. Bunratty Castle and Folk Park

Bunratty Castle and Folk Park is one of the most complete and authentic fifteenth-century medieval castles in Ireland. It has a long and bloody history. The castle is a combination of earlier Norman castles and the later Gaelic Tower Houses. It is furnished with a fine collection of medieval furniture, artwork and ornate carvings. Tours are available during the day. A four-course medieval banquet and entertainment with performers in traditional costume is offered in the evenings.

The Folk Park is a reconstructed nineteenth-century village with a variety of buildings, including a school, thatched cottages, grocery store, craft shop, coffee shop, pub and agricultural machinery on display. The Folk Park is a living museum where animals are tended to and bread is baked. Country style meals are served and entertainment is offered, with story telling, music, dance and story telling.

4. Blarney Castle

Blarney Castle in County Cork was built by Dermot McCarthy, King of Munster in 1446. The castle is located on 1,000 acres of beautiful woodland, and is partially hidden by trees, some up to 1,000 years old. The castle has been witness to the triumph and turmoil of Irish chiefs and enemy armies. By the 1700s the castle no longer functioned as a fortress.

Queen Elizabeth coined the term 'Blarney' when she wrote to Cormac McCarthy, Lord of Blarney. She had wanted the castle for herself. He would stall her requests by responding with letters overflowing with flattery, ovations of devotion and loyalty to the crown, without addressing the issue. Lore has it that when one kisses the Blarney Stone, you acquire the gift of the gab, 'eloquent speech'.

To reach the Blarney Stone, you climb 120 steps to the roof of Blarney Castle. The stone is built into the outer face of a gap in the battlements. One legend says that this stone is part of the 'Stone of Destiny', the Stone of Scone, on which the Scottish monarchs were crowned. The castle is five miles from Cork city and very popular with tourists.

5. Fota Wildlife Park

Fota Wildlife Park is on one of the three islands in Cork Harbour, and features 90 different species of wildlife, where animals roam in their natural habitat. Cheetahs are the only caged animals. The park is the largest breeder of cheetahs in the world. The animals come from five continents. The arboretum has many exotic plants and trees. It is one of the best in Europe. A train around the grounds is used to take visitors on a guided tour.

The complex also includes the Fota Island Golf Course and Fota House, an architecturally unique residence dating from the early 1800s.

6. Kinsale

Kinsale is a quaint fishing and resort town in County Cork, with a picture perfect harbour. There are wonderful narrow streets lined with colourfully painted buildings. It is renowned for its art galleries and gourmet restaurants.

Kinsale is considered the Gourmet Capital of Ireland. There is an abundance of accommodation to choose from, ranging in price and amenities. Kinsale is a very popular tourist attraction, especially during the high season.

There are many sites to enjoy around Kinsale. These include the Harbour, the Courthouse, Desmond Castle, James Fort and Charles Fort. There are also a variety of walking tours on offer. From May to October, there are a variety of festivals and events. Many of the pubs offer traditional Irish music.

7. Galway Irish Crystal Heritage Centre

Galway Irish Crystal Heritage Centre is a short, five-minute drive from the city. In the Hall of Tribes you learn of the merchants, seafarers and artists who made up the original fourteen tribes. You can discover the history of the Claddagh village and the famous claddagh ring, learn the story of glass craft, and watch craftspeople at work. The facility has a restaurant and showroom.

8. Connemara
Connemara is located north of Galway city, at the western tip of the county. Connemara is known for its wild beauty. There are islands, beaches and harbours. It is one of the most unspoiled regions of Ireland. Connemara is a vibrant Irish-speaking area. One is never too far from a view of the Twelve Bens mountain range. There are regattas and water sports. Galway's traditional fishing vessel is known as a hooker. Connemara National Park covers 2000 hectares of mountains, bogs, heaths, and grasslands. Glanmore (meaning large glen), forms the centre of the park. The Visitors Centre has 3-D models and displays. There are megalithic court tombs, some 4,000 years old, to be found in it. Ruined houses and old walls are all that remains of the past.

9. Kylemore Abbey
Kylemore Abbey, completed in 1868, is also in Connemara. It is currently home to the Benedictine Nuns and their international girls' boarding school. There is a restored Gothic church, lake walk and craft shop, with pottery made by the nuns and also a restaurant.

10. Clifden
Clifden founded in 1812 by John D'Arcy, is known as the capital of Connemara and offers beautiful beaches, unique shops and antiques.

11. Roundstone
Roundstone is a fishing village situated in the heart of Connemara. It offers fine beaches and it is the home of 'Roundstone Musical Instruments', which are handmade by Malachy Kearn. The movie *The Matchmaker* (1997) was filmed in this quaint village.

12. Killarney

Killarney (Irish: *Cill Airne*, meaning 'church of the sloes'), dating back to 1604, is an area that now caters to the tourist. There are a multitude of places to shop, stay and enjoy a drink. Killarney is famed for its natural beauty in the mountains, lakes, and landscape.

Killarney National Park encompasses 25,000 acres of land with an oceanic climate of high humidity and mild winters. Some of the finest examples of natural plant life thrive here. This is the oldest national park in Ireland and was established in 1932 when Muckross Estate was donated to the public. The estate consists of Muckross House and G ardens, Muckross Traditional Farms and Muckross Abbey. Muckross House serves as the centre of the park and the Visitor Center is now located in the house.

The lakes of Killarney comprise almost a quarter of the park's area; they are the Upper, Middle (Muckross) and Lower Lakes. The lakes meet at what is known as 'The Meeting of the Waters'.

13. Knock

On 21 August 1879, an apparition of the Blessed Virgin Mary, St Joseph, and St John the Evangelist, all appeared at St John the Baptist parish church in Knock in County Mayo for approximately two hours. A group of townspeople described a bright golden light in which appeared Mary, Joseph and John in prayer. All figures were above ground, with Mary slightly higher. The group of fifteen witnesses ranged in age from six to 70 years old. Soon the news of this miracle spread throughout Ireland. Many miracles have occurred at the shrine since the apparition and today over 1.5 million people a year visit the the National Shrine of Our Lady of Knock to pray, seek solace or request a miracle. Pope John Paul II visited the shrine in August 1979 in celebration of the one-hundredth anniversary. Mother Theresa was also a visitor.

14. Newgrange

Newgrange is the most famous prehistoric monument in Ireland. It was originally built around 3,100 BC and accidentally discovered in the seventeenth century. The site consists of a huge stone and turf mound, approximately 280 feet in diameter and 44 feet high. Large boulders, 8 feet high, form a ring around the monument and at the base are horizontal stones with uniquely carved spiral, concentric circles, triangles, zigzags, and human face designs. On the inside of Newgrange are similar designs. There are guided torchlight tours through a single passage, 82.5 feet in length, that leads to a cruciform chamber. Here one finds side chambers, ornamental stone basins, and prehistoric human bones. The ceiling of the chamber has vaulted, interlocked stone slabs that have kept the chamber dry for 5,000 years. Above the entrance is a slit in the stonework and a roof box. On winter solstice, the sunrays shine through the box to the centre of the tomb for about seventeen minutes. The tomb is then beautifully enveloped with golden light.

15. Clonmacnoise

Clonmacnoise is located at Shannonbridge, on the banks of the River Shannon in County Offaly. It is one of the world's most famous monastic sites. Clonmacnoise began as an isolated monastery founded by St Ciaran in 545 AD. It is an ecclesiastical site, with ruins of a cathedral, eight churches, and three high crosses, one of which is a carved 'Cross of the Scriptures'. There are two round towers: the O'Rourke Round Tower that was hit by lightning in the tenth century; and the McCarthy Tower from the twelfth century, which is still in excellent condition. Also part of the ruins is a castle, two holy wells and ancient cemeteries, in one of which the last high king of Ireland is buried, Rory O'Connor.

16. Rock of Cashel

The Rock of Cashel (County Tipperary) dates back 1,000 years before St Patrick. It was the stronghold of Brian Boru, High King of Ireland in the tenth century. The ruin consists of a large cathedral, ancient round tower and Cormac's Chapel. It is situated on the top of a rocky hill. Bru Boru is the interpretive centre at the foot of the Rock of Cashel. Along with telling the history of the area, the centre incorporates folk theatre, a craft centre, genealogy site and an information centre.

17. Ulster American Folk Park
The Ulster American Folk Park, County Tyrone, is located three miles north of Omagh, in Camphill. The Folk Park is an open-air living history museum and explores Ulster's links to the many famous Americans who trace their ancestry to the North of Ireland. The park is comprised of an indoor gallery with information on the causes and patterns of immigration. Outside are a variety of reconstructed buildings of eighteenth- and nineteenth-century Ireland.

18. County Wicklow
County Wicklow is often referred to as the 'garden of Ireland'. It has some of the most breathtaking scenery in all of Ireland, with spectacular views of mountains, valleys, lakes and coastline. Wicklow is located just south of Dublin and makes for a wonderful day trip or overnight stay.

Glendalough is a sixth-century monastic site that was founded by St Kevin. It is nestled into the heart of the Wicklow Mountains and offers a truly spectacular setting. It has a stone tower that stands 110 feet tall, several churches, a cathedral and many other monastic buildings, ruins and sites. There is a visitors centre and guided tours are available.

Wicklow National Park is an unspoiled natural wonder with nearly 50,000 acres of natural beauty. The drive through the Wicklow Gap from Glendalough to Hollywood is regarded as one of the most beautiful in Ireland.

19. Ring of Kerry

The Ring of Kerry is regarded by tourists as part of the mystical and unspoilt Ireland that has always attracted visitors. It is spectacularly beautiful is beyond question and is a natural centre for outdoor pursuits including golf, watersports, cycling, walking, riding and fishing. The Ring of Kerry has some of the finest beaches in Europe that provide all the facilities for a traditional seaside holiday.

Above all, the Ring of Kerry provides an insight into the ancient heritage of Ireland: its Iron Age forts and stones, old Monasteries and a landscape carved out of rock by the last Ice Age, 10,000 years ago.

20. Waterford Crystal

Waterford Crystal is a trademark brand of crystal glassware produced in Waterford by the company Waterford Wedgwood plc. A crystal business was originally founded in the city in 1793 by George and William Penrose, it produced extremely fine crystal that became world famous. A visit to their visitor centre is a must.

Twenty-two Festivals and Events

March
1. St Patrick's Festival, Dublin

The festival is a five day party offering an exciting programme of free entertainment highlighting some of the best artistry and flair the country has to offer. Over the five days audiences can look forward to music, fireworks, street theatre and dance. There's also a treasure hunt, visual art exhibitions, family fun and, of course, the best and most eagerly anticipated St Patrick's Day Parade in the world.

May
2. Bantry International Mussel Fair, County Cork

The fair features open air concerts, street theatre, marching and pipe bands, food events and fireworks. This event promotes the mussel industry, with the bars around town providing locally grown mussels.

May
3. Fleadh Nua, Ennis, County Clare

This Comhaltas Ceoltoiri Eireann festival attracts thousands of people from all parts of Ireland. It includes musicians, singers, dancers, wrenboys, biddy boys, strawboys, all together in a rich cultural environment. Local Clare music and musicians integral to the event.

4. Wexford Opera Festival

The Wexford Opera Festival has been hailed as one of the world's great parties. The town becomes the centre of the operatic world, presenting three major productions and over 40 other events in a festival programme which has drawn artists and audiences from all over the world.

June

5. Listowel Writers' Week, County Kerry

The Listowel Writers' Week is one of Ireland's leading literary festivals, featuring readings, lectures, seminars and art and drawing workshops. It is popular among both budding and established writers. With a competition to suit everybody aged seven to 97, there is something for everyone in the family, with an extensive children's programme available.

June

6. Bloomsday Festival, Dublin

This festival is a celebration of James Joyce and his literary masterpiece, *Ulysses*. There are readings, re-enactments, music, theatre, street theatre and many unofficial activities which take place throughout the city. Make sure to take the book with you.

July

7. Willie Clancy Summer School, Miltown Malbay, County Clare

This summer school has been taking place for many years and attracts thousands of musicians and music lovers. There are classes for up to a 1,000 students of all ages in the mornings, afternoon lectures and evening workshops. There are lecturers participating from Ireland and overseas. Events at the summer school include lectures, recitals, *céili*, piping, whistle and flute classes, accordion, concertina and fiddle classes, dancing classes and singing classes. There are lectures and workshops on a wide variety of subjects.

July

8. Galway Arts Festival

The Galway Arts Festival can rightfully claim to be one of Europe's biggest and most exciting cultural events. This unique event is a truly international celebration of the performing and visual arts -

but with a distinctive west of Ireland flavour. It is founded on a consistent policy of presenting the best in national and international theatre, music, street spectacle films and exhibitions.

Late July / early August
9. Galway Races
The Galway Races follow on the heels of the Galway Arts Festival. It is an enormously fun week with first class horseracing. It draws people from all over the island. There are restaurants, bars, funfairs and banking facilities available at the races. Ladies Day is a fashion spectacle and fun for the whole family. There is a regular bus service from Eyre Square, and a variety of taxi services to the racecourse on race days.

August
10. Dublin Horse Show – Royal Dublin Society (RDS)
This horse show is one of the world's top equestrian events, attracting the top national and international showjumpers. National competitions are an important part of the show, with over 1,500 horses.

August
11. Kilkenny Arts Festival
The festival is presented against the stunning backdrop of Ireland's medieval capital, with its narrow walkways and authentic shop fronts. During the festival every corner and crevice pulses with artistic activity and it presents a fabulous opportunity to see the city at its most attractive and vibrant.

August
12. Puck Fair, Killorglin, County Kerry
Puck Fair is an ancient annual festival. It has developed into an entertaining family festival with fifteen hours of free entertainment daily. The main events include the horse fair, the busking competi-

tion, the parade and coronation of a wild goat as King Puck, open air concerts, fireworks display, children's competitions, street entertainment and Irish dancing displays.

August
13. Rose of Tralee International Festival, County Kerry
The Rose of Tralee Festival is an opportunity for young women around the world, of Irish ancestry, to compete in a variety of categories, which culminates at the festival. The festival is a celebration of the art of being Irish, with family entertainment and a host of activities.

August
14. *Fleadh Cheoil na hEireann*, Clonmel, County Tipperary
At *Fleadh* weekend, men and women flock to the chosen town where for three days, they do little but play, talk, sing and dance or listen to traditional Irish music. This is a unique experience. This premier traditional music event attracts over 220,000 visitors and 10,000 performers each year. These include 4,000 competitors in the 150 or so traditional competitions.

August
15. Tralee Races, Ballybeggan Park, County Kerry
The Tralee August meeting is the centre-piece of the International Rose of Tralee Festival. Racing takes place for six days, it has developed into a great day out for the entire family.

August
16. Oul' Lammas Fair, Ballycastle, County Antrim
Ireland's oldest traditional market fair, dating back to the seventeenth century. In days of old, flowers and fruit were offerings made at holy wells. This was done to mark the end of summer and the beginning of the harvest. This fair is always held on the last Monday

and Tuesday in August. Today thousands of visitors enjoy the fair, with livestock sales, horse trading, street entertainment, competitions and market stalls selling a multitude of items and the fair's traditional 'Dulse and Yellowman', a mixture of edible purple seaweed and toffee. Traditional Irish music and dance takes place in the pubs and on the streets.

September
17. Galway International Oyster Festival, the Claddagh
The Galway International Oyster Festival is the home of the Guinness world oyster Championship and has been voted one of the twelve greatest shows on earth. It comprises of a weekend of non-stop entertainment that features national and international top class artists, cabaret and dancing.

September
18. Dublin Theatre Festival
The Dublin Theatre Festial was founded in 1957, and has since produced a two-week season of theatre each autumn. It takes place at various venues throught the city and usually about 300 artists, well over 50,000 tickets are sold to audiences from Ireland and abroad. In addition to the main programme, the festival co-produces a season of children's theatre with The Ark, presents numerous lectures and workshops and hosts a wide range of parallel events and conferences.

October
19. Corona Cork International Film Festival
The Corona Cork International Film Festival is Ireland's oldest film event. It was established in 1956 to bring to Irish audiences the best of international cinema and to serve as a platform for new Irish film.

October
20. Cork Jazz Festival

The Cork Jazz Festival has been running since 1977 and has played host to some jazz legends like Ella Fitzgerald, Oscar Peterson and Dizzie Gillespie. All forms of jazz are performed from afternoon to late evening in venues throughout the city.

October
21. Belfast Festival at Queens
The Belfast Festival at Queens has been runing since 1962 and is one of the largest arts festivals in Ireland, with participation from world-class artistes covering everything from theatre, dance, classical music, literature, jazz, comedy, visual art, folk music and popular music, attracting over 50,000 visitors.

October
22. Dublin City Marathon
2007 is the twenty-eighth year of the Dublin City Marathon so it is one of the oldest runs around. It takes place through the historic Georgian streets of Dublin.

Fifteen Facts about Guinness

1. **Guinness** Brewery was established in 1756.

2. **Guinness** is now owned by Diageo.

3. **Guiness'** annual production is approximately 100 million litres.

4. **Guinness** stout is made from four natural ingredients: water, barley, hops and yeast.
   The barley is roasted to give Guinness its dark colour and characteristic taste.

5. Despite the 'meal in a glass' or 'liquid bread' reputation **Guinness** has among some non-Guinness drinkers, Guinness only contains 198 calories (838 kilojoules) per imperial pint (1460 kJ/l), less than an equal-sized serving of skimmed milk or orange juice.

6. Draught **Guinness** and its canned namesake contain nitrogen (N2) as well as carbon dioxide (CO2). Unlike carbon dioxide, nitrogen does not dissolve in water, which allows the beer to be put under high pressure without making it fizzy. The high pressure is required to force the draught beer through fine holes in a plate in the tap, which causes the characteristic 'surge' (the widget in cans and bottles achieves the same effect).

7. Draught **Guinness** is considered at its best flavour when served cool, although not necessarily cold. Many consider the ideal serving temperature of Guinness to be as high as 13°C (55°F), although this is often disputed. Others consider the desired temperature for serving Guinness is between 6°C and 8°C, which is much warmer than

many other beers (usually between 3°C and 5°C).

8. **Guinness** should be poured slowly at a 45° angle; about three-quarters is poured and left to settle before the rest is added. The tap handle should be pushed forward, rather than pulled, when the beer is topped off. This creates the characteristic creamy head that lasts until the last sip.

9. Advertising campaigns have stated that 'it takes 119.5 seconds to pour the perfect pint' of Guinness. The perfect pint should have a head just proud of the rim of the glass and no overspill.

10. Another myth is that **Guinness** is brewed using water from the River Liffey, which flows through Dublin, close to St James' Gate. It actually comes from the Wicklow Mountains; specifically, Lady's Well.

11. A long-time subject of bar conversations has been the observation that gas bubbles travel downwards in a pint glass of **Guinness**. The effect is attributed to drag; bubbles which touch the walls of a glass are slowed in their upwards travel. Bubbles in the centre of the glass are, however, free to rise to the surface, and form a rising column of bubbles. The rising bubbles create a current by the entrainment of the surrounding fluid. As beer rises in the centre, the beer near the outside of the glass falls. This downward flow pushes the bubbles near the glass towards the bottom. Although the effect occurs in any liquid, it is particularly noticeable in dark nitrogen stout, as the drink combines dark-coloured liquid and light-coloured bubbles.

12. Nigeria is the third largest and fastest-growing **Guinness** market in the world. However, as the cultivation of barley is restricted in Nigeria, the local version is made primarily from sorghum.

13. **Guinness** uses the Brian Boru, or Trinity College Harp, as their trademark. This c. fourteenth-century harp which is still visible at Trinity College, Dublin has been used as a symbol of Ireland since the reign of Henry VIII in the sixteenth century.

14. **Guinness** fans can visit the Guinness Storehouse in Dublin, which has been described as Disneyland for the beer (or, perhaps, more accurately, stout) lover. Located on the site of the St James' Gate brewery, the Storehouse is an interactive, multimedia experience, taking you through all things Guinness.

15. The grandson of the original Arthur **Guinness**, Sir Benjamin Guinness, was lord mayor of Dublin in 1851.

Eleven interesting Facts about Irish Dancing

1. The **dancing** tradition probably grew in tandem with Ireland's rich tradition in music. The very first roots were in Pre-Christian Ireland, but Irish dance was also heavily influenced by dance forms on the continent, especially the quadrille dances and ballet. Travelling dancing masters taught all over Ireland.

2. The Catholic Church and English authorities both frowned on **dancing**, the former as immoral and the latter as subversive, but the tradition never truly disappeared.

3. Many folk tales exist to explain the practice of keeping the arms stiff at one's side while **dancing**, a practice which is nearly unique in the world of dance. One folk tale originated when the practice of Irish culture, including dance, was forbidden in Ireland under British rule. When people wanted to dance, they would just move their feet, and if anyone happened to look in the window, they would see only the motionless upper body and think nothing of it.

Another explanation relates to the stage. In order to get a hard surface to dance on, people would often unhinge doors and lay them on the ground. Since this was clearly a very small stage, there was no room for the movement of the arms.

Yet another explanation has to do with venue. Irish dance was usually performed in pubs or in small barns where, because of the restricted space, moving the arms could be hazardous to both the dancer and the audience.

But perhaps the most likely explanation is a practical one. The solo dances are characterised by quick, intricate movements of the feet. Movement of the upper body would only distract from the precise movements, and hence is kept to a minimum.

4. Three types of shoes are worn in competitive step **dancing**: hard shoes and two kinds of soft shoe. The hard shoe ('heavy shoe', 'jig shoe') is often mistaken for a tap shoe, but the taps on the sole of the shoe are made of wood, fibreglass, or resin, rather than of metal. The first hard shoes did have metal taps.

5. It was common practice in the seventeenth and eighteenth centuries to hammer nails into the soles of a **dancing** shoe in order to increase the life of the shoe. Dancers used the sounds created by the nails to create the rhythms that characterise hard-shoe dancing. Later, the soles were changed into resin or fibreglass to reduce the weight.

6. Each **dancing** shoe has eight striking surfaces: the toe, bottom and sides of the front tap and the back, bottom, and sides of the back tap (the heel).

7. The actual steps in Irish step **dance** are usually unique to each school. Steps are developed by Irish dance teachers for students of their school. Each dance is built out of the same basic elements, or steps, but the dance itself is unique, and new dances are being choreographed all the time. For this reason, choreography can be closely guarded and videotaping of competitions is forbidden under the rules of the World Irish Dance Commission.

8. The group **dances**, or the *céilí*, vary widely throughout Ireland and the rest of the world. There are a group of *céilí* dances which have been standardised, called the 'book' dances. A *céilí* may be performed with as few as two people and as many as sixteen. The *céilí* dances are also called party dances; they are meant more for socialising and fun than as an athletic and competitive form. But the *céilí*s are still fast paced and complicated.

9. An organised step **dance** competition is referred to as a *feis*, plural *feiseanna*. The word *feis* means 'festival' in Irish and, strictly speaking, is also composed of competitions in music and crafts. *Feile* is a more correct term for the dance competition but the terms may be used interchangeably. Many annual dancing *feiseanna* are becoming fully-fledged festivals, by adding competitions in music, art, baking, etc.

10. Rules for *feiseanna* are set by the World Irish Dance Commission (*An Coimisiún le Rincí Gaelacha*). Dancers are judged by adjudicators certified by *An Coimisiún*. This certification is known as the ADCRG (*Ard Diploma Choimisiuin Le Rinci Gaelacha* or Highest Diploma in Gaelic Dancing. It is awarded to those who have passed the exams set by the *An Coimisiún*. Local organisations may add additional rules to the basic rule set.

11. Annual 'national' **dancing** championship competitions are held in Ireland (known as the 'All-Ireland' competition), North America (including Canada and the United States), Australia and Europe.

Annual World Championship competitions have been held in the Republic of Ireland, Northern Ireland and Scotland. The World Championship competitions (called the *Oireachtas Rince na Cruinne*) are held around Easter each year.

Seventeen Irish Gardens

1. Altamont Gardens, Tullow, County Carlow

Known as the most romantic garden in Ireland, Altamont is an enchanting blend of formal and informal gardens located on a 100-acre estate. Whilst still little known, it ranks in the top ten of Irish gardens and is often referred to as 'the jewel in Ireland's gardening'. A fascinating walk through the Arboretum, Bog Garden and Ice Age Glen, with its canopy of ancient oaks, leads to the majestic River Slaney. Along the river walk, you may see salmon and trout rising, perhaps even an otter, and throughout the garden, an abundance of birds and butterflies. On your return via the hill walk, there are wonderful views of the Blackstairs and Wicklow Mountains, and Mount Leinster.

2. Anne's Grove, Castletownroche, County Cork

A creeper-covered eighteenth-century house and walled garden form part of this wild garden, which began in the 1700s and was mentioned then in Arthur Young's tour of Ireland. The later garden was the creation of R.A. Grove Annsley, grandfather of the present owner. Three areas of contrast comprise the 30 acres; the walled garden, the glen and the riverside garden. The Robinsonian garden in the glen contains some of the earliest Kingdon Ward rhododendron introductions to Ireland, many of them grown from seed.

Rhododendrons and azaleas cover the area much as they would in a Himalayan setting, perfuming the air and growing amid tall trees. The river garden leans more to the tropical and contains such specimens as *Primula florindae* grow to tremendous size. Rustic bridges cross the river, constructed by pre-World War Two British soldiers stationed at Fermoy barracks. A central path flanked by herbaceous borders comprises a key feature of the walled garden. Here, scarlet-flowered *Tropaeolum* (creeping nasturtium) climbs through yew hedges. A summer house is complemented by a pond surrounded by water-loving plants.

3. Birr Castle Demesne, County Offaly
These gardens are over 100 acres in extent. There are formal gardens, designed around a seventeenth-century plan, and the tallest box hedges in the world. Birr has one of the world's greatest collections of trees and shrubs and is particularly strong in species of Chinese and Himalayan origin.

4. Creagh Gardens, Skibbereen, County Cork
A garden for the romantic; quiet and peaceful, of woodlands, sloping down to a sea estuary, with interesting and varied wild life. There are over 8 hectares of informal gardens based on a number of woodland glades and a serpentine mill pond, amid a scene reminiscent of the background of a Douanier Rousseau painting by which it was inspired. Many rare plants are lovingly maintained as the life work of Gwendoline and Peter Harold-Barry, who purchased Creagh in 1945. The large, walled garden dating from the Regency period has been restored as a traditional and organic kitchen garden.

5. Dereen Gardens, Killarney, County Kerry
The luxuriant woodlands of Dereen Gardens give glimpses of the sea and the surrounding wild, majestic country. Mossy paths and lichen-encrusted rocks, tunnels in deep shade through the rhododendrons, towering eucalyptus and groves of bamboo all contribute to the making of this fine, sub-tropical garden.

Dereen is also famous for its tree ferns, *Dicksonia antarctica*, azaleas, rhododendrons (some rising as high as 60 feet), and the Maddenii and Sinograndes.

6. Fernhill Gardens, Sandyford, County Dublin

The giant Wellingtonian redwoods in the broadwalk at Fernhill form a cathedral-like aisle. Beyond them stretches the Victorian laurel lawn and a magnificent springtime blaze of colour from rhododendrons and azaleas. Many of these specimens were introduced from the Himalayas by the William Hooker (a famous English botanist) expedition. At Fernhill you can see an increasingly rare example of an enclosed Victorian vegetable and flower garden. Many of the trees in the estate date back 200 years and the work of Judge William Darley, who collected plants from all over the world, has been continued by the Walker family.

7. Fota Arboretum, Carrigtwohill, County Cork

Fota Arboretum is primarily a collection of trees and shrubs. The tradition of planting exotic trees and shrubs, started by James Hugh Smith-Barry, still continues, extending the history of tree planting in the gardens over 150 years.

Fota is also noteworthy for the large number of rare plants that flourish there, such as tree ferns, *Pinus montezumae* and dwarf fan palm (*Chamaerops humilis*). Several factors distinguish Fota from other large gardens in Ireland and the most significant of these factors are: the age of the gardens, the availability of good historical records due, in part, to the fact that the gardens were managed with little interruption since their establishment, the wide spacing of the plants and the number of large trees that have reached their full stature.

8. Glenveagh Castle Gardens, Glenveagh National Park, Churchill, County Donegal

The gardens, created by Henry McIlhenny from Philadelphia, are made up of wood gardens and pleasure grounds, Italian and Belgian gardens, terraces with antique sculpture and terracotta pots, and all these different themes have been skilfully interwoven against the wild Donegal landscape. This, one of the most celebrated Irish gardens, contains an important collection of trees and shrubs, some rare.

The National Park covers 40,000 acres and takes in a beautiful valley occupied by Lough Veagh and the Poisoned Glen, a marshy valley enclosed by dramatic cliffs. The park also protects the largest herd of red deer in the country. Glenveagh Castle stands on the southern shores of Lough Veagh and is reached only by a healthy hike or by the park-supplied shuttle bus.

9. Heywood Garden, Ballinakill, County Laois

Considered the finest Lutyens-designed garden in Ireland, Heywood's historical interest combines a romantic eighteenth-century garden with a spectacular hillside setting and gothic features. Terraces and elliptical beds encircle a pool and fountain, the whole of which is sheltered by a circular, pierced wall. The garden is divided into four parts, a sunken garden linked with a formal lawn, an alley of pleached limes backed by stone walls decorated with niches and classical urns, a series of herb gardens and a terraced pergola that overlooks the largest of the ornamental lakes. In 1941, the Silesian Order purchased the house and estate; it is now in the hands of the Office of Public Works which is handling the restoration of the garden.

10. Hotel Dunloe Castle Gardens, Beaufort, Killarney, County Kerry

The Dunloe Castle Gardens contain one of the most fascinating and important collections of trees and shrubs in Ireland. In fact, there are trees gowing here that are rarely, if at all found, in Britain or indeed Europe. The most ancient trees are the two yews known as Adam and Eve in the walled garden which are between 300 and 350 years old. Most others, however, have been planted this century, the majority during the 1920s by Howard Harrington, an American who lived in the old house at Dunloe Castle for almost twenty years.

11. Ilnacullin, Glengarriff, County Cork

Perhaps the most magical setting a garden could have is to be on an island, bathed in the warm waters of the gulf stream, surrounded by scenery of great natural beauty; such is the situation of Ilnacullin. The Italian garden designed by Harold Peto, the Martello tower, the clock tower, a Grecian temple overlooking the sea, flights of steps and magnificent pedimented gateways: all these superb architectural features are brilliantly integrated with a plant collection of worldwide repute. The island is reached by licensed boats from Glengarriff.

12. Kilruddery, Bray, County Wicklow

Laid out in the seventeenth century by a French gardener called Bonet who worked at Versailles, Kilruddery is regarded as one of the finest French classical gardens in Ireland. Among its important features are romantic parterres, a pair of long canals in a setting of grass and trees, a high beech hedge encircling a pool and fountains, a good collection of statues, many of which are Victorian, and a very fine mid nineteenth-century conservatory. The sylvan theatre, a small enclosure surrounded by a bay hedge, is the only known example of its kind in Ireland.

13. Lodge Park Walled Garden, Straffan, County Kildare

The restoration of this eighteenth-century walled garden adjoining Lodge Park, a Palladian house of 1773, started in 1980. The old, brick-faced walls look much as they did when it was built, and here fruit, flowers and vegetables are grown for the house. The garden is divided into different sections but the design is dictated by the long, box-edged axis path, with regularly spaced clipped yew trees. It comprises a south-facing shrub border, herbaceous border, different coloured gardens, vegetable area, decorative salad garden with a walkway of sweet peas, and a rosarie which is at its best in June and July. The garden is beside the Steam Museum.

14. National Botanic Gardens, Glasnevin, Dublin

The National Botanic Gardens, Glasne vin, founded by the Royal Dublin Society in 1795, is now administered by the Department of Arts, Culture and the Gaeltacht. The Gardens, 19.5 hectares on the south bank of the Tolka River, contain many attractive features including: an arboretum, rock garden and burren areas, large pond, extensive herbaceous borders, student garden and annual display of decorative plants including a rare example of Victorian carpet bedding. Glasshouses include: the beautifully restored curvilinear range designed and built by Richard Turner between 1843 and 1869, a large palm house, new alpine house and the complex for ferns, tropical water plants and succulents.

15. National Garden Exhibition Centre, Kilquade, County Wicklow

There are unique displays of sixteen permanent gardens ranging from town-house gardens to rose gardens to large water and woodland gardens. These gardens were designed and built by some of Ireland's leading designers and landscapers. The exhibition offers inspiriation to both the new and experienced gardener.

16. Mount Usher Gardens, Ashford, County Wicklow

These lovely gardens, laid out along the banks of the Vartry River, represent the Robinsonian style, that of informality and natural design. Trees and shrubs introduced from many parts of the world are planted in harmony with woodland and shade-loving plants. The Gardens cover 20 acres and contain approximately 5,000 different species of plants and trees including many rhododendrons, magnolias, camellias, eucryphia and shrubs.

17. Powerscourt, Enniskerry, Bray, County Wicklow

Powerscourt is one of the world's great gardens situated 20km south of Dublin in the foothills of the Wicklow Mountains. The gardens were begun by Richard Wingfield, Viscount Powerscourt, in the 1740s. The word garden belies the magnitude of this creation which stretches out over 20 hectares. It is a sublime blend of formal gardens, sweeping terraces, statuary and ornamental lakes with secret hollows, rambling walks, walled gardens and over 200 variations of trees and shrubs. The eighteenth-century house, which was gutted by fire in 1974, has an innovative new use, incorporating a terrace restaurant overlooking the garden, speciality shops and an exhibition on the history of the estate.

FIFTEEN BASIC IRISH WORDS AND PHRASES

1. *Dia Dhuit*   Hello (literally, God to you)

2. *Dia's Muire dhuit*   Reply (literally, God and Mary to you)

3. *Cén t-ainm atá ort?*   What is your name? (male)

4. *Cad is ainm duit*   What is your name? (female)

5. *Éamonn atá orm.*   My name is Éamonn.

6. *Síle is ainm dom.*   My name is Síle.

7. *Conas tá tú?*   How are you?

8. *Tá mé go maith.*   I am good.

9. *Tá mé go hiontach.*   I am wonderful.

10. *Tá mé go dona.*   I am (feeling) bad.

11. *Cá bhuil tú i do chónaí?* Where do you live?

12. *Tá mé i mo chónaí i gCorcaigh.* I live in Cork.

13. *Slán agat.*   Goodbye (said by person leaving).

14. *Slán leat.*   Goodbye (said by person staying).

15. *Slán abhaile.*   Have a safe trip home.

WORDS

Ten Quotes about the Irish

1. In Ireland the inevitable never happens and the unexpected constantly occurs. *Sir John Pentland Mahaffy*

2. St Patrick's Day is an enchanted time – a day to begin transforming winter's dreams into summer's magic. *Adrienne Cook*

3. This is one race of people for whom psychoanalysis is of no use whatsoever. *Sigmund Freud*

4. Ireland is rich in literature that understands a soul's yearnings, and dancing that understands a happy heart. *Margaret Jackson*

5. The problem with Ireland is that it's a country full of genius, but with absolutely no talent. *Hugh Leonard*

6. Only Irish coffee provides in a single glass all four essential food groups: alcohol, caffeine, sugar and fat. *Alex Levine*

7. I'm troubled, I'm dissatisfied. I'm Irish.
Marianne Moore, Spenser's Ireland

8. There is no language like the Irish for soothing and quieting.
John Millington Synge

9. Every St Patrick's Day every Irishman goes out to find another Irishman to make a speech to. *Shane Leslie*

10. In order to find his equal, an Irishman is forced to talk to God.
Stephen Braveheart

SEVEN REVOLUTIONARY QUOTES

1. It is not those who can inflict the most but those that can suffer the most who will conquer.   *Terence MacSwiney*

2. You cannot put a rope around the neck of an idea; you cannot put an idea up against the barrack-square wall and riddle it with bullets; you cannot confine it in the strongest prison cell your slaves could ever build.   *Sean O'Casey*

3. To gain that which is worth having, it may be necessary to lose everything else.   *Bernadette Devlin McAliskey*

4. Let no man write my epitaph; for as no man who knows my motives dare now vindicate them, let not prejudice or ignorance asperse them. Let them rest in obscurity and peace! Let my memory be left in oblivion, my tomb remain uninscribed, until other times and other men can do justice to my character.   *Robert Emmet*

5. Irishness is not primarily a question of birth or blood or language; it is the condition of being involved in the Irish situation, and usually of being mauled by it.   *Conor Cruise O'Brien*

6. Everyone, Republican or otherwise, has their own particular part to play. No part is too great or too small, no one is too old or too young to do something.   *Bobby Sands*

7. You cannot conquer Ireland. You cannot extinguish the Irish passion for freedom. If our deed has not been sufficient to win freedom, then our children will win it by a better deed.   *Padraig Pearse*

Twelve Quotes by Oscar Wilde

Oscar Wilde (1854–1900), Irish poet and dramatist, penned witty, elegant dramas such as *The Importance of Being Earnest* and *Lady Windermere's Fan* and one novel, *The Picture of Dorian Gray*.

1. Bigamy is having one wife too many. Monogamy is the same.

2. I love acting. It is so much more real than life.

3. I sometimes think that God, in creating man, somewhat overestimated his ability.

4. Imagination is a quality given a man to compensate him for what he is not, and a sense of humour was provided to console him for what he is.

5. My experience is that as soon as people are old enough to know better, they don't know anything at all.

6. It is only the modern that ever becomes old-fashioned.

7. To lose one parent may be regarded as a misfortune ... to lose both seems like carelessness.

8. Men always want to be a woman's first love. Women have a more subtle instinct: what they like is to be a man's last romance.

9. Never speak disrespectfully of society. Only people who can't get into it do that.

10. Rich bachelors should be heavily taxed. It is not fair that some men should be happier than others.

11. Work is the curse of the drinking classes.

12. Moderation is a fatal thing – nothing succeeds like excess.

Eighteen Literary Quotes

Samuel Beckett (1906–1989)

Irish playwright, novelist. He is best known for his play *Waiting for Godot*, 1952; and he won the Noble Prize Literature in 1969

1. Ever tried. Ever failed. No matter. Try Again. Fail again. Fail better.
2. We are all born mad. Some remain so.
3. I have my faults, but changing my tune is not one of them.
4. Nothing is funnier than unhappiness, I grant you that. Yes, yes, it's the most comical thing in the world.

Brendan Behan (1923–1964)

Irish dramatist, author. His humorous, vibrant books captured the spirit of Irish nationalism. He is best known for his autobiographical *Borstal Boy*, 1958.

5. New York is my Lourdes, where I go for spiritual refreshment ... a place where you're least likely to be bitten by a wild goat.
6. It's not that the Irish are cynical. It's rather that they have a wonderful lack of respect for everything and everybody.
7. I have a total irreverence for anything connected with society except that which makes the roads safer, the beer stronger, the food cheaper, and the old men and old women warmer in the winter and happier in the summer.
8. Critics are like eunuchs in a harem; they know how it's done, they've seen it done every day, but they're unable to do it themselves.
9. I was court-martialled in my absence, and sentenced to death in my absence, so I said they could shoot me in my absence.

James Joyce (1882–1941)

Irish novelist, poet, playwright. Subtle, frank portraits of human nature were his forte. He is best known for *A Portrait of the Artist As a Young Man*, 1914; and *Ulysses*, 1922.

10. A man of genius makes no mistakes. His errors are volitional and are the portals of discovery.

11. The artist, like the God of the creation, remains within or behind or beyond or above his handiwork, invisible, refined out of existence, indifferent, paring his fingernails.

12. No pen, no ink, no table, no room, no time, no quiet, no inclination.

13. Whatever else is unsure in this stinking dunghill of a world a mother's love is not.

Sean O'Casey (1880-1964)

Irish playwright, renowned for realistic dramas of the Dublin slums in war and revolution, in which tragedy and comedy are juxtaposed in a new way. He is best known for his plays, *The Shadow of a Gunman, Juno and the Paycock* and *The Plough and the Stars*.

14. The hallway of every man's life is paced with pictures; pictures gay and pictures gloomy, all useful, for if we be wise, we can learn from them a richer and braver way to live.

15. Laughter is wine for the soul – laugh soft, or loud and deep, tinged through with seriousness. Comedy and tragedy step through life together, arm in arm ... Once we can laugh, we can live.

16. Wealth often takes away chances from men as well as poverty. There is none to tell the rich to go on striving, for a rich man makes the law that hallows and hollows his own life.

William Butler Yeats (1865-1939)

Irish poet, dramatist. He was the leader of the Irish literary renaissance. He won the Nobel Prize for Literature in 1923 for 'inspired poetry' and founded the Abbey Theatre, Dublin.

17. The problem with some people is that when they aren't drunk, they're sober.

18. Do not wait to strike till the iron is hot; but make it hot by striking.

EIGHTEEN GEORGE BERNARD SHAW QUOTES
(1856-1950)

Irish playwright, essayist, political activist, lecturer, novelist, philosopher, revolutionary evolutionist, and the most prolific letter writer in literary history.

1. Martyrdom is the only way a man can become famous without ability.

2. Life would be tolerable but for its amusements.

3. Find enough clever things to say, and you're a prime minister; write them down and you're a Shakespeare.

4. I enjoy convalescence. It is the part that makes the illness worthwhile.

5. I never thought much of the courage of a lion tamer. Inside the cage he is at least safe from people.

6. The government who robs Peter to pay Paul can always depend on the support of Paul.

7. If history repeats itself, and the unexpected always happens, how incapable must man be of learning from experience!

8. We have not lost faith, but we have transferred it from God to the medical profession.

9. But a lifetime of happiness! No man alive could bear it: it

would be hell on earth.

10. The things most people want to know about are usually none of their business.

11. Imagination is the beginning of creation. You imagine what you desire; you will what you imagine; and at last you create what you will.

12. If women were as fastidious as men, morally or physically, there would be an end of the race.

13. A life spent making mistakes is not only more honourable , but more useful than a life spent doing nothing.

14. Money is the most important thing in the world. It represents health, strength, honour, generosity and beauty as conspicuously as the want of it represents illness, weakness, disgrace, meanness and ugliness.

15. The people who get on in this world are the people who get up and look for the circumstances they want and, if they can't find them, make them.

16. A pessimist is a man who thinks everybody is as nasty as himself.

17. Better keep yourself clean and bright. You are the window through which you must see the world.

18. When I was a young man I observed that nine out of ten things I did were failures. I didn't want to be a failure, so I did ten times more work.

Twelve Irish Toasts

1. May your glass be ever full.
May the roof over your head be always strong.
And may you be in heaven
half an hour before the devil knows you're dead.

2. Here's to you and yours
And to mine and ours.
And if mine and ours
Ever come across to you and yours,
I hope you and yours will do
As much for mine and ours
As mine and ours have done
For you and yours!

3. Here's a toast to your enemies' enemies!

4. Here's to a long life and a merry one.
A quick death and an easy one.
A pretty girl and an honest one.
A cold beer – and another one!

5. Here's to our wives and girlfriends:
May they never meet!

6. There are four things you must never do: lie, steal, cheat or drink.
But if you must lie, lie in the arms of the one you love.
If you must steal, steal away from bad company.
If you must cheat, cheat death.
And if you must drink, drink in the moments that take your breath away.

7. May your grass always be green
May your skies forever blue
May God Bless the Irish
And may God bless you!

8. Always remember to forget the troubles that passed away.
But never forget the blessings that come each day.

9. May you both live as long as you want.
And never want as long as you live.

10. May your troubles be less and your blessings be more.
And nothing but happiness come through your door.

11. May your right hand always be stretched out in friendship, and
never in want.

12. May God be with you and bless you,
May you see your children's children,
May you be poor in misfortune, rich in blessings.
May you know nothing but happiness from this day forward.

Eleven Quotes about Ireland and its People

1. Love is never defeated and, I could add, the history of Ireland proves it.
Pope John Paul II to the people of Galway, September 1979

2. A nation reveals itself not only by the men it produces but also by the men it honours, the men it remembers.   *John F. Kennedy*

3. Too young to die. Too drunk to live.
Renee McCall of the Daily Express *on the passing of Brendan Behan in 1964 at the age of 41*

4. Real vision is the ability to see the invisible.   *Jonathan Swift*

5. When anyone asks me about the Irish character, I say look at the trees. Maimed, stark and misshapen, but ferociously tenacious.
Edna O'Brien

6. I want peace and quiet. I want it so much I'd die for it.
Michael Collins

7. The contest on our side is not one of rivalry or vengeance, but of endurance. It is not those who can inflict the most, but those who can suffer the most who will conquer.
Inaugural speech of Cork mayor Terence MacSwiney who died on hunger strike, 25 October,1920

8. When I look back on my childhood I wonder how I managed to survive at all. It was, of course, a miserable childhood: the happy childhood is hardly worth your while. Worse than the ordinary miserable childhood is the miserable Irish childhood, and worse yet is

the miserable Irish Catholic childhood.

Frank McCourt – Angela's Ashes

9. We are ready to die and shall die cheerfully and proudly ... You must not grieve for all of this. We have preserved Ireland's honour and our own. Our deeds of last week are the most splendid in Ireland's history. People will say hard things of us now, but we shall be remembered by posterity and blessed by unborn generations.

Pádraig Pearse, Easter Uprising, 24 April 1916

10. Our greatest glory is not in never falling, but in rising every time we fall. *Oliver Goldsmith*

11. Some men see things as they are and ask why. Others dream things that never were and ask why not. *George Bernard Shaw*

Eleven slang words

1. Banjaxed or knackered — *Tired / broken*

2. Sound — *Nice / fine*

3. A bowsie — *A trouble maker*

4. The black stuff — *Guinness*

5. Craic — *Fun*

6. A chiseller — *A child*

7. A redneck/culchie/bogger — *Anyone from outside of Dublin*

8. A nixer — *A job done without paying any tax*

9. A cabbage — *A stupid person*

10. A hooley — *A party*

11. Langers/paralytic/stocious — *Drunk*

Seventeen Proverbs

1. You've got to do your own growing, no matter how tall your grandfather was.

2. When the apple is ripe, it will fall.

3. There is not a tree in heaven higher than the tree of patience.

4. Least said soonest mended.

5. You'll never plow a field by turning it over in your mind.

6. The thief is no danger to the beggar.

7. The full stomach does not understand the empty one.

8. As the old cock crows the young cock learns.

9. You are better off alone than in bad company.

10. It's for her own good that the cat purrs.

11. You never miss the water till the well has run dry.

12. Those who get the name of rising early may lie all day.

13. When the fruit is scarcest, its taste is sweetest.

14. Good as drink is, it ends in thirst.

15. If you do not sow in the spring you will not reap in the autumn.

16. There is no need like the lack of a friend.

17. Thirst is the end of drinking and sorrow is the end of drunkenness.

Eight Irish Blessings

1. May the road rise to meet you. May the wind be always at your back. May the sun shine warm upon your face, the rains fall soft upon the fields. And, until we meet again, may God hold you in the palm of his hand.

2. May you be poor in misfortune, rich in blessings. Slow to make enemies, quick to make friends. But rich or poor, quick or slow, may you know nothing but happiness from this day foward.

3. Always remember to forget the troubles that passed away. But never forget to remember the blessings that come each day ...

4. May you have warm words on a cold evening, a full moon on a dark night, and the road downhill all the way to your door.

5. May the light of friendship guide your paths together. May the laughter of children grace the halls of your home. May the joy of living for one another trip a smile from your lips, a twinkle from your eye.

6. May your pockets be heavy and your heart be light, may good luck pursue you each morning and night.

7. Friends and relatives, so fond and dear, 'tis our greatest pleasure to have you here. When many years this day has passed, fondest memories will always last. So we drink a cup of Irish mead and ask God's blessing in your hour of need.' The guests respond: 'On this special day, our wish to you, the goodness of the old, the best of the new. God bless you both who drink this mead, may it always fill your every need.'

8. May your blessings outnumber the shamrocks that grow, and may trouble avoid you wherever you go.

1. A Nation Once Again

When boyhood's fire was in my blood
I read of ancient freemen
Of Greece and Rome, who bravely stood
Three hundred men and three men
And then I prayed I yet might see
Our fetters rent in twain
And Ireland long a province, be
A nation once again .

Chorus
A nation once again
A nation once again
And Ireland long a province, be
A nation once again

So from the time through wildest woe
That hope has shone a far light
Nor could love brightest summer glow
Outshine that solemn starlight
It seemed to watch above my head
In forum, field and fane
It's angle voice rang round my bed
A nation once again
Repeat Chorus

So as I grew from boy to man
I bent me to that bidding -
The spirit of each selfish plan
And cruel passions ridding

For thus, I hoped some day to aid –
Oh, can such hope be vain?
When my dear country shall be made
A nation once again
Repeat Chorus

2. The Fields of Athenry

By the lonely prison wall
I heard a young girl calling,
Michael, they are taking you away,
For you stole Trevelyn's corn,
So the young might see the morn,
Now a prison ship lies waiting in the bay.

Chorus
Low, lie the fields of Athenry,
Where once we watched the small free birds fly,
Our love was on the wing,
We had dreams and songs to sing,
It's so lonely round the fields of Athenry.

By a lonely prison wall
I heard a young man calling,
Nothing matters Mary when you're free,
Against the Famine and the Crown,
I rebelled they ran me down,
Now you must raise our child with dignity.
Repeat chorus

By a lonely harbour wall
She watched the last star falling
And that prison ship sailed out against the sky

Sure she'll wait in hope and pray
For her love in Botany Bay,
It's so lonely round the fields of Athenry.
Repeat chorus

3. The Cliffs of Dooneen

You may travel far, far from your own native home,
Far away o'er the mountains, far away o'er the foam,
But of all the fine places that I've ever been,
There is none can compare with the cliffs of Dooneen.

It's a nice place to be on a fine summer's day,
Watching all the wild flowers that ne'er do decay,
Oh, the hare and the pheasant are plain to be seen,
Making homes for their young round the cliffs of Dooneen.

Take a o'er the mountains, fine sights you'll see there,
You'll see the high rocky mountains on the west coast of Clare,
Oh, the towns of Kilkee and Kilrush can be seen,
From the high rocky slopes around the cliffs of Dooneen.

Fare thee well to Dooneen, fare thee well for a while,
And although we are parted by the raging sea wild,
Once again I will wander with my Irish colleen,
Round the high rocky slopes of the cliffs of Dooneen.

4. Danny Boy

Oh, Danny Boy, the pipes, the pipes are calling,
From glen to glen and down the mountain side.
The summer's gone and all the leaves are falling,
It's you, it's you must go and I must bide.

But come ye back, when summer's in the meadow,
and all the valley's hushed and white with snow.
It's I'll be here in sunshine or in shadow,
Oh, Danny Boy, Oh, Danny Boy, I love you so!

But when ye come, and all the flowers are dying
If I be dead, as dead I well may be.
Then come and find the place where I am lying,
And kneel and say an *Ave* there for me.

And I shall hear, though soft your tread above me,
And all my grave will warmer, sweeter be.
And you shall bend, and tell me that you love me,
And I shall sleep in peace until you come to me.

5. **Dirty Old Town**
I met my love, by the gas works wall.
Dreamed a dream, by the old canal.
Kissed my girl by the factory wall,
Dirty old town, dirty old town.

I heard a siren from the dock
Saw a train set the night on fire.
Smelled the spring in the smoky wind
Dirty old town, dirty old town.

Clouds are drifting across the moon
Cats are prowling on their beat
Spring's a girl in the street at night
Dirty old town, dirty old town.

I'm going to make a good sharp axe

Shining steel, tempered in the fire
We'll chop you down like an old oak tree
Dirty old town, dirty old town.

6. Galway Bay

If you ever go across the sea to Ireland
Then maybe at the closing of your day
You will sit and watch the moon rise over Claddagh
And see the sun go down on Galway Bay

Just to hear again the ripple of the trout stream
The women in the meadows making hay
And to sit beside a turf fire in the cabin
And watch the barefoot gosoons at their play.

For the breezes blowing over the seas from Ireland
Are perfumed by the heather as it blows
And the women in the uplands diggin' praties
Speak a language that the strangers do not know.

For the strangers came and tried to teach us their way
They scorn'd us just for being what we are
But they might as well go chasing after moonbeams
Or light a penny candle from a star.

And if there is going to be a life hereafter
And somehow I am sure there's going to be
I will ask my God to let me make my heaven
In that dear land across the Irish sea.

7. The Irish Rover

On the fourth of July, eighteen hundred and six,
We set sail from the sweet cove of Cork,
We were sailing away with a cargo of bricks,
For the grand city hall in New York.
'Twas an elegant craft, she was rigged fore and aft,
And how the wild wind drove her,
She could stand a great blast in her 27 masts,
And we called her the *Irish Rover*.

We had one million bags of the best Sligo rags,
We had two million barrels of stones,
We had 3 million sides of old blind horses' hides,
We had 4 million barrels of bone,
We had 5 million hogs, 6 million dogs,
Seven million barrels of porter,
We had 8 million bales of old nanny goat tails,
In the hold of the *Irish Rover*.

There was Barney McGee from the banks of the Lee,
There was Hogan from County Tyrone,
There was Johnny McGuirk who was scared stiff of work,
And a chap from Westmeath called Malone.
There was Slugger O'Toole who was drunk as a rule,
And fighting Bill Tracey from Dover,
There was Dolan from Clare, just as strong as a bear,
All aboard on the *Irish Rover*.

We had sailed seven years when the measles broke out,
And our ship lost its way in the fog.
Then the whole of the crew was reduced down to two,
Just myself and the captain's old dog.
The ship struck a rock, Lord what a shock,

The boat, it was flipped right over,
Turned nine times around, and the poor old dog was drowned,
I'm the last of the *Irish Rover*.

8. Molly Malone

In Dublin's fair city, where the girls are so pretty
I first set my eyes on sweet Molly Malone,
As she wheeled her wheel barrow, through streets broad and narrow,
Crying cockles and mussels a-live a-live oh

Chorus
A-live, a-live oh, a-live a-live oh,
Crying cockles and mussels a-live a-live oh

She was a fishmonger, and sure 'twas no wonder,
For so were her father and mother before
And they both wheeled their barrows, through streets broad and narrow,
Crying cockles and mussels a-live a -live oh
Repeat chorus

She died of a fever, and no one could save her
And that was the end of sweet Molly Malone
But her ghost wheels her barrow through streets broad and narrow,
Crying cockles and mussels a-live a -live oh
Repeat chorus

9. Raglan Road

On Raglan Road of an autumn day I saw her first and knew
That her dark hair would weave a snare that I might one day rue
I saw the danger and I passed along the enchanted way
And I said let grief be a fallen leaf at the dawning of the day

On Grafton Street in November we tripped lightly along the ledge
Of the deep ravine where can be seen the worth of passion's play
The Queen of Hearts still making tarts and I not making hay
Oh I loved too much and by such by such is happiness thrown away

I gave her gifts of the mind I gave her the secret signs
That's known to the artists who have known the true gods of sound and stone
And words and tint without stint, I gave her poems to say
With her own game there and her own dark hair, like clouds over fields of May.
On a quiet street where old ghosts meet I see her walking now
Away from me so hurriedly my reason must allow
That I had loved not as I should a creature made of clay
When the angel woos the clay he'll lose his wings at dawn of day

10. Rare Ould Times

Raised on songs and stories, heroes of renown,
The passing tales and glories, that once was Dublin town,
The hallowed halls and houses, the haunting children's cries,
That once was part of Dublin, in the Rare Ould Times.

Chorus
Ring a Ring a rosie,
As the lights decline,
I remember Dublin city,
In the rare ould times.

I courted Peggy Diagnam, as bonnie as you please,
A gentle child of Mary, from the rebel Liberties,
I lost her to a student chap, with skin as black as coal,
When he took her off to Birmingham, she took away my soul.

Repeat chorus

So fare thee well my Anna Liffey, no longer can I stay,
And watch the great glass cages, grow up along the quay,
My mind's too full of wandering, to listen to new chimes,
I'm a part of what was Dublin, in the Rare Ould Times.
Repeat chorus

11. She Moved Through the Fair

My young love said to me 'My mother won't mind,
And my father won't slight you for your lack of kind.'
As she turned away from me and this did say,
'It will not be long love, 'til our wedding day'.

She stepped away from me and she moved through the fair,
And fondly I watched her move here and move there,
And then she turned homeward with one star awake,
As the swan in the evening moves across the lake.

Last night I dreamt, my dead love came in,
So softly she came that her feet made no din.
And she laid her hand on me and this did say,
'It will not be long love, 'til our wedding day'.

12. Spancil Hill

Last night as I lay dreaming of pleasant days gone by
My mind been bent on rambling to Ireland I did fly
I stepped on board a vision and followed with a will
Til next I came to anchor at the cross in Spancil Hill.

It been on the twenty-third of June the day before the fair
When Ireland's sons and daughters and friends assembled there

The young, the old, the brave and the bold came their duty to fulfil
At the parish church in Clooney, a mile from Spancil Hill.

Delighted by the novelty, enchanted by the scene.
Where in my early boyhood often I had been.
I thought I heard a murmur. I think I hear it still.
It's the little stream of water that flows down Spancil Hill.

To amuse a passing fancy, I laid down on the ground.
And all my school companions, they shortly gathered round.
When we were home returning, we danced with bright good will
To Martin Monahan's music, at the cross at Spancil Hill.

I went to see me neighbours to see what they might say
The old ones were all dead and gone, the young ones turning grey
But I met the tailor Quigley, he's as bold as ever still
Ah, he used to make me britches when I lived at Spancil Hill.

I paid a flying visit to my first and only love
She's as white as any lily, gentle as a dove
And she threw her arms around me, saying Johnny I love you still
Ah, she's now a farmer's daughter and the pride of Spancil Hil.

I dreamt I knelt and kissed her as in the days of yore
Ah, Johnny you're only joking as many the times before
Then the cock he crew in the morning, he crew both loud and shrill
I awoke in California, many miles from Spancil Hill.

13. The Spanish Lady
As I went out through Dublin city at the hour of twelve at night,
Who would I see but the Spanish lady
Washing her feet by candle light

First she washed them then she dried them
O'er a fire of amber coals
In all my life I ne'er did see a maid so sweet about the soul.

Chorus
Whack fol de turalura ladie
Whack fol de turalureley
Whack fol de turalura ladie
Whack fol de turalureley

As I came back through Dublin city at the time of half past eight
Who would I see but the Spanish lady
Brushing her hair so trim and neat
First she teased it then she brushed it.
On her lap was a silver comb
In all my life I ne'er did see so fair a maid since I did roam.
Repeat chorus

As I went round old Dublin city when the sun began to set
Who would I spy but the Spanish lady
Catching a moth in a golden net
When she saw me quick she fled me
Lifting her petticoats over her knee
In all my life I ne'er did see a maid so shy as the Spanish lady.
Repeat chorus

I stopped to look but the watchman passed says he 'Young fella
now the night is late
Along with you now or I will wrestle you
Straight way throught the Bridewell Gate.'
I blew a kiss to the Spanish lady
Hot as a fire of my angry coals
In all my life I ne'er did see a maid so sweet about the soul.

Repeat chorus

As I went out through Dublin city as the hour of dawn was over
Who should I see but the Spanish lady
I was lonely and footsore
First she coaxed me then she chid me
Then she laughed at my sad plight
In all my life I ne'er did see a maid so sweet as on that night.
Repeat chorus

I've wandered north and I've wandered south through Stoneybatter
and Patrick's Close
Up and around by the Gloucester Diamond
Round by Napper Tandy's house
Old age had laid her hand on me
Cold as a fire of ashey coals
But where is the lovely Spanish lady, neat and sweet about the soul.
Repeat chorus

14. The Town I loved So Well
In my memory I will always see
The town I have loved so well
Where our school played ball by the gas yard wall
And we laughed through the smoke and the smell
Going home in the rain, running up the dark lane
Past the jail and down behind the fountain
Those were happy days, in so many ways
In the town I loved so well.

In the early morning a short factory horn
Called women from Creggan, The Moor and The Bog
While the men on the dole played a mother's role

Fed the children, and then trained the dogs
And when times got tough there was just about enough
But they saw it through without complaining
For deep inside was a burning pride
In the town I loved so well.

There was music there in the Derry air
Like a language that we could all understand
I remember the day, when I earned my first pay
As I played in the small pick-up band
Then I spent my youth, and to tell you the truth
I was sad to leave it all behind me
For I'd learned about life and I'd found me a wife
In the town I loved so well.

But when I returned, how my eyes were burned
To see how a town could be brought to its knees
By the armoured cars and the bombed out bars
And the gas that hangs on to every breeze
Now the army's installed by the old gas yard wall
And the damned barbed wire gets higher and higher
With their tanks and guns, oh my God what have they done
To the town I loved so well.

Now the music's gone, but they still carry on
Though their spirit's gone, but never broken
They will not forget for their hearts are all set
On tomorrow, and peace once again
For what's done is done, and what's won is won
And what's lost is lost and gone forever
I can only pray for a bright brand new day
In the town I love so well.

15. Whiskey in the Jar

As I was a-goin' over the Cork and Kerry Mountains
I met with Captain Farrell, and his money he was countin'.
First I drew my pistols and then I drew my rapier,
Sayin' 'Stand and deliver, for I am your bold deceiver.'

Chorus
Musha rain dum-a-doo dum-a-da, ha, ya
Whack fol the daddy-o,
Whack fol the daddy-o,
There's whiskey in the jar.

He counted out his money and it made a pretty penny;
I put it in my pocket to take home to ' Jenny.
She sighed and swore she loved me and never would deceive me,
But the devil take the women, for they always lie so easy!
Repeat chorus

I went into me chamber all for to take a slumber,
To dream of gold and girls, and of course it was no wonder:
Me Jenny took me charges and she filled them up with water,
Called on Captain Farrell to get ready for the slaughter.
Repeat chorus

Next mornin' early, before I rose for travel,
Up came a band of footmen and likewise Captain Farrell.
I goes to draw my pistol, for she'd stole away my rapier,
But I couldn't shoot for water, so a prisoner I was taken.
Repeat chorus

They put me into jail with a judge all a-writin':
For robbin' Captain Farrell on Gilgarra Mountain.
But they didn't take me fists and I knocked the jailer down

And bid me a farewell to this tight-fisted town.
Repeat chorus

I'd like to find me brother, the one who's in the army;
I don't know where he's stationed, be it Cork or in Killarney.
Together we'd go roamin' o'er the mountains of Kilkenny,
And I swear he'd treat me fairer than my darlin' sportin' Jenny!
Repeat chorus

There's some that takes delight in the carriages and rollin',
Some that takes delight in the hurley or the bollin',
But I takes delight in the juice of the barley,
Courtin' pretty maids in the mornin', o so early!
Repeat chorus

16. Wild Rover

I've been a wild rover for many a year
I've spent all my money on whiskey and beer
Now I'm returning with gold in great store
And I swear that I'll play the wild rover no more.

Chorus
And its no, nay, never
No, nay, never, no more
Will I play the wild rover
No, never, no more.

I went into an ale house I used to frequent
And I told the landlady me money was spent
I asked her for credit she answered me nay
Such a custom as yours I can get any day
Repeat chorus

I took from me pocket ten sovereigns bright
And the landlady's eyes opened wide with delight
She said I have whiskey and wines of the best
And the words that I said were only in jest
Repeat chorus

I'll go home to my parents confess what I've done
And ask them to pardon their prodigal son
And then they'lll caress me as oft times before
And I never will play the wild rover no more.
Repeat chorus

17. The Rose of Tralee

The pale moon was rising above the green mountain
The sun was declining beneath the blue sea
When I strayed with my love to the pure crystal fountain
That stands in the beautiful vale of Tralee.

Chorus
She was lovely and fair as the rose of the summer
Yet, 'twas not her beauty alone that won me
Oh no! 'Twas the the truth in her eye ever beaming
That made me love Mary, the Rose of Tralee.

The cool shades of evening their mantle were spreading
And Mary all smiling was listening to me
The moon through the valley her pale rays was shedding
When I won the heart of the Rose of Tralee.
Repeat chorus

18. The Banks of My own Lovely Lee

How oft do my thoughts in their fancy take flight
To the home of my childhood away,
To the days when each patriot's vision seem'd bright
Ere I dreamed that those joys should decay.
When my heart was as light as the wild winds that blow
Down the Mardyke through each elm tree,
Where I sported and play'd 'neath each green leafy shade
On the banks of my own lovely Lee.

And then in the springtime of laughter and song
Can I ever forget the sweet hours?
With the friends of my youth as we rambled along
'Mongst the green mossy banks and wild flowers.
Then too, when the evening sun's sinking to rest
Sheds its golden light over the sea
The maid with her lover the wild daisies pressed
On the banks of my own lovely Lee

'Tis a beautiful land this dear isle of song
Its gems shed their light to the world
And her faithful sons bore thro' ages of wrong,
The standard St Patrick unfurled.
Oh! would I were there with the friends I love best
And my fond bosom's partner with me
We'd roam thy banks over, and when weary we'd rest
By thy waters, my own lovely Lee.

Oh what joys should be mine ere this life should decline
To seek shells on thy sea-girdled shore.
While the steel-feathered eagle, oft splashing the brine
Brings longing for freedom once more.
Oh all that on earth I wish for or crave

Is that my last crimson drop be for thee,
To moisten the grass of my forefathers' grave
On the banks of my own lovely Lee
To moisten the grass of my forefathers' grave
On the banks of my own lovely Lee.

IRISH TRIVIA

1568 – Three ships of the Spanish Armada run aground at Streedagh, County Sligo.

1720 – The Royal Cork Yacht Club is established in Crosshaven, Cork (one of the oldest in the world).

1729 – Laying of foundation stone for new Parliament House (now Bank of Ireland), College Green, Dublin.

1773 – Foundation stone laid at the King's Hospital – the Blue Coat School (now the premises of the Incorporated Law Society of Ireland).

1779 – First St Patrick's day parade in New York City.

1783 – A glass factory is established in Waterford by George and William Penrose (the beginnings of Waterford Crystal).

1786 – Foundation stone laid for the Four Courts, Dublin.

1791 – First Irish transported convicts arrive in New South Wales, Australia.

1796 – First ever Orange celebrations on 12 July – the Protestant victory of the Battle of the Boyne.

1800 – First priests ordained at Maynooth College.

1812 – Galway Court House is built.

1817 – Act of Parliament establishes first public lunatic asylums in Ireland.

1818 – The Salmon Weir Bridge in Galway is built.

1830 – Dublin Zoo opens.

1832 – First burial in Glasnevin Cemetery, Dublin.

1834 – Opening of St Vincent's Hospital, Dublin.

1841 – First published edition of the *Cork Examiner*.

1844 – First female graduates conferred by the Royal University of Ireland.

1850 – Queen's Colleges in Belfast, Cork (now University College Cork), Galway (now National University of Ireland Galway) established.

1852 – Submarine telegraph cable from Holyhead to Howth links Britain and Ireland for the first time.

1853 – Announcement of proposal to introduce first Irish income tax.

1854 – Catholic University (now University College Dublin) opens.

1855 – Completion of the Dublin–Belfast railway line.

1859 – First publication of *The Irish Times*.

1861 – Opening of the Mater Hospital, Dublin.

1862 – The Harland and Wolff shipyard in Belfast is founded.

1863 – St Stephen's Green, Dublin, first opens to the public.

1866 – Completion of the transatlantic telegraph cable from Valentia Island, County Kerry, to Newfoundland.

1870 – Belfast Castle is built by the Marquis of Donegal.

1872 – A horse-drawn tram is introduced to Cork by Cork Tramway Company.

1876 – The People's Park in Limerick is designed.

1890 – Belfast Public Library is built.

1893 – Cork's first purpose-built fire station is opened in Sullivan's Quay at a cost of £1,800.

1896 – First use of X-rays in Ireland at Dr Steeven's Hospital, Dublin.

Twelve Important Years in
Twentieth-century Ireland

1907 – Marconi wireless service begins between Clifden, County Galway, and Cape Breton, Canada.

1907 – Opening of Tara Street fire station, Dublin.

1911 – Launch of the *Titanic* from Harland and Wolff shipyard, Belfast.

1947 – Shannon airport becomes the world's first duty free airport.

1951 – Dr E.T.S. Wilson of Trinity College Dublin wins the Nobel prize for Physics.

1961 - Raidió Telifís Éireann television begins broadcasting.

1973 - Irish continental line begins their Rosslare–Le Havre car ferry service.

1974 – Sean MacBride wins the Nobel prize for peace.

1978 – RTÉ2 TV launched.

1979 - RTÉ Radio 2 (now 2FM) goes on the air for the first time.

1979 – Pope John Paul II begins the first ever Papal visit to Ireland.

1985 – Live Aid concert, organised by Bob Geldof, raises £45 million for third world famine countries.

EIGHT FACTS ABOUT ST PATRICK

1. **St Patrick**'s Day marks the Roman Catholic feast day for Ireland's patron saint, who died in the fifth century. St Patrick (Patricius in Latin) was not, however, born in Ireland, but in Britain.

2. Irish brigands kidnapped **St Patrick** at sixteen and brought him to Ireland. He was sold as a slave in Antrim and served in bondage for six years until he escaped to Gaul, in present-day France. He later returned to his parents' home in Britain, where he had a vision that he would preach to the Irish. After fourteen years of study, Patrick returned to Ireland, where he inspired the building of many churches and spread the Christian faith for some 30 years.

3. Many myths surround **St Patrick**. One of the best known – and most inaccurate – is that Patrick drove all the snakes from Ireland into the Irish Sea, where the serpents drowned, (some still say that is why the sea is so rough). But snakes have never been native to the Emerald Isle. The serpents were likely a metaphor for druidic religions, which steadily disappeared from Ireland in the centuries after St Patrick planted the seeds of Christianity on the island.

4. Colonial New York City celebrated the first official **St Patrick**'s Day parade in 1762, when Irish immigrants in the British colonial army marched down city streets. In subsequent years Irish fraternal organisations also held processions to St Patrick's Cathedral in New York. The various groups merged some time around 1850 to form a single, grand parade which still takes place on St Patrick's Day each year.

5. Today New York's **St Patrick**'s Day parade is the longest running civilian parade in the world. Each year nearly three million specta-

tors watch the spectacle and some 150,000 participants march.

6. Dublin's **St Patrick**'s Day parade is little more than 75 years old and draws around 400,000 spectators.

7. By law, pubs in Ireland were closed on **St Patrick**'s Day, a national religious holiday, as recently as the 1970s.

8. Chicago is famous for dyeing the Chicago River green on **St Patrick**'s Day. The tradition began in 1962, when a pipe fitters' union – with the permission of the mayor – poured 100 pounds (45 kilogrammes) of green vegetable dye into the river. Today only 40 pounds (18 kilogrammes) of dye are used, enough to turn the river green for several hours. According to the Friends of the Chicago River, a local environmental group, more people are likely to view the Chicago River on St Patrick's Day than on any other day.

Fifteen Symbols of Ireland

1. A pint of Guinness

2. Newgrange

3. The potato

4. Irish flag

5. The All-Ireland finals in Croke Park

6. Neutrality

7. The Angelus

8. Tayto crisps

9. Harp

10. Claddagh ring

11. Banshees

12. Leprechauns

13. Shamrock

14. Celtic cross

15. St Patrick

Nine World Records Relating to Ireland

1. Largest Attendance In Gaelic Football
The record crowd for Gaelic Football is 90,556, when Down played rivals Offaly in the final at Croke Park, Dublin, in 1961. Down beat Offaly 3-6 to 2-8.

2. Worst Yacht Racing Disaster
Between 13–15 August 1979, nineteen people died during the 28th Fastnet Race, when 23 boats sank or were abandoned in a Force 11 gale. Of the 316 boats that started the race, only 128 finished. Thirty-six people were saved by air-sea rescue units.

3.. Largest *Ceilí*
A total of 8,371 people danced a *ceilí* (a traditional Irish dance, pronounced kay-lee) for five minutes in Cork city on 11 September 2005. Participants entered the *Guinness Book of Records* and the event was witnessed by Michael Flatley, star of *Riverdance* and *The Lord of the Dance*.

4. The longest palindrome
The longest palindrome in the *Oxford English Dictionary* is the twelve-letter tattarrattat, a nonce word (invented for a particular event or occasion) meaning rat-a-tat. The Irish author James Joyce used the word in *Ulysses* (1922): I knew his tattarrattat at the door'.

5. Most Isle Of Man TT Race Wins
Joey Dunlop (Ireland) had a record 26 victories in the Isle of Man Tourist Trophy races between 1977 and 2000.

6. Tallest Box Hedge
The tallest box hedge is 11m (36 ft) high, and grows at Birr Castle,

County Offaly. It is at least three centuries old.

7. Largest permanent hedge maze

The world's largest permanent hedge maze is the Peace Maze at Castlewellan Forest Park, County Down, Northern Ireland, which has a total area of 11,215m (2.771 acres), a total path length of 3.515km (2.184 miles) and opened on 12 September, 2001. The maze was designed by Beverley Lear (UK) and created by Northern Ireland and members of the public.

8. Fastest Time To Pluck a Turkey

Vincent Pilkington of Cootehill, County Cavan plucked a turkey in 1 minute 30 seconds on 17 November, 1980. His past best time was 2 minutes 44 seconds. Vincent is so enthusiastic about his skills that he even carried out 24 hours of turkey plucking to raise funds for his local Holy Family School. In this time he plucked 244 turkeys.

9. Country With Most Eurovision Song Contest Wins

The country with the most Eurovision Song Contest wins is Ireland, winning seven times. The winners were:

1970 Dana, 'All Kinds of Everything'

1980 Johnny Logan, 'What's Another Year?'

1987 Johnny Logan, 'Hold me Now'

1992 Linda Martin, 'Why Me?'

1993 Niamh Kavanagh, 'In Your Eyes'

1994 Paul Harrington and Charlie McGettigan, 'Rock 'n' Roll Kids'

1996 Eimear Quinn with 'The Voice'

Nine Inventions

1. Submarine
Phillip John Holland left his native County Clare in 1872 for the United States where in 1899, he invented the world's first submarine.

2. Harpoon Gun
Thomas Nesbitt invented the harpoon gun in 1760.

3. Atom Bomb
Developed (at least, indirectly) by Ernest Walton of Dungarvan, County Waterford.

4. Hypodermic Syringe
Francis Rynd developed the hypodermic syringe specifically for the injection of morphine.

5. Shorthand
John Gregg from Monaghan invented shorthand writing in 1893, basing the system on the natural movements of the hand.

6. Armoured Tank
In 1915, Walter Gordon Wilson invented the armoured tank on the commission of Winston Churchill.

7. Aircraft Ejector Seat
James Martin of County Down perfected his invention in 1944 and the first successful ejection from a moving aircraft was made in 1946.

8. Monorail
Louis Brennan of Castlebar, County Mayo, invented the world's first

monorail in 1907. The first time Brennan's design was put into use was on the Listowel to Ballybunion route in County Kerry.

9. Colour Photography
The engineer, geologist and physicist, John Joly of Hollywood, County Offaly invented the first practical system of colour photography in 1894.

Seventeen Pieces of Trivia about Dublin

1. **Dublin**'s O'Connell Bridge was originally made of rope and could only carry one man and a donkey at a time. It was replaced with a wooden structure in 1801. The current stone bridge was built in 1863 and was first called 'Carlisle Bridge'.

O'Connell Bridge is the only traffic bridge in Europe which is wider than it is long and Dublin's second O'Connell Bridge is in St Stephen's Green.

2. **Dublin** was originally called *Dubh Linn* meaning Black Pool. The pool to which the name referred is the oldest known natural treacle lake in Northern Europe and currently forms the centrepiece of the penguin enclosure in Dublin Zoo.

3. None of the so-called **Dublin** Mountains is high enough to meet the criteria required to claim mountain status. The Sugarloaf is the tallest 'Dublin Mountain' yet measures a mere 1,389 feet above sea level.

4. The headquarters of the national broadcaster RTÉ in Montrose was originally built for use as an abattoir.

5. The Temple Bar area is so called because it housed the first Jewish temple built in Ireland. The word 'bar' refers to the refusal of Catholics to allow the Jewish community to enter any of the adjoining commercial premises.

6. Tiny Coliemore Harbour beside the Dalkey Island Hotel was the main harbour for **Dublin** from the fifteenth to the seventeenth century.

7. Harold's Cross got its name because a tribe called the Harolds lived in the Wickow Mountains and the Archbishop of **Dublin** would

not let them come any nearer to the city than that point.

8. Leopardstown was once known as Leperstown because of the leper hospital that used to be there.

9. There are twelve **Dublin**s in the United States and six in Australia.

10. Buck Whaley was an extremely wealthy gambler who lived in **Dublin** in the 1700s. Due to inheritance, he had an income of £7,000 per year (not far off £7 million a year at today's prices). He lived in a large house near St Stephen's Green which is now the Catholic University of Ireland. He went broke and he had to leave Ireland due to gambling debts. He swore he would be buried on Irish soil but is buried in the Isle of Man in a shipload of Irish soil which he imported for the purpose.

11. The converted Ford Transit used for the Pope's visit in 1976 was upholstered using the most expensive carpet ever made in **Dublin**. The carpet was a silk and Teflon weave and rumoured to have cost over £950.00 per square metre.

12. There are 46 rivers in **Dublin** city. The river flowing through Rathmines is called the River Swan (beside the Swan Centre). The Poddle was once known as the 'Tiber' and was also known as the River Salach (dirty river), which is the origin of the children's song 'Down by the river Saile'. It is also the river whose peaty, mountain water causes the Black Pool.

13. St Valentine was martyred in Rome on 28 February 1,800 centuries ago. He was the Bishop of Terni. His remains are in a cask in Whitefriar Street Church, **Dublin**. He is no longer recognised as a saint by the Vatican.

14. Nelson's Pillar was blown up in 1966 by the IRA to mark the fiftieth annivarsary of the 1916 rising. Its remains now lie in a heap in a valley in County Wicklow.

15. Leinster House in **Dublin** was originally built as a private home for the Duke of Leinster. At that time, the most fashionable part of Dublin was the north side and he was asked why he was building on the south side. He said 'Where I go, fashion follows me ...' and to this day the most fashionable part of Dublin is the south side.

16. Tallaght is one of the oldest placenames in Ireland and it means 'the plague cemetery'.

17. There are five areas in **Dublin** whose names end in the letter 'O', Rialto, Marino, Portobello, Phibsboro and Pimlico.

Nine Facts about the Irish Flag

1. The national **flag** is the tricolour of green, white and orange.

2. The **flag** is divided into three equal stripes and its width is equal to twice its height.

3. It is used as the civil and state **flag** and as the civil and naval ensign.

4. GREEN – The green stripe represents those of native Irish descent. It also signifies Irish Catholics and the Republican cause.

5. ORANGE – The orange stripe represents the descendants of seventeenth-century British colonists (who supported William of Orange in the War of the Two Kings, 1689-91). It also represents the Protestants in Northern Ireland.

6. WHITE – represents the hope for peace between the two groups.

7. The oldest known reference to the use of the three colours (green, white and orange) as a nationalist emblem dates from September 1830 when tricolour cockades were worn at a meeting held to celebrate the French revolution of that year – a revolution which restored the use of the French tricolour.

8. However, the earliest attested use of a tricolour **flag** was in 1848 when it was adopted by the Young Ireland movement under the influence of the French revolution.

9. The tricolour was publicly unveiled by Thomas Francis Meagher, a leader of the Young Ireland movement, at a meeting in his native city of Waterford on 7 March 1848.

Seven Irish Whiskeys

1. Tullamore Dew

Tullamore no longer exists as a distillery. However, its name lives on in its most famous whiskey. It is now produced for Tullamore Dew Co., by the Irish Distillers Group, at the Midleton Distillery, County Cork.

Tullamore Due is probably the grainiest of the popular Irish whiskeys. With its smooth sweet flavour, it makes a good aperitif.

2. Black Bush

Now owned by the Pernod Ricard group and part of the Irish Distillers Group Bushmills Distillery promotes itself as being the oldest licensed distillery in the world, remembered by having the year of 1608 displayed on every bottle produced.

Black Bush is a premier blended whiskey, with a malty nose, whose nutty flavours are rounded off by a sherry sweet finish.

3. Bushmills Sixteen-year-old Single Malt

A new addition to the stable of Bushmills, this offering was first released in 1996. Notable for its 'Three wood finish' (referring to the fact that the whiskey has been influenced by three different types of cask during the maturation process).

An excellent malt whiskey and a must for any connoisseur, it is a rich whiskey with a subtle sweetness not to be missed.

4. Bushmills Original

No one knows for certain just how long Bushmills 'Original', or 'White Bush' as it is sometimes known, has been available. The Old Bushmills Distillery lost most of its records during the Irish War of Independence when their offices were burned. It is the best known of the Bushmills brands.

It is a blended, light, fresh-bodied whiskey with a pleasant malty sweet finish.

5. Paddy Old Irish Whiskey

Produced by the Cork Distillers Company, Paddy Old Irish Whiskey carried the rather unwieldy name of 'Cork Distilleries Company Old Irish Whiskey' originally. It was renamed after Paddy Flaherty, a sales rep for the company.

Paddy Old Irish Whiskey is light and fresh, being one of the softest of all Irish whiskeys, due to the low percentage of pot still content.

6. Powers

John Power and sons began production in 1791 in 1886 they were one of the first to start to bottle their whiskeys. Until then almost all drinks were sold from the barrel. Powers is probably the best-know Irish whiskey sold in Ireland. Originally a pure pot still, it is now produced at the Midleton Distillery in County Cork as a blend of pot still and grain whiskeys.

Powers is an Irish favourite with its fruity and spicy flavours giving way to a lingering finish.

7. Locke's Irish Whiskey

Locke's Irish Whiskey is made at the distillery at Kilbeggan. Although distilling began in 1757, Locke's Irish Whiskey is named after the nineteenth-century family who took over the running of the distillery in 1843. The distillery finally closed in the early 1950s and was literally turned into a pigsty. Today it is managed by the Kilbeggan Development Association.

Locke's is a smooth, quality, blended whiskey, its malty sweet taste being complemented by dryer fresh notes.

THE TEN MOST POPULAR BOYS' NAMES AS PER THE CENTRAL STATISTICS OFFICE (2006)

1. Sean
2. Jack
3. Conor
4. Adam
5. James
6. Daniel
7. Cian
8. Luke
9. Michael
10. Aaron

THE TEN MOST POPULAR GIRLS' NAMES AS PER THE CENTRAL STATISTICS OFFICE (2006)

1. Emma
2. Katie
3. Sarah
4. Amy
5. Aoife
6. Ciara
7. Sophie
8. Chloe
9. Leah
10. Niamh

Nine Contributors to Science

1. Barry, Vincent (1908–1975)
Corkman Vincent Barry led a medical research team that discovered a compound (B663) that ultimately led to a treatment for leprosy. The team were working on a cure for tuberculosis at the time.

2. Bull, Lucien (1876–1972)
Lucien was a prolific Dublin innovator responsible for pioneering high-speed photography in order to view images in slow motion. Bull was also patented an improved version of the electrocardiogram (ECG) in 1938.

3. Coffey, Aeneas (1780–1852)
Dublin man Aeneas Coffey invented the world's first heat-exchange device in 1830. Coffey's patent still was a very efficient apparatus that led to many advances in whiskey distilling.

4. Collis, Robert (1900–1975)
Collis was a Dublin doctor who pioneered the technique for feeding premature infants via a nasal tube as opposed to spoon feeding. He also invented a simple, but affordable, incubator for premature infants.

5. Drumm, Dr James (1896–1974)
County Down man Dr James Drumm invented the nickel-zinc rechargeable battery in 1930. Having been successfully tested on a train in 1931, Drumm's traction batteries had many advantages over their predecessors – especially their ability to discharge and recharge rapidly.

6. Ferguson, Harry (1884–1960)
Nicknamed the 'mad mechanic', Harry Ferguson designed and built

a new plough which was coupled to the tractor in three-point linkage, so that both formed a single unit. This Ferguson System, patented in 1926, was to revolutionise farming. Ferguson also designed and built his own motorcycle, racing car and aeroplane - becoming the first Irishman to fly in 1909.

7. Mallet, Robert (1810-1881)
Explosion seismology was born in 1851, when Dublin man Robert Mallet used dynamite explosions to measure the speed of elastic waves in surface rocks - pioneering and coining the word 'seismology'.

8. Mitchell, Alexander (1780-1868)
Dublin-born blind engineer Alexander Mitchell was the inventor and patentee of the 'Mitchell Screwpile and Mooring' - a simple yet effective means of constructing durable lighthouses and ship moorings in deep water, mud banks and shifting sands.

9. Stokes, George (1819-1903)
Born in Skreen, County Sligo, it was in Cambridge between 1845 and 1850 that he determined the movement of a body through viscous fluids of various densities - Stokes' law (between 1909 and 1913 an American physicist, Robert Millikan, used Stokes' law as a basis for solving his experiment involving the charge on the electron). In 1852 George Stokes received the Rumford Medal for the first explanation of fluorescence. In the same year, he produced one of his most important contributions to mathematics while analysing elliptically polarised light - Stokes' parameters. To this day Stokes' parameters is used to describe light emitted in an experiment within atomic and optical physics.

Nine Irish Recipes

1. Potato Soup
Ingredients
1kg potatoes
3 onions
3 cups of milk
3 cups of water
Chives or parsley
Rashers (streaky)
Salt and pepper
1 cup of light cream.

Cooking
Chop all ingredients into chunks and put them into a large pot with the milk. Cover and simmer gently until it becomes a pulp.

Put the pulp in a blender and purée, then add cream.

Reheat; place parsley or chives on top. Fried crispy bacon is added to the top on serving.

2. Coddle
Ingredients
Ham or bacon slices
2 onions
Chopped parsley
4 large potatoes
Salt and pepper
2lbs pork sausages

Cooking
Cut ham/bacon into small pieces. Cut potatoes into quarters.

Cut onions into quarters, if large, or leave whole.

Put all ingredients into large saucepan. Cover with water. Simmer until it becomes soupy

3. Irish Stew
Ingredients
4lbs beef or lamp cutlets
2lbs potatoes
4 large onions
Parsley and thyme mixes
Salt and pepper

Cooking
Cut meat into medium pieces
Peel and slice the potatoes and onions. Layer potatoes in the pan, add herbs, salt and pepper. Then add a layer of meat and a layer of onions. Repeat as long as the ingredients last.
Cover with water, then foil and add the lid.
Simmer until every thing is cooked through.

4. Potato Cakes
Ingredients
2 cups of self-raising flour
1½ cups of mashed potato
¼ cup of milk
2 heaped tablespoons of butter or fat
Salt

Cooking
Mix butter or fat into flour. Add salt to taste.
Mix in the mashed potato and milk to make a soft dough. Roll out on a floured table. Cut into cakes.
Bake in a hot oven for 20 to 30 minutes.
Serve hot with butter

5. Corned Beef and Cabbage
Ingredients
3lbs corned beef
5 sliced carrots
1 large cabbage
2 onions
Cloves
Parsley and thyme
Salt and pepper

Cooking
Place all the ingredients, bar the cabbage, in a saucepan.

Cover with water and bring to the boil. Cover and simmer for forty-five minutes.

Cut cabbage up into manageable lumps. Place in pan with the other ingredients. Cook for a further 45 minutes. Serve with a plate of spuds.

6. Fried Bread
Ingredients
Bread
Left over grease from rashers, sausages, kidney, liver, etc.

Cooking
Melt the grease in a solid-bottomed pan. Dip each slice of bread into the grease and allow it to soak up the grease.

Place each slice of bread on a plate. Turn up the heat on the pan. Place each grease-soaked slice back in the pan until golden brown. Garnish with salt

Pour a cup of tea and enjoy each unhealthy slice.

7. Guinness Beef Stew
Ingredients
4lbs stewing steak
4 large onions
5 carrots
Soaked prunes (soak in Guinness)
Parsley
Water
1 cup of Guinness
Salt and pepper

Cooking
Cut meat into smallish pieces. Chop carrots and onions. Place all in a pot. Cook until all ingredients are tender. Add prunes just before serving.

8. Soda Bread
Ingredients
500g flour
½ teaspoon breadsoda
275ml buttermilk
Pinch of salt

Cooking
Flour a baking tin. Sieve flour, salt and breadsoda into a bowl. Add 200ml of buttermilk. Mix to a loose dough. Add remaining buttermilk if necessary

Knead on board until smooth. Shape dough into a circular shape, and mark a cross on the top. Place on a floured tin.

Bake for 40 to 45 minutes at 200°C.

9. Irish Tea Brack – three-way mix

Ingredients

At least 2 pints of strong black tea
1kg mixed dried fruit
1 cup of brown sugar
3 eggs, lightly beaten
enough white self raising flour
3 or 4 teaspoon mixed spice and/or cinnamon

Preparation

Preheat oven (middle shelf gas) at 350°C. Use 3 1lb loaf tins.

Put fruit, sugar and mixed spice into a large bowl, pour tea over and leave overnight.

Next morning, add beaten egg and mix in with a large fork. Fold in the flour. Place in three greased tins to make three cakes.

Cooking

Bake for 1½ hours approximately. Leave for 10 minutes in the tin after cooking, then turn out. The brack will keep in the freezer for ages.

Six Well-known Irish Retailers

1. Arnotts

Arnotts is the oldest and largest department store in Dublin. Established in 1843, the main store occupies much of the block behind the General Post Office to the west of O'Connell Street, between Henry Street and Abbey Street. The main entrance is on the pedestrianised Henry Street.

Arnotts is privately owned by a consortium, Nesbitt Acquisitions, comprising of about 50 members of the Nesbitt family. Led by Richard Nesbitt, the store was bought out of public ownership by the consortium on 20 June 2003.

2. Clerys

Clerys is a prestige department store on O'Connell Street in Dublin. It is part of a retail group, also called Clerys, which is what the Guineys group rebranded to after purchasing the store in 1940; this is due to Clerys' prestige status outweighing Guineys discount status.

They operate two homewares-only stores in Blanchardstown and Leopardstown, under the brand name 'At Home With Clerys'.

3. Dunnes Stores

Dunnes Stores is a supermarket and clothing retail chain. It primarily sells food, clothes and household wares. In addition to its main customer base in the Republic of Ireland and Northern Ireland, the chain has operations in Scotland, England and Spain. The chain's stores are unusual in that most combine a full supermarket with a clothes department store. The company is famous for its St Bernard label, and its slogan 'Dunnes Stores, always better value'. Both of these have declined in usage in recent years, however, with 'St Bernard' largely being replaced by 'Dunnes Stores' on product labels.

The chain was founded in 1944 in Cork by Ben Dunne, Senior,

as a clothing retailer. The food side of the business began in the 1960s. The company opened the first Irish out-of-town shopping centre at Cornelscourt, Stillorgan, County Dublin, in 1968.

4. Easons

Easons is a major Irish distributor of newspapers and magazines, both in the Republic of Ireland and Northern Ireland. The chain is headquartered in Dublin and employs almost 2,000 staff.

The company was originally founded in 1819 as Johnston & Co. It was in the heady days of Parnell and the Land League that Charles Eason and his son acquired the business from W.H. Smith in 1886. During the nineteenth century, the company was directly involved in the industrial and literary revolutions occurring throughout the country.

Under the clock at Easons' largest store (on O'Connell Street, Dublin) is a well-known meeting spot for Dubliners.

5. Guineys

Guineys (or Micheal Guineys) is a discount chain of department stores with shops in Dublin, Limerick, Waterford, Tralee and Cork. It is well known for having its three Dublin stores within sight of each other – one on North Earl Street and two on Talbot Street, which run directly into each other off O'Connell Street.

In 1940 the Guineys group purchased Clerys and changed the corporate name to Clerys, although they did not rebrand any of their stores. Clerys' single store is close to Guineys' Dublin stores.

6. Superquinn

Superquinn is an Irish supermarket chain. The company was, until 2005, privately held by the Quinn family. It is now a subsidiary of Select Retail Holdings Limited. The company operates eighteen supermarkets under the 'Superquinn' brand and two convenience stores under the 'Superquin Select' brand. Its own brand is

Euroshopper. Superquinn is known for having a high level of customer service compared to other supermarket chains.

The business was founded in 1960 as 'Quinns Supermarkets' in Dundalk. It was set up by Fergal Quinn, and the company headquarters were later moved to Sutton, Dublin. Since 1991, Fergal's son, Eamon Quinn, took a key management role as deputy chairman.

In January 2005, it was announced that Superquinn was to be sold to the Select Retail Holdings consortium and the sale was completed in August that year.

Twelve Facts about Aer Lingus

Aer Lingus is the national airline of Ireland. Based in Dublin, it operates over 40 aircraft serving Europe and the United States. Aer Lingus is a member of the Oneworld airline alliance.

1. On 28 April 1958 Aerlínte Éireann operated the first transatlantic service from Shannon to New York. On 1 January 1960 Aerlínte Éireann was renamed **Aer Lingus** – Irish International Airlines.

2. The **Aer Lingus** callsign is a shamrock.

3. **Aer Lingus** Teoranta was registered as an airline on 22 May 1936.

4. The name, **Aer Lingus,** is an anglicisation of the Irish *Aer Loingeas* which means Air Fleet.

5. In January 1940 a new airport was completed in the Dublin suburb of Collinstown and **Aer Lingus** moved their operations to the new aviation centre. From this point on Aer Lingus planes were painted in a silver and green livery, and the airline's first flight attendants were introduced.

6. In 1956 **Aer Lingus** introduced a new, green top livery with a white lighting flash down the windows and the Irish flag displayed on each plane's fin.

7. **Aer Lingus** entered the jet-age on 14 December 1960 when three Boeing 720s were delivered for use on the New York route, as well as for the newest Aer Lingus destination, Boston.

8. A new livery was adopted in the same year, with a large white

shamrock on the fin and titles of **Aer Lingus**-International just above the plane's windows.

9. **Aer Lingus** suffered its only air crash in 1968 when a Vickers Viscount aircraft en route from Cork to London crashed near Tuskar Rock in the waters off the south-east coast of Ireland. All 57 passengers and four crew perished. The crash is generally known as the Tuskar Rock Air Disaster. The cause of the crash is still unknown, with some suggesting that British missile tests were to blame.

10. In 1968, **Aer Lingus** flights from Belfast to New York began. The service proved successful in the beginning but it was soon suspended due to the beginning of the troubles in Northern Ireland.

11. In 1974 a new livery was unveiled and the word International disappeared from the fuselage titles on **Aer Lingus** planes. The livery included two different colours of blue and one green, plus the white shamrock on the tail/fin.

12. In September 1979 **Aer Lingus** became the first airline other than Alitalia to be used by Pope John Paul II. The pontiff flew aboard a specially modified Boeing 747 (EI-ASI or *St Patrick*) from Rome to Dublin and later from Shannon to Boston.

Thirteen Facts about the Irish Government

1. The **government** of Ireland is based on the constitution of 1937, as amended. This document proclaims Ireland a sovereign, independent, democratic state.

2. The constitution also defines the national territory as the whole of Ireland. The country became a republic in 1949. Executive power under the Irish constitution is vested in the **government**, consisting of about fifteen members.

3. The **government**, responsible to the lower house of the national legislature, is headed by the Taoiseach, or prime minister. This official is nominated by the lower house and appointed by the president.

4. The members of the **government** head the various administrative departments, or ministries. They are nominated by the prime minister and, subject to the approval of the lower house, appointed by the president.

5. Legislative authority within the **government** is vested in a bicameral legislature known as the Oireachtas. This is composed of a 166-member lower house, or Dáil Éireann, and a 60-member Senate, or Seanad Éireann.

6. The members of Dáil Éireann are elected for terms of up to five years by proportional representation.

7. Eleven members of the Senate are selected by the prime minister and six members are elected by the universities. The remaining 43 members of the senate are elected by members of Dáil Éireann, senators and local councillors.

8. The elected members of the Senate are chosen from candidates representing national culture, labour, agriculture and fisheries, public administration and social services, and commerce and industry.

9. The Senate may not veto legislation enacted by the Dáil and is otherwise restricted in authority.

10. Judicial authority in Ireland is vested in a supreme court, a high court, a court of criminal appeal, and circuit and district courts. All the judges of these courts are appointed by the president on the recommendation of the **government**.

11. The system of proportional representation by which members are elected to the Dáil favours a multiplicity of political parties representing special interests. In recent years, however, four parties have emerged as the most powerful: Fianna Fáil, Fine G ael, the Progressive Democrats and Labour.

12. Local **government**: county councils, county borough corporations, borough corporations, urban district councils and town commissioners are charged with responsibility for most locally administered services, including health and sanitation, housing, water supply and libraries. Members are elected to these local bodies by popular vote, generally for five-year terms.

13. Local executive organisation is based on the manager system. A central appointments commission in Dublin chooses the executive manager of local authorities by examination. Local government generally is supervised by the department of local government.

NINE PROMINENT DATES

1. 6 January
Feast of the Epiphany. Also known as 'Little Christmas' or 'Women's Christmas', when the women in house took a rest from their chores.

2. 1 February
St Brigid's Day. Irish saint of healing and smiths but particularly of fertility.

3. 14 February
St Valentine's Day. In honour of the patron saint of love.

4. 17 March
St Patrick's Day in honour of Ireland's patron saint.

5. 1 April
April's fool day. A day associated with practical jokes.

6. 16 June
Bloomsday. Relating to the James Joyce novel *Ulysses*

7. 1 August
Festival of Lughnasa. Lugh was the handsome sun god and this festival was related to the yearly harvest.

8. 31 October
Hallowe'en. A pagan festival that marks the end of one pastoral year and the beginning of another.

9. 8 December
Feast of the Immaculate Conception (traditional shopping day for Christmas).

ART
AND
LITERATURE

Twenty Significant Years for Irish Art and Literature

1742 – First performance of Handel's *Messiah* in Fishamble Street, Dublin.

1785 – First meeting of the Irish Academy for the Sciences and Humanities – (Royal Irish Academy from 1786).

1871 – Opening of the Gaeity Theatre, Dublin.

1890 – Opening of the National Library of Ireland.

1895 – First performance of Oscar Wilde's *The importance of being Earnest.*

1896 – First sceening of a moving film in Ireland at Dan Lowrey's Star of Erin Palace of Varieties, Dame Street, Dublin (now the Olympia Theatre).

1904 – The Abbey Theatre, Dublin, opens

1907 – First night of J.M. Synge's *Playboy of the Western World* at the Abbey Theatre.

1909 – Ireland's first cinema, the Volta, opens in Mary street, Dublin. It was managed by the writer, James Joyce.

1914 – Publication of James Joyce's *A Portrait of an Artist as a Young Man.*

1923 – W.B. Yeats wins the Nobel prize for literature.

1925 – George Bernard Shaw wins the Nobel prize for Literature.

1926 – First performance of Sean O'Casey's T*he Plough and the Stars* at the Abbey Theatre, Dublin, leads to rioting three nights later.

1934 – World premiere of Robert Flaherty's film *Man of Aran.*

1951 – Fire destroys the old Abbey Theatre in Dublin.

1951 – First Wexford Opera Festival opens.

1954 – First performance of the *Quare fella* by Brendan Beehan.

1957 – First Dublin Theatre Festival opens.

1969– Samuel Beckett wins the Nobel prize for Literature.

1970 – Dana (Rosemary Brown) from Derry is Ireland's first winner of the Eurovision song contest singing 'All Kinds of Everything'.

Twelve Famous Irish Novels of All Time

1. *Ulysses* by James Joyce

2. *Gulliver's Travels* by Jonathan Swift

3. *At Swim-Two-Birds* by Flann O'Brien

4. *Amongst Women* by John McGahern

5. *Dr Copernicus* by John Banville

6. *The Sea* by John Banville

7. *The Master* by Colm Toibin

8. *The Land of Spices* by Kate O'Brien

9. *Death and Nightingales* by Kate O'Brien

10. *How Many Miles to Babylon* by Jennifer Johnston

11. *Paddy Clarke Ha Ha Ha* by Roddy Doyle

12. *Dracula* by Bram Stoker

Twenty Facts about Michael Flatley
and *Riverdance*

Riverdance is a theatrical show, consisting of traditional Celtic step dancing, notable for its rapid leg movements, while body and arms are kept largely stationary.

1. **Riverdance** was first performed during the interval of the 1994 Eurovision Song Contest, on 30 April, in a seven-minute format, performed by dancers **Michael Flatley** and Jean Butler.

2. The music accompanying **Riverdance** was composed by Bill Whelan, and featured the Irish choral group Anúna, the RTÉ Concert Orchestra and traditional musicians.

3. The music from **Riverdance** was released as a single in Ireland, where it went straight to number one and remained there for eighteen weeks.

4. In November 1994, tickets were sold in Dublin for the first full-length show of **Riverdance**, which opened at the Point Theatre on 9 February 1995, with both of the original dancers.

5. **Riverdance** ran for five weeks and was a sell-out. Later in 1995, the show enjoyed another sell-out run of six weeks at the Point Theatre, and two sell-out runs of four and eighteen weeks at the Hammersmith Apollo in London.

6. **Riverdance** continues to be performed all over the world. Each production company is named after an Irish river; examples include the Boyne in the United States and the Avoca and Foyle in Europe.

7. Since **Riverdance** opened in 1995, it has been performed over 8,000 times.

8. **Riverdance** has been seen live by over 18 million people in over 250 venues worldwide, throughout 30 countries across four continents

9. The **Riverdance** show has travelled over 500,000 miles (or to the moon and back!).

10. **Riverdance** has played to a global television audience of close to 2 billion people.

11. There have been over 2.5 million copies of the Grammy Award-winning CD of the music from **Riverdance** sold.

12. There have been over 9 million copies of **Riverdance** videos/DVD sold.

13. In October 1995, **Michael Flatley**, who had been with the show since it opened, quit the production due to 'creative differences' over its direction. He went on to produce his own shows, *Lord of the Dance* and *Feet of Flames*.

14. In March 1996, **Michael Flatley**'s show, *Lord of the Dance* was performed in the United States for the first time – at Radio City Music Hall in New York City – where it sold out eight times. Between March 2000 and August 2001, the show was performed on Broadway at the Gershwin Theatre.

15. In 1989 **Michael Flatley** tapped his way into the *Guinness Book of Records* with an incredible 28 taps per second. In 1998, he broke that record by tapping 35 taps per second.

16. **Michael Flatley**'s legs were, at one stage, insured for $40 million.

17. **Michael Flatley** was the first American to win the World Irish Dancing Championships.

18. **Michael Flatley** took boxing lessons after being bullied as a child and in 1975, he won the Chicago Gold en Glove Amateur Boxing Championship.

19. **Michael Flatley** used to lose up to 7lbs in weight during a performance of *Lord of the Dance*, burning up to 4,000 calories during each show.

20. **Michael Flatley** also plays flute and won the All-Ireland Flute championship in 1975.

TEN SUCCESSFUL FILMS RELATED TO IRELAND

1. The Quiet Man (1952)
An American boxer returns to his native Ireland and falls in love with a spirited lass - but has to deal with local customs (including the payment of a dowry) and the young woman's bullheaded brother. The film's appeal is assisted by beautiful scenery and music. Directed by John Ford. Cast: John Wayne, Maureen O'Hara, Barry Fitzgerald, Victor McLaglen, Ward Bond.

2. Ryan's Daughter (1970)
Simple love story blown by gargantuan proportions in Kerry, where a young woman marries a simple plodding, school teacher and then conducted an affair with a British soldier stationed in town. Mills won an Oscar in his supporting role as a hunchback Directed by David Lean. Cast: Robert Mitchum, Trevor Howard, Sarah Miles, Christopher Jones, John Mills, Leo McKern.

3. The Field (1990)
Set in the rugged west of Ireland where the land is rocky and infertile, this film explores the land lust of those left behind when the rest of the inhabitants went to seek 'greener pastures'. Filled with righteous indignation and contempt for the emigrants, the people of the west struggle to regain and keep their land, though they can barely scratch out a living from it.

'Bull' McCabe's family has farmed a field for generations, sacrificing endlessly for the sake of the land. And when the widow who owns the field decides to sell in a public auction, McCabe knows that he must own it. But while no one in the village would dare bid against him, an American regarded as an outsider, steps and decides that he wants to purchase the land. The Bull and his son decide to convince the American to give up bidding on the field, but things go horribly wrong. Cast: Richard Harris, John Hurt, Tom Berengar, Sean Bean, Brenda Fricker, Brendan Gleeson.

4. My Left Foot (1990)
The film is based on the autobiography of Christy Brown (1932–1981), the Dublin-born writer and painter. Brown suffered cerebral palsy from birth, yet lived to be one of the thirteen surviving children out of 22 of this poor Irish Catholic family. The details of life, like sleeping four to a bed, give the audience a real appreciation of what life was like in such a large family. Though Brown wrote of his isolation from society, he always found acceptance with his family, who refused to place him in a home. Cast: Daniel Day-Lewis, Brenda Fricker, Fiona Shaw, Ray McAnally, Owen Sharp.

5. The Commitments (1991)
Enormously satisfying tale of an ambitious young Dubliner who takes on the challenge of assembling and managing a band made up of other working class Dubliners who sing 60's style soul music. The film was a co-production between companies in Ireland, the UK and the US. Cast: Robert Arkins, Michael Aherne, Angeline Ball, Maria Doyle Kennedy, David Finnegan, Bronagh Gallagher, Feilim Gormley, Glen Hansard, Dick Massey, Johnny Murphy, Kenneth McCluskey, Andrew Stong, Colm Meaney, Anne Kent, Andrea Corr.

6. In The Name of the Father (1993)
Here we see Irishmen as victims of British oppression. This is the story of the 'Guildford Four' who were wrongly convicted of bombing an English pub in 1974. Believed to be members of the IRA, the four were railroaded into confessing and sent to prison. Their families and the press kept hope alive for years until the convictions were overturned. Cast: Daniel Day-Lewis, Pete Postlethwaite, Emma Thompson.

7. Michael Collins (1996)

This film features Ireland's struggle for independence from 1916 to 1922. After the disastrous Easter Rebellion against British troops, Michael Collins, an Irish nationalist leader of Sinn Féin, transformed the Irish army into guerrilla fighters, who later became the IRA. The film clearly shows the ambivalence of the nationalists, many of whom wanted independence but would accept no compromise Collins and his men, through perseverance, brought about a treaty with England and the establishment of the Irish Free State. Cast: Liam Neeson, Aidan Quinn, Julia Roberts, Alan Rickman.

8. The Boxer (1997)

The story focuses on Danny Flynn, a promising boxer who had been imprisoned at the age of eighteen for his part in IRA activities. After serving a fourteen-year sentence, he returns to his Belfast neighbourhood at a time when local IRA leader Joe Hamill is attempting to negotiate a peace treaty with the British government. Despite having no further interest in IRA rivalries, Danny finds himself at the centre of political and emotional turmoil when he is reunited with his former girlfriend. Cast: Daniel Day-Lewis, David McBlain, Emily Watson, Brian Cox.

9. The Butcher Boy (1998)

In a small town in Northern Ireland in the early 1960s, 12-year-old Francie Brady retreats into a fantasy world and has visions of the Virgin Mary. This film shows us a boy who cannot shed his hatred for another boy. Francie's alcoholic father and long-suffering mother are only the beginning of his troubles. He lives in a world of 'haves' and 'have nots', and when confronted by those he perceives as haves, he cannot control his rage. Unable to be helped by family or the clergy (who don't understand him and cannot even solve their own problems) Francie descends into violence and madness. Cast: Stephen Rea, Fiona Shaw, Eamonn Owens, Alan Boyle, Aisling O'Sullivan.

10. Angela's Ashes (1999)

An adaptation of Frank McCourt's book which details his early life in the lanes of Limerick and later emigration to America. We see life in Limerick through a child's eyes. Though there is poverty, there is also humour and though there is tragedy, there is also triumph. Cast: Emily Watson, Robert Carlyle, Joe Breen, Ciaran Owens, Michael Legge, Ronnie Masterson, Pauline McLynn.

11. Bloody Sunday (2002)

Documentary-style drama showing the events that led up to the tragic incidents on 30 January, 1972 in Northern Ireland when a protest march led by civil rights activist Ivan Cooper was fired upon by British troops, killing thirteen protesters and wounding fourteen more. Cast: James Nesbitt, Allan Gildea, Gerard Crossan, Mary Moulds.

Seven Points of Interest about Irish Television

1. RTÉ stands for Radío Telefís Éireann. RTÉ One went on the air in 1961 as Telefís Éireann and is the most popular television channel in Ireland.

2. The two most popular programmes on RTÉ One are the long running *Late Late Show* and the soap, *Fair City*.

3. RTÉ 2 is RTÉ's second channel. RTÉ 2 carries all RTÉ's sports and children's programming and is intended to have a bias towards 'youth' (anyone under 45).

4. Television came to Ireland when the BBC opened their Belfast transmitter in 1953, just in time for the coronation of Britain's Queen Elizabeth.

5. RTÉ gave its first colour transmissions in 1969. The purchase of a colour telecine unit meant that colour films could be broadcast in colour. However, it was to be another six years before RTÉ were fully in colour. The first programme made in colour by RTÉ was a Seven Days documentary special, *John Hume's Derry*.

6. The next phase was colour outside broadcasts, and the first was the 1971 Eurovision Song Contest, the first of many such productions by RTÉ.

7. In 1973, a colour televison licence was introduced, allowing RTÉ to pick up extra funding.

Fifteen Well-known Musicians/Bands

1. U2
U2 was formed in 1978 by Larry Mullen (drums), Adam Clayton (bass), The Edge (guitar) and Bono (vocals), while they were all still students at Dublin's Mount Temple School. The teenage U2 made a local name for themselves in their native Dublin and released a three-track EP on CBS called U23 in 1979. In January 1980, a readers' poll in the Irish rock magazine *Hot Press* gave U2 the top spot in five categories. In April, they signed with Island Records and in May released their first single, '11 O' Clock Tick Tock'. U2's worldwide record sales are now in excess of 70 million.

2. The Corrs
With their unique blend of contemporary and traditional Irish music, the Corrs, have established themselves as true originals. The band consists of siblings Jim (keyboards/guitars/vocal), Andrea (lead vocals, tin whistle), Caroline (drums, bodhrán, vocals) and Sharon (violin, vocals).

3. Enya
Eithne Ní Bhrasnáin (Enya) was born on 17 May 1961. She comes from the small village of Dore (*Dobhar* in Irish) in the Gweedore (*Gaoth Dobhair*) region of County Donegal. She now lives in Killiney, in south Dublin, and in London. She is a four-time Grammy-Award-winning singer, ac Academy-Award-winning songwriter and Ireland's best-selling solo artist.

4. The Dubliners
Formed in 1962 under the name of The Ronnie Drew Folk Group, The Dubliners have had ten members altogether. Of the original group of Ronnie Drew, Barney McKenna, Luke Kelly, Ciaran Bourke and John

Sheehan, Barney McKenna is the only member still in the group. Luke Kelly died in 1984, Ciaran Burke died in 1988 and Ronnie Drew now has a solo career. The present line up includes Paddy Reilly, John Sheahan, Barney McKenna and Eamonn Campbell.

5. Boyzone

Boyzone was an Irish boy band from the 1990s, comprising of Keith Duffy, Michael Graham, Ronan Keating, Shane Lynch & Stephen Gately. They formed on 18 November, 1993 with their first appearance on the *Late Late Show*, where their 'dance routine' has been aired repeatedly as an embarrassing clip. Their managers were Louis Walsh and Mark Plunkett and they went on to score sixteen top ten singles and four number one albums. The vast majority of their hits were cover versions of older hit songs.

6. The Chieftains

The Chieftains are an Irish musical group founded in 1962, known for performing and popularising Irish traditional music. The band has recorded many albums of instrumental Irish folk music, as well as multiple collaborations with popular musicians of many genres, including country music, Galician traditional music, Cape Breton and Newfoundland music, and rock and roll. They have performed with Van Morrison, Elvis Costello, Tom Jones, Sinéad O'Connor, James Galway, and numerous country-western artists.

They have won six Grammy Awards and have been nominated eighteen times. In 2002 they were given a Lifetime Achievement Award by the UK's BBC Radio 2.

7. The Cranberries

The Cranberries are an Irish rock band that became popular in the 1990s. They disbanded in 2004. They comprised of Mike Hogan, Noel Hogan, Fergal Lawlor and Dolores O'Riordan.

Noel and Mike Hogan, two brothers from Limerick, formed the

band with drummer Fergal Lawlor in 1990. The band was originally named The Cranberry Saw Us, a pun on cranberry sauce. Dolores O'Riordan auditioned for and won the role of lead singer and wrote the lyrics for 'Linger'. Her voice was the distinctive element of the band's sound.

The Cranberries signed with Island Records. Their second single, 'Linger', and debut album, *Everybody Else Is Doing It, So Why Can't We?*, became a huge hit first in the the United States and later in the UK.

8. Bob Geldof

Robert Frederick Xenon Geldof, KBE (born 5 October, 1951 in Dún Laoghaire, County Dublin) is a singer, songwriter, actor and political activist, known simply as Bob Geldof.

He shot to fame in the mid-1970s as leader of the Boomtown Rats, a rock group closely linked with the punk movement. In 1978, they had their first number one single, 'Rat Trap'. A follow-up, 'I Don't Like Mondays', was equally successful.

By 1984 the Boomtown Rats' career had declined sharply. In November Geldof saw a BBC news report by Michael Buerk on the famine in Ethiopia and vowed to do something. He called Midge Ure from another band, Ultravox, and together they wrote the song, 'Do They Know It's Christmas?' They put together a group called Band Aid, consisting of leading British and Irish rock and pop musicians, all of whom were at the top of the industry.

The single was released just before Christmas 1984 with the aim of raising money for the relief of the famine. Geldof's somewhat cautious hope was for £70,000. Ultimately, however, the song raised millions The song was re-recorded and released in 1989 under the Band Aid II banner, featuring more contemporary artists such as Kylie Minogue and Jason Donovan. It was re-recorded again just before Christmas 2004 with a new group of musicians called Band Aid 20.

9. Ronan Keating

Ronan grew up in Bayside, Dublin. He joined the band Boyzone at sixteen, after being discovered by Louis Walsh; and he later briefly co-managed fellow Irish boy band Westlife. Despite Boyzone never officially disbanding, they have not released a single since 1999 and he continued with his own solo career, clocking up a total of twelve top ten singles, as well as three number one albums in addition to his previous success with the group.

Ronan presented the Eurovision Song Contest in 1997, and also presented the MTV Europe Music Awards in 1997 and 1999.

10. Luke Kelly

Luke Kelly (17 November 1940-30 January 1984) was an Irish singer and folk musician from Dublin, most famous as a member of The Dubliners. Kelly was one of the best-known figures of the Irish folk music movement of the 1960s and 1970s. Kelly emigrated to Britain in 1958. There he became involved in the growing international folk music scene. In 1962 Luke Kelly returned to Dublin and became a central figure in the city's burgeoning folk music community, playing in sessions in O'Donoghue's pub on Merrion Row with the likes of Ronnie Drew, Barney McKenna and The Fureys. Not long after, he formed a folk group with Drew, McKenna, Ciaran Bourke and John Sheahan, which he named The Dubliners.

Luke remained a politically engaged musician, and many of the songs he recorded dealt with social issues, the arms race and war, workers' rights and Irish nationalism.

Luke Kelly was diagnosed with a brain tumour in 1980, and died in 1984. He remains a Dublin icon and his music is widely regarded as one of the city's cultural treasures.

11. Shane MacGowan

Shane MacGowan is a singer and one-time leader of The Pogues, an Anglo/Irish indie-rock/punk/folk band popular in the 1980s.

MacGowan drew on his Irish heritage to create the band. He has written songs of astonishing beauty. Many of his songs are influenced by Irish republicanism and history. MacGowan has often cited the nineteenth-century Irish poet James Clarence Mangan as an influence.

Since leaving The Pogues, he has formed a new band, Shane MacGowan and The Popes, and still records and tours.

12. Christy Moore

Christy Moore (born 7 May 1945) is a popular Irish folk singer and guitarist, well known as one of the primary members of Planxty. His first album, *Paddy on the Road* (a minor release of 500) was recorded with Dominic Behan (brother of Brendan) in 1969. The following year brought his first major release, *Prosperous* (named after the town in County Kildare where the album was recorded), which brought together the four musicians who thereafter formed Planxty: Liam O'Flynn, Andy Irvine and Donal Lunny. For a time they called themselves 'CLAD', an acronym of their names, but soon decided on Planxty.

After leaving Planxty in 1975, Moore continued his solo career (reforming his old band on occasion) which he has been doing ever since. He is also a member of the band Moving Hearts with Lunny and five other musicians and in 2000 he published his autobiography, *One Voice*.

13. Van Morrison

George Ivan 'Van' Morrison is originally from Belfast. He plays a variety of instruments, including the guitar, harmonica, keyboards and saxophone.

Morrison first rose to prominence as the singer of the British/Irish band Them, penning their seminal 1966 hit 'Gloria'. A few years later, Morrison left the band for a successful solo career.

Morrison was inducted into the Rock and Roll Hall of Fame and the Songwriters Hall of Fame. In 2000, Morrison ranked number 25 on American cable music channel VH1's list of the 100 Greatest Artists of Rock and Roll.

14. Sinead O'Connor
Sinéad Marie Bernadette O'Connor is a Grammy-Award-winning singer and songwriter. She is Ireland's second biggest selling female artist (behind Enya). Sinead ranks among the most distinctive and controversial pop music stars of the 1990s.

15. Westlife
Westlife is an Irish boy band and was formed in July 1998, with the members Shane Filan, Kian Egan, Mark Feehily, Nicky Byrne, and Bryan McFadden.

The bands' origins are in Sligo in northwest Ireland. They were named Westside. That conflicted with another band of the same name so their name was changed to Westlife. Boyzone singer Ronan Keating was brought in to co-manage the band with Louis Walsh. The band have had fourteen UK number one singles between 1999 and 2007, the fourth-highest such total of all time (trailing only Elvis Presley, The Beatles and Cliff Richard). Their first seven singles released reached number one, a record (once held earlier for two decades by Gerry and the Pacemakers), and furthermore, each of these singles entered the charts at number one.

Westlife have had success all over the world, especially Scandinavia and South East Asia, but also throughout Europe, Canada, Latin America and Australia.

PEOPLE

1. Theobald Wolfe Tone

Theobald Wolfe Tone, the eighteenth-century Protestant lawyer, was one of the few leaders of his time who was well-respected by the governing parties in both Dublin (nationalist) and Belfast (unionist). In autumn 1791, he called for Irish independence and a rapprochement between Protestants and Catholics. Tone was involved in the creation of the Society of United Irishmen, which had chapters in Belfast and Dublin. In 1798, the Irish nationalists rose against British occupation in the belief that a French invasion was imminent. The rebellion was crushed by British forces. Tone was captured and sentenced to be hanged but he chose suicide over submitting to British justice, and slit his own throat.

2. Michael Collins

Michael Collins was born on 16 October 1890 at Sam's Cross outside Clonakilty, County Cork. He was a member of the Irish Republican Brotherhood and an elected MP for Cork South, and went on to become the director of intelligence for the Irish Republican Army. He took part in the 1916 Easter Rising in Dublin and was responsible for organising resistance to British rule in Ireland. His tactics are said to be the basis for all guerrilla warfare. In 1921 Collins was a signatory to a Treaty to bring to an end the war for Irish independence between Britain and Ireland. This treaty was not to the liking of all Irishmen and a civil war broke out. Collins said after the signing 'I may have signed my actual death warrant.' He was killed in an ambush at Béal na mBlath in County Cork on the 22 August 1922.

3. Eamon de Valéra

Eamon de Valéra was born in Manhattan, New York, on 14 October

1882, son of a Spanish immigrant father and an Irish immigrant mother. He was a commandant in the 1916 Rising and had his death sentence commuted because the British authorities were unsure of his nationality and wanted to avoid an international incident with the United States. Elected as a Sinn Féin MP for East Clare in July 1917, he was later elected as president of Ireland on 25 June 1959 at the age of 76, and held office until 24 June 1973. He had been re-elected on 1 July 1966. He died on 29 August 1975 at the age of 92.

4. Padraig Pearse

Born in Dublin in 1879, Padraig Pearse was a leader of Irish nationalism, poet and teacher. He was the first president of the Provisional Government of the Irish Republic and was Commander-in-Chief of the Irish forces on Easter Monday 1916, when the 1916 rising began. After surrendering to British forces he was sent for court-martial and executed in Kilmainham jail on 3 May 1916.

5. Mary Robinson

Mary Robinson was elected as president of Ireland in 1990 – a milestone event in Irish society – not only was she the first woman president of Ireland, she was, at the time, one of only three female heads of state in the world. She resigned the presidency on 12 September 1997, eleven weeks short of her full seven-year term, to accept the position of United Nations High Commissioner for Human Rights. Prior to serving as president, she was an elected member of the Irish Senate for twenty years. She had started her career as a barrister.

6. Mary McAleese

Mary McAleese is the second female and current president of the Republic of Ireland and the first to be born in Northern Ireland. Born in 1951 into a Catholic Belfast family, Ms McAleese grew up in a Protestant area, near Ardoyne. She moved to Dublin in 1975 to take up a professorship of law at Trinity, aged only 24. Four years later she left Trinity to join RTÉ and worked for two years as a reporter on the *Frontline* and *Today Tonight* television programmes.

7. Daniel O'Connell

Daniel O'Connell was born near Cahirciveen, Kerry, in 1775. Statesman and Irish leader in the British House of Commons. He was known in Ireland as 'The Liberator'. By his overwhelming victory in an election he forced the British to accept the Emancipation Act of 1829, by which Roman Catholics were permitted to sit in parliament and hold public office.

8. Charles Stuart Parnell

Charles Stuart Parnell was born in 1846 in Avondale, County Wicklow. An Irish nationalist leader in the late nineteenth century, he was elected to parliament in 1875. He became president of the Irish Land League in 1879. He organised massive land agitation as well as obstruction of Parliamentary business. His latter years saw him deposed as party leader and involved in a divorce scandal. He died suddenly in 1891.

9. Roger Casement

Roger Casement was born in Dun Laoghaire, County Dublin in 1864. Casement gained international fame when he revealed the atrocities being committed against the natives in the Congo and was awarded a knighthood in 1914. He attempted to recruit Irish prisoners of war in Germany to fight against England. He was arrested in 1916 after being put ashore from a German submarine near Tralee in County Kerry. He was convicted of treason and hanged.

10. Michael Davitt

Michael Davitt was born in Straide, County Mayo on 25 March 1846, the second of five children. When Michael was six years old, his parents, Martin and Sabina Davitt, were evicted. In 1865, he joined the

Irish Rrepublican Brotherhood and two years later gave up his job to become organising secretary of the Fenians in Northern England and Scotland. In 1892 he was elected MP for Mayo but disliked the institution of parliament and became increasingly impatient with the inability or unwillingness to right injustice. He left the House of Commons in 1896 with the prophetic prediction that 'no just cause could succeed there unless backed by physical force'.

Davitt died in Dublin in 1906. By the time of his death in 1906, the land for the people had largely become a reality, prison reform had begun, and he himself had become an international champion of liberty.

11. Oliver Plunkett
Oliver Plunkett was born in 1692 in Loughcrew, County Meath and was the Archbishop of Armagh and the Roman Catholic Primate of Ireland. He maintained his duties in the face of English persecution and was eventually arrested and tried for treason. He was hanged, disembowelled and quartered at Tyburn. His preserved head can be seen in Drogheda.

12. Monsignor Hugh O'Flaherty
Monsignor Hugh O'Flaherty was an Irish priest in the Vatican who, during the Second World War developed a rescue service whereby he made it possible for over 6,000 members of the Allied Expeditionary Force to be safely transported to Switzerland so that they could be returned to their military units. (These 6,000 Allied Military Personnel represented those who were shot down over Italy and/or became prisoners of war who escaped.) Many of these allied soldiers and sailors were members of the Jewish faith. One of his other activities was his use of many churches in Rome to protect Jews by having Baptismal Certificates made out in their names.

13. Arthur Guinness

It was in 1759 that young Arthur Guinness, then 34 and already an experienced brewer, decided to set up business in Dublin. His new premises covered a mere one acre at St James' Gate on the banks of the Liffey. Small beginnings certainly, but that did not deter Mr Guinness' ambition, if the lease is anything to judge by. It was for 9,000 years, at £45 per annum. The economic climate of the time did not encourage optimism and competition was stiff as a result of English imports. Yet, in spite of it all, the Guinness brewery flourished and grew.

14. Thomas John Barnardo

Thomas John Barnardo was born Dublin in 1845. He was a pioneer in social work who founded many homes for destitute children. From the foundation of the homes in 1867 to the date of Barnardo's death, nearly 60,000 children had been assisted. The work of Thomas Barnardo is continued today by the charity Barnardo's.

15. Robert Erskine Childers

Robert Erskine Childers was born 25 June 1870 in London and died 24 November 1922 in Beggar's Bush, County Dublin He was a writer and Irish nationalist agitator and was executed because of his support for the republican cause in the civil war that followed the establishment of the Irish Free State.

A first cousin of the English politician Hugh Childers, he was a clerk in the House of Commons from 1895 to 1910.

Despite his position on British rule in Ireland, Childers served the British in the First World War as an intelligence and aerial-reconnaissance officer. But by the end of the war he supported a wholly independent Irish republic. In 1921 he was elected to Dáil Éireann as a Sinn Féin deputy from County Wicklow and became the Dáil's minister of propaganda. Later that year he was secretary to the Irish delegation to the Anglo-Irish treaty conference. He was captured by the Free State forces in the Civil War and executed by firing squad in 1922.

Childers was the author of *The Riddle of the Sands* (1903), a popular spy story involving an imaginary German raid on England.

Seven Famous Irish Explorers

Among the Irish explorers to venture to the Antarctic are famous names such as Ernest Shackleton and Tom Crean. There were others as well who braved the extremes of the southern continent. Here is a brief summary of the best-known Irish Antarctic explorers, men who displayed great courage and ability.

1. Ernest Shackleton

Ernest Shackleton was a superb leader of men. Born in Ballytore, County Kildare, in 1874, to a Quaker family, the young Ernest joined the merchant Navy and worked his way up through the ranks. Shackleton's first experience of the Antarctic was in 1902 as a member of Scott's *Discovery* expedition, when he first met his fellow countryman, Tom Crean. Shackleton returned to Antarctica in 1907 with his own expedition, when he got within 97 miles of the Pole, 360 miles closer than anyone previously.

After Amundsen reached the pole, Shackleton was determined to be the first to cross the continent and returned with the ill-fated *Endurance* in 1914 to disaster and an epic escape to South Georgia. Shackleton could not get the Antarctic out of his blood and returned once more in 1922 but only made it to South Georgia this time where he died and is buried.

Shackleton is remembered alongside Scott and Amundsen as the greatest Antarctic explorers. The British Antarctic Survey's logistics vessel RRS *Ernest Shackleton* is named in his honour.

2. Tom Crean

Tom Crean played a major role in three of the greatest Antarctic expeditions. On his second trip to the Antarctic in 1911, Crean was a member of the tragic Scott expedition who were narrowly beaten in the race to the South Pole by the Norwegian, Amundsen. Crean retrieved the bodies of Scott's polar party, frozen only 11 miles from a food depot. In 1914 Crean was back in the Antarctic for a third time, on this occasion with old friend Ernest Shackleton, on the ill-fated *Endurance* expedition.

Tom Crean was a Kerryman, born in 1877 just outside Annascaul. At the age of fifteen he ran away and joined the Navy as a Boy 2nd Class. Crean was a tall, strong explorer, always assigned to the more demanding tasks and operations. One contemporary wrote 'Crean is a man who wouldn't care if he got to the Pole and God Almighty was standing there – or the Devil'.

Crean returned to Ireland and opened a pub – The South Pole Inn which remains in Annascaul to this day. He married Ellen Herlihy and had two daughters. Tom Crean died on 27 July 1938 at the age of 63. Crean is commemorated by Mount Crean in Victoria Land, Antarctica and the Crean Glacier in South Georgia (east of the Falkland Islands).

3. Edward Bansfield

Edward Bansfield was born in Cork in 1783. Bansfield was the first European to sight Antarctica. As a merchant seaman, he was pressed into the British Navy and took part in the blockade of Brest (1813–14) during the Napoleonic Wars. By 1815 he had risen to be a master, the highest rank available to him. From 1829 to 1821 he explored and charted the South Shetland Islands (as named by him). In 1819 he discovered Trinity Land, the north-western tip of the Antarctic peninsula. Bransfield Island, Bransfield Straight, Bransfield Rocks and Mount Bransfield are named after him.

4. Francis Crozier

Francis Crozier was born in Banbridge, County Down, in 1796. Crozier joined the British Navy in 1810. He made three Arctic voyages with Parry between 1821 and 1827. He explored the Antarctic as second in command to Ross from 1839 to 1843 and took over command of Franklin's Arctic expedition in 1847 when Franklin died.

Cape Crozier on King William Island, Canada, is named after him.

5. Robert McClure

Robert McClure was born in Wexford in 1807. McClure entered the British Navy in 1824 and was involved in the Arctic expeditions of 1836 and 1848. In 1851 he discovered the Northwest Passage, the sea route along the northern coast of Canada, connecting the Atlantic to the Pacific via the Arctic Ocean. McClure Straight is now the name of the final link of the Northwest Passage.

6. Francis McClintock

Francis McClintock was born in Dundalk in 1819. McClintock entered the British Navy in 1831 and between 1848 and 1852 he made several Arctic voyages – his first as captain in 1852. He made a number of long journeys by sledge across the Arctic and developed methods that were widely adopted. In 1859 McClintok found the remains of Franklin's expedition and the grave of Crozier and his men. Mount McClintock in Antarctica is called after him.

7. Henry Kellett

Henry Kellett was born in Clonacody, County Tipperary in 1806. Kellett became a vice admiral in the British Navy and took part in four Arctic voyages between 1848 and 1853. In 1949, he was the first European to sight and chart Ostrov Vrangelya (Wrangel Island) in the Chukchi Sea, north of eastern Siberia. Cape Kellett, on the easternmost point of Banks Island in Canada is named after him.

Ten Irish Heroes Overseas

1. Daniel Joseph Keogh

Born near Drumlish, County Longford, in 1928, he emigrated to America when he was twenty. He was later called up to serve in the Korean war. A massive, closely-fought battle took place on the strategically important Hill 355. Danny fought bravely during the battle but was killed on St Patrick's Day. He became an American war hero and was awarded the Purple Heart and the Gold Star for bravery. A street in Nevada was also named after him.

2. John Boyle O'Reilly

O'Reilly was born at Dough Castle, County Meath, in 1844. He was a huge Fenian supporter who had been imprisoned and sent to Australia for his actions. However, he managed to escape during his term.

A few years later he plotted a heroic mission to rescue six Irish heroes from their prison in Australia. They broke free from a chain gang and were ferried to a ship that had been organised by O'Reilly. They then outwitted the British Navy and made good their escape. O'Reilly became known as an Irish-American champion of the free.

3. Thomas Sweeney

Sweeney was born in Cork in 1820 and emigrated to New York with his family when he was twelve. He joined the army when he was eighteen and, during a battle in 1846 in the USA-Mexico war, his right arm was shattered by a musket ball. This led to the arm being amputated. He became known as 'Fighting Tom' and was regarded as a one-man fighting machine.

He went on to become brigadier general in the American army and was an inspirational leader. He was wounded several times but never defeated.

Even after all his wars against the Mexicans, the Indians and the civil war, he raised an army of several thousand Fenian supporters and tried to drive the British army out of Canada.

4. John 'Dagger' Hughes

The Irish bishop of New York from County Tyrone (Liam Neeson's character in the film *Gangs of New York* is based on Hughes. He got his name from the type of crucifix he wore) became a living legend in Irish-American history for standing up for justice. He resolved gang tension in New York in the 1860s when riots gripped the city. He also won a huge battle in the school's system where they had only taught the Protestant faith. He introduced Catholicism and stood up for the Irish working class in their newly-adopted country.

5. Robert Blair Mayne

Mayne was born in 1915 at his family home in Mountpleasant, Newtownards, County Down. He was the Irish heavyweight boxing champion during his time in Queen's University. He also played rugby for Ireland and for the British and Irish Lions on their tour of South Africa in 1938.

When the Second World War broke out, he joined the Special Air Service (SAS) where he served in South Africa. He went on to become commanding officer of the elite regiment that struck German airfields and fuel dumps at night. He rose to the rank of lieutenant-colonel and won many medals. He played a key part in helping defeat the Germans in the vicious conflict across North Africa in 1942.

6. Chaim Herzog

Herzog was born into an Irish-Jewish family in Belfast and moved to Dublin in 1931. His father was the chief Rabbi in Ireland.

He served as an Intelligence officer for the British army during World War Two, where he helped track down Heinrich Himmler, the feared Nazi leader who, with Hitler, had plotted the extermination of the Jewish race.

After the Second World War, he joined the Intelligence Service in Palestine and later the Israeli Defence Force, as well as being the commander of an armoured brigade.

He also helped establish 'Moss Ad', the crack Israeli intelligence unit that tracked down Nazis and enemies of the State. He went on to achieve the rank of major-general.

Later, he was Israel's ambassador to the UN and in 1983, he went on to become Israel's sixth president – a position he held for ten years.

7. Edward 'Mick' Mannock

Mannock was born in Ballincollig, County Cork, but moved to England when he was twelve and became one of Britain's top fighter pilots in World War One. He was credited with shooting down 73 German planes.

Before he joined the British airforce, he had been imprisoned in Turkey while working as an engineer where he was brutally treated by Germany's ally.

A few years later, after gaining release from prison, he developed into a fearless fighter and brilliant leader. He was awarded the military cross and promoted to acting captain. Unfortunately, he lost his life when he was shot down over France in 1918.

8. Monsignor Hugh O'Flaherty

Hugh O'Flaherty was born in Killarney, County Kerry, and went on to become known as the Irish Oscar Schindler – the German industrialist who helped save the lives of thousands of Jews.

During the Second World War, Pope Pius XII appointed O'Flaherty as Head of the Holy Office's Intelligence and Humanitarian Relief Operation. He became a key figure in the European-wide Catholic network that saved thousands of Jews from the death camps. He hid them in monasteries, convents and his own Vatican residence – ironically the German College.

After the war, the monsignor was made a Notary of the Holy Office, the first Irishman to earn this honour.

9. Edward J. Landers

Landers was born in Oola, County Tipperary, in 1937 and emigrated to America when he was twenty. He joined the army and ended up as a captain in the Vietnam war. He had the honour of becoming the most highly-decorated Irish-born soldier fighting for America during the conflict.

He led a unit trying to stop an advance on Saigon. His courage enabled dozens of his men to escape almost certain death by giving them the time needed to retreat to the helicopters. For his actions, Landers won the Silver Star for Gallantry in Action, the Bronze Star for Meritorious achievements against hostile forces and the Purple Heart for wounds received in action.

10. John Barry

Barry was born in Our Lady's Island, County Wexford. He emigrated to America and grew up to help found the American Navy during the War of Independence. He was known as 'The Father of the Navy'. He was a courageous captain and sank many British ships.

In 1797, President Washington made him the Commodore of the Navy and gave him his own vessel, the flagship christened *The United States*. He became one of the most powerful men in the world, with hundreds of ships under his control.

A huge statue of Barry stands in Philadelphia, from where he sailed during the war.

Eleven Well-known Irish Artists

1. George Barret (1732–1784)

Born and educated in Dublin, George Barret moved to London in 1763 and joined the Royal Academy five years later. Working in oils and watercolour, he preferred to paint landscapes, the most famous of which is a panoramic view of the Lake District in Surrey. In later years he suffered financial difficulties, but was helped by wealthy friends and was appointed as master painter of Chelsea Hospital, a a post he held until his death in 1784.

2. James Barry (1741–1806)

James Barry received his first break in 1763 upon meeting Irish writer and statesman, Edmund Burke. Burke encouraged Barry to move to London and also paid for his stay abroad from 1766 to 1771, most of this time spent in Rome. Inspired by the allegorical work of the Renaissance masters, Barry was adamant about creating historical art, despite the domination of portraiture in the British art market. In 1782, he was appointed professor of painting at the Royal Academy but was dismissed in 1799 for slandering his colleagues. Barry died in poverty in 1612 and was buried in St Paul's Cathedral.

3. Francis Danby (1793–1861)

Danby was born in Ireland but worked in Bristol for the first part of his career, where his landscapes and scenes of rustic life made him the best-known member of the Bristol School. In 1824 he moved to London where he concentrated on painting large-scale Biblical subjects and fantasy landscapes, rivalling those of John Martin. After his wife left him in 1829 he moved to Switzerland and Paris. He returned to London in 1838 but his paintings became increasingly unfashionable.

4. Charles Jervas (1675-1739)

Born in Ireland, Charles Jervas studied with Kneller before spending a decade in Italy. He settled in London in 1709 and spent the majority of his career there. In 1723, he became the principal painter to George II. Much of his fame also owed to his friendship with a number of prominent literary figures that spread praise for his work through their writing. Jervas was also a writer, translating Cervantes' *Don Quixote*, published in 1742 after Cervantes' death.

5. Sir John Lavery (1856-1941)

John Lavery was orphaned at three, and lived with relatives in Scotland. He began a career of retouching photographs but, when his studio burned down, he used the insurance money to attend art schools in London and Paris. In 1885, he founded the Glasgow School, which used French Impressionist techniques. As well as landscapes and genre scenes, Lavery painted portraits, notably of Queen Victoria's visit to Glasgow in 1888. He was knighted in 1918 and worked in diplomacy between England and Ireland for much of the rest of his career.

6. Daniel Maclise (1806-1870)

Born in Ireland, Daniel Maclise began working as a caricaturist and painter in London after 1827. He was a successful history painter, receiving impressive commissions for places such as the House of Lords. In caricature, he is remembered for his series of portraits of literary men and women. He also painted some traditional portraiture, such as the painting of Charles Dickens located in the National Portrait Gallery in London.

7. William Mulready (1786-1863)

Irish painter, William Mulready, began as a drawing master and illustrator of children's books. After 1809 he devoted himself to genre subjects and gained a considerable reputation. His popular paintings show the influences of Sir David Wilkie and of the Dutch school. Well-known examples are *The Sonnet* and *First Love* (both displayed in Victoria and Albert Museum, London and *Snow Scene* (Tate Gallery, London). Mulready illustrated Goldsmith's *Vicar of Wakefield*.

8. Sarah H. Purser (1848-1943)

Irish artist, Sarah Purser earned a reputation as a society portraitist but she was influential in other areas of art. Beginning in 1911, she held social gatherings for the leaders in Irish academia in her home, Mespil House. In 1924, she began the Friends of the National Collections of Ireland, campaigning to bring artwork by Irish artists back into the country. She also founded the stained-glass studio, *An Tur Gloine* (the Tower of Glass) that remained open in Dublin from 1903 to 1944.

9. Sean Scully (1945-)

Irish born, Sean Scully was raised in England and studied at the Croydon College of Art between 1965 and 1968. He then studied at Harvard University and settled in the United States in 1975. His work combines his varied influences in a conglomeration of minimalism, conceptual art, and abstract expressionism. At first glance, his paintings seem minimalist because of their simple patterns of contrasting colors. However, a closer look reveals Scully's attention to detail and layering, incorporating interesting textures and colours

10. Jack Butler Yeats (1871-1957)

Jack Butler Yeats was the son of the artist, John Butler Yeats, and the brother of the poet W.B. Yeats, and was born in London in 1871. Educated in County Sligo, he moved to England where he studied art under Frederick Brown at the Westminster School of Art.

Yeats wrote and illustrated stories for books and magazines. In 1894 he produced the first cartoon strip version of Sherlock Holmes.

He contributed to several newspapers and journals including the *Manchester Guardian*, the *Daily Graphic*, *The Sketch*, *Cassell's Saturday Journal* and *Punch Magazine*, where he used the pseudonym, W. Bird. He also edited and illustrated two monthly publications, *Broadsheet* (1902-03) and *Broadside* (1908-15). After the First World War Yeats moved back to Ireland where he concentrated on painting and writing. Jack Butler Yeats died in Dublin in 1957.

11. Louis le Brocquy (1916-)
Born in Dublin, Ireland, Louis le Brocquy is one of the foremost Irish painters of the twentieth century. His work has received much international attention and many accolades in a career that spans seventy years of creative practice.

Acknowledged by museum retrospectives worldwide, the artist's work is represented in numerous public collections, from the Guggenheim in New York City to the Tate Gallery in London. In Ireland, he is honoured as the first and only living painter to be included in the Permanent Irish Collection of the National Gallery.

Fourteen Famous Irish-Americans

1. Mariah Carey

Carey is the third and youngest child of Patricia Hickey, a Catholic opera singer and voice coach of Irish-American ethnicity, and Alfred Roy Carey (né Núñez), an aeronautical engineer of Afro-Venezuelan descent.

2. Alec Baldwin

Alexander Rae Baldwin III (born 3 April 1958, in Massapequa, Long Island, New York, USA) is the oldest and best known of the 'Baldwin brothers', with brothers Daniel, Stephen and William all being actors. He is of three-quarters Irish and one quarter French descent.

3. George Clooney

Clooney is the son of Nina Bruce Warren and Cincinnati news anchor and TV host Nick Clooney, a nephew of actress and singer Rosemary Clooney, and a cousin of actor Miguel Ferrer. His paternal ancestors, Nicolas Clooney and Bridget Byron, emigrated to the United States from Ireland.

4. Mia Farrow

Mia Farrow (born on 9 February 1945 in Los Angeles, California) is an Irish-American actress. Farrow was christened Maria de Lourdes Villiers Farrow but has always been known as Mia. She is the daughter of the late Australian-born director John Farrow and his wife, the late Irish-born actress Maureen O'Sullivan.

5. Harrison Ford

Ford was born in Chicago, Illinois. His mother, Dora Nidelman (born in 1917 in New Jersey to Harry Nidelman and Anna Lifschutz) was Jewish; his father, Christopher Ford (born in 1906 in New York to John Fitzgerald Ford and Florence Veronica Niehaus was

Irish/German and a Catholic, as well as a former actor.

6. Grace Kelly
Grace Kelly was born in Philadelphia, Pennsylvania, to John Brendan Kelly Sr (4 October 1889-20 June 1960) and Margaret Katherine Majer, a Catholic convert from Lutheranism. Kelly's father's Irish Catholic family (originally from Kidney Lake, Newport, County Mayo) were new but prominent figures in Philadelphia society.

7. Bill Murray
Murray is the fifth of nine children in a large, Irish Catholic family. Three of Murray's siblings are also actors: John Murray, Joel Murray, and Brian Doyle-Murray. All four Murray brothers appeared in the 1988 film *Scrooged*.

8. Conan O'Brien
Conan Christopher O'Brien was born in Brooklyn, Massachusetts, a suburb of Boston. He is the third of six children in an Irish-American family, one of four boys. His father's family hail from Cork. His father, Dr Thomas O'Brien, was a research physician at Brigham and Women's Hospital and an associate professor at Harvard Medical School, specialising in infectious disease. His mother, Ruth Reardon O'Brien, is a former partner of the Boston law firm of Ropes and Gray.

9. Mickey Rourke
Rourke, born to an Irish Catholic family, grew up in the tough neighbourhoods of Liberty City in Miami. He is an actor who has primarily appeared in drama, action and thriller movies. He had a short period as a professional boxer in the 1990s but retired before winning a world title. While boxing, he suffered serious facial injuries and required several operations to repair the damage to his face.

10. Brooke Shields

Brooke Shields' parents are the late Francis Alexander Shields and Maria Theresia Schmonn, who married in 1964. Her paternal grand-parents are Francis Xavier Shields, of Irish descent, and Italian princess Donna Marina Torlonia di Civitella-Cesi, who was a sister of Don Alessandro Torlonia, 5th Prince di Civitella-Cesi, the husband of the Spanish Infanta Beatrix of Bourbon-Battenberg (aunt of King Juan Carlos I of Spain).

11. Billy Bob Thornton

Billy Bob Thornton (born 4 August 1955, in Hot Springs, Arkansas, to a father of Irish descent and an Italian/Choctaw Native American mother) is an American actor, and also an occasional director, play-wright, screenwriter and singer.

12. John Travolta

John Joseph Travolta (born 18 February 1954) is an American actor and singer. Travolta was born in Englewood, New Jersey, the son of Salvatore Travolta, an Italian American semi-professional footballer turned tyre salesman, and Helen Cecilia Burke, (whose family emi-grated from the west of Ireland) an actress and singer who had appeared in radio vocal group The Sunshine Sisters, and acted and directed before becoming a high school drama teacher.

13. John McEnroe

Tennis star John McEnroe was born on 16 February 1959 in Wiesbaden, Germany, where his father was stationed with the US Air Force. He is of Irish Catholic descent. When he was less than a year old, his family moved to New York City, and he grew up in Douglaston, Queens.

14. Henry Ford

Ford was born on a prosperous farm in Springwells Township (now in the city of Dearborn, Michigan) owned by his parents, William Ford (1826-1905) and Mary Litogot (c.1839-1876), immigrants from County Cork, Ireland. He was the founder of the Ford Motor Company and father of modern assembly lines used in mass production. His introduction of the Model T automobile revolutionised transportation and American industry.

Thirteen Irish Scientists

1. Robert Boyle

Robert Boyle (1627-1691) was born at Lismore Castle, County Waterford. Boyle, sometimes called the Father of Chemistry, is a ??? in the history of science. In 1661 he published *The Sceptical Chemist*. Alchemy, the pseudo-scientific predecessor of chemistry, was questioned by Boyle, who taught that the proper object of chemistry was to determine the composition of substances. He coined the term 'analysis'. In 1662 he formulated Boyle's Law which states that the pressure and volume of a gas are inversely related at constant temperature.

2. William 'Guillermo' Bowles

William 'Guillermo' Bowles (1720-1780) was born near Cork and spent most of his life in continental Europe. He studied law in England and natural history, chemistry and metallurgy in Paris. He wrote the first modern scientific description of Spain. He helped establish Spain's Natural History Museum and became its principal scientist. In 1775 he published his *Introduction to the Natural History and Physical Geography of Spain*.

3. Francis Beaufort

Francis Beaufort (1774-1857) was born in Navan, County Meath, and became the British Navy's greatest hydrographer and mapmaker. He is best known as the author of the table which classifies the velocity and force of winds at sea – The Beaufort Scale. He also developed a system of classifying the weather's various states by letters of the alphabet.

4. Reverend Nicholas Callan

Reverend Nicholas Callan (1799-1864) was born near Ardee, County Louth. He was appointed Professor of Natural Philosophy at

Maynooth in 1826. Callan acquired a great interest in electrical phenomena and his most notable contribution was the invention of the induction coil, the forerunner of the modern step-up voltage transformer.

5. William Parsons

William Parsons, Third Earl of Rosse (1800-1867), was born in York, England, and brought up at Birr Castle, County Offaly. In 1845 Parsons built the then-largest telescope in the world at Birr, a distinction retained for 70 years. A main purpose in building the telescope was to study the status of the sun and the star system (galaxy) in which it lies. The construction of the telescope, particularly of the 72-inch mirror, was a wonderful feat of engineering. The telescope could see further into space than any other instrument of the time and Parsons discovered that many galaxies are spiral in shape.

6. George Boole

George Boole (1815-1864), born in Lincoln, England, was the first Professor of Mathematics at Queen's College, Cork (University College Cork today). Boole, sometimes called the Father of Computer Science, developed his system of Boolean Algebra while in Cork. This is used today in the design and operation of electronic computers and electronic hardware responsible for modern technology.

7. William Rowan Hamilton

William Rowan Hamilton (1805-1864), born in Dublin, became Professor of Astronomy at TCD and Royal Astronomer of Ireland. At the age of nine he knew thirteen languages. Hamilton introduced the terms scalar and vector into mathematics and he invented the method of quanternions as a new algebraic approach to 3-D geometry, which turned out to be the seed of much modern algebra.

8. John Tyndall

John Tyndall (1820-1893) was born in County Carlow and he became one of greatest scientists of nineteenth century. Professor of Natural Philosophy (Physics) at The Royal Institution, he did pioneering work on radiant heat, germ theory of disease, glacier motion, sound and diffusion of light in the atmosphere. He was the first to explain how scattering of light in the atmosphere causes the blue colour in the sky. He explained how the gases in the atmosphere trap heat and keep the earth warm. He invented the light pipe which later led to the development of fibre optics.

9. William Thomson

William Thomson (1824-1907) (Lord Kelvin) first, Baron Kelvin (1866) was born in Belfast. Professor of Natural Philosophy (Physics) at Glasgow University, he became a world-renowned physicist. He introduced the absolute scale of temperature - the Kelvin scale. His work on the conversion of energy led to the Second Law of Thermodynamics. He was also closely involved in laying the first successful transatlantic telegraph cable under sea between Ireland and Newfoundland in 1866.

10. George Francis Fitzgerald

George Francis Fitzgerald (1851-1901) was born in Dublin and became Professor of Natural and Experimental Philosophy at Trinity College Dublin. He is best remembered for his proposal that a moving body contracts in the direction of its motion, but that this contraction cannot be measured because moving rulers shrink in the same proportion. This was a significant step towards Einstein's Special Theory of Relativity.

11. George Johnstone Stoney

George Johnstone Stoney (1826-1911) was born in Dun Laoghaire and became Professor of Natural Philosophy at Queen's College,

Galway (NUI Galway today). His most notable scientific work was his conception and calculation of the magnitude of the 'atom' of electricity, for which he proposed the name 'electron'.

12. J.D. Bernal

J.D. Bernal (1901-1971) was born in Nenagh, County Tipperary and became Professor of Physics, Birbeck College, University of London. he developed the technique of modern X-ray crystallography and led a group that used the technique to work out the 3-D structure of proteins, nucleic acids and viruses.

13. Ernest Walton

Ernest Walton (1903-1997), born in Dungarvan, County Waterford, was a pioneer nuclear physicist and is Ireland's only science Nobel Laureate. He built the first successful particle accelerator with John Cockroft at Cambridge with which they disintegrated lithium ('split the atom') in 1931. Walton became Professor of Natural and Experimental Philosophy at Trinity College Dublin in 1947. He shared the 1951 Nobel Prize for physics with Cockroft, a British physicist.

TWELVE FANTASTIC PIECES OF TRIVIA

1. Smallest Irishman
David Jones, Lisburn, County Antrim, was born 28 April 1903, and measured an unconfirmed 2 feet 2 inches at his death on 28 March 1970. His weight of 4 stone, however, suggests a height of approximately 3 feet.

2. Tallest Irishman
Although Jim Cully, Tipperary is, at 7 feet 2 inches, the best-known tall man, Patrick Cotter O'Brien of Kinsale, County Cork is said to have measured 8 feet 7.75 inches. Porthumous calculations, however, put his height at 7 feet 10.86 inches.

3. Smallest Irishwoman
Catherine Kelly who died in Norwich, England, in October 1785 was recorded at being 34 inches in height. Weighing 1 stone 8 pounds she was nicknamed 'The Irish Fairy'.

4. Oldest Mother
Mrs Mary Higgins, Cork city, who was born on 7 January 1876, gave birth to a baby girl on St Patrick's Day 1931 when aged 55 years and 69 days.

5. Tallest Corpse
The preserved body of an 8-foot tall Crusader may be seen at St Michan's Vaults, Dublin where, due to unique atmospheric conditions, bodies do not decompose.

6. Oldest Triplets
Anthony, Joseph and Edmund McMahon were born in Coore East, County Clare in 1898 and all three lived into their eighties.

7. Shot Before Birth

Catherine Anne Gilmore was dellivered by Caesarean section three months prematurely in July 1976. Her mother had been shot in the Ardoyne district of Belfast and a bullet had lodged in her baby's back. It was removed and the child was released from hospital eight months later.

8. Longest Skip

On 25 June 1977 a Waterford boxer, Paddy 'Flutter' Reilly, kept up a non-stop skipping routine for 5 hours, 41 minutes to make an Irish and world record.

9. Strongest Man

The late Michael 'Butty' Sugrue from Killorglin, County Kerry, was Ireland's strongest man. Among his feats of strength was the pulling of a passenger-laden double decker bus.

10. Gulp and Croak

John McNamara, Scariff, County Clare won the first frog-swallowing championship of Ireland at Ballycomber, County Offaly, in 1975 swallowing five live frogs in 1 minute 5 seconds.

11. US Crossing

Tom McGrath, Eddery, County Fermanagh, ran 3,046 miles from New York to San Francisco in September-October 1977. His record time of 53 days 7 minutes was made during his honeymoon.

12. Oldest Married Couple

James P. Hanlon died in Massachusetts., America at the age of 109, two years after his wife of 80 years, the former Florence Gillon, passed away. She was 101. Hanlon died at the Annemark Nursing Home in Revere. According to the book 'Living to 100', the odds of a married couple both living more than a century are about 6 million to 1.

Hanlon was born in Ireland in 1891, when Queen Victoria was on the throne in England. He emigrated to the United States as a young man. Asked about his longevity he said, 'The secret is to keep it simple, be true to yourself and walk kindly with God'.

FOURTEEN PEOPLE WHO HAVE APPEARED ON STAMPS IN THE REPUBLIC OF IRELAND

1. 1929: **Daniel O'Connell**

2. 1937: **Saint Patrick**

3. 1939: **George Washington**

4. 1948: **Wolfe Tone**

5. 1953: **Robert Emmet**

6. 1959: **Arthur Guinness**

7. 1965: **W.B. Yeats**

8. 1966: **Padraig Pearse**

9. 1967: **Jonathan Swift**

10. 1968: **Countess Markievicz**

11. 1969: **Mohandas (Mahatma) Gandhi**

12. 1977: **Jack B. Yeats**

13. 1979: **Pope John Paul II**

14. 1980: **Oscar Wilde**

Nine Well-Known Irish People and their Previous Jobs

1. Bertie Ahern
Current Irish Taoiseach was an accountant, Mater Hospital, 1974.

2. Gay Byrne
Broadcaster, managed a cinema and ran a car-hire business.

3. Steve Collins
Former middleweight champion of the world was an electrician with Guinness Brewery, 1981-1986.

4. Joe Duffy
Broadcaster, was a probation social worker with the department of Justice 1984-1988.

5. Brian Kerr
Ex-Irish football manager, was a laboratory technician in University College Dublin, 1970-1997.

6. Michael Murphy
Broadcaster, was an apprentice draper with Crowe Wilson, 1959-1961.

7. Fergal Quinn
Founder of Superquinn supermarkets, worked in the family-owned 'Red Island' holiday camp.

8. John Rocha
Designer, was a state registered psychiatric nurse, Banstead Hospital.

9. Sharon ní Bheolain
RTÉ News presenter, used to be a secondary school teacher.

Seven Well-Known Irish Women and their Maiden Names

1. **Darina Allen**   **Darina O'Connell**
Cookery school owner, chef, author, TV presenter

2. **Twink**   **Adele Condron-King**
Entertainer

3. **Michelle de Bruin**   **Michelle Smith**
Irish swimmer

4. **Margaret Heffernan**   **Margaret Dunne**
Dunnes Stores family

5. **Mary McAleese**   **Mary Leneghan**
Current Irish president

6. **Mary Robinson**   **Mary Bourke**
Previous Irish president/United Nations High Commissioner for Human Rights

7. **Rosemary Scallan (Dana)**   **Rosemary Brown**
Eurovison Song Contest winner/previous member of the European Parliament

THIRTEEN FAMOUS IRISH ACTORS

1. Pierce Brosnan
Born 1952, County Meath, Brosnan was educated at the Drama Centre, England. Off-hand charm and self-deprecating comic timing were two of the qualities this dashing Irish-born leading man brought to his winning portrayal of the sophisticated, often inept, conman/private investigator *Remington Steele* on the long-running television series in the 1980s. Brosnan received his cinematic license to kill in 1994 when he was named as the new 007. He proved an elegant yet hard-edged Bond in *Golden Eye* (1995) *Tomorrow Never Dies* (1997), *The World is Not Enough* (1999) and *Die Another Day* (2002).

2. Gabriel Byrne
Born in Dublin, the son of a cooper, Byrne is the eldest of six. It was not until he was 29 that he gave any thought to a career in acting, having spent his younger adulthood as an archaeologist, school-teacher, short-order cook. He even trained as a bullfighter while teaching English in Spain.

3. Colm Meaney
Dublin-born actor Colm Meaney is best known as Chief Engineer Miles O'Brien on the hit syndicated series *Star Trek: Deep Space Nine*. Meaney started acting at the Abbey Theatre in Dublin. Meaney and his wife then moved to Los Angeles, where he soon made his feature debut in an obscure action thriller feature, *Omega 7* (also known as *Omega Syndrome*). This genre would prove to be Meaney's television home for many years when he was cast on *Star Trek: The Next Generation* (1987-92), the hugely successful syndicated follow-up to the legendary *Star Trek* television series.

4. Brenda Fricker

Born in Dublin in 1945, she gained experience in Irish theatre and with the National Theatre, the Royal Shakespeare Company and the Court Theatre Company in Great Britain before receiving acclaim for her Oscar-winning, supporting performance as the determined mother of a son afflicted with cerebral palsy in *My Left Foot* (1989). Venturing to Hollywood in the 1990s, Fricker played a homeless woman befriended by kid-on-the-loose Macaulay Culkin in the sequel film *Home Alone 2: Lost in New York* (1992) and followed up with a more zany mother role in *So I Married an Axe Murderer* (1993). Having acted on English television in the BBC series *Casualty*, Fricker began conquering US television with roles in the American Playhouse presentation *Lethal Innocence* (1991) and the mini-series *The Sound and the Silence* (1993).

5. Liam Neeson

Born on 7 June 1952 in Ballymena, Northern Ireland, Liam joined the Belfast Lyric Players Theatre and made his professional debut in *The Risen People*. Two years later he joined Dublin's Abbey Theatre to perform the classics. Director John Boorman spotted him and Liam became a member of the *Excalibur*-cast. His films include *The Mission, Suspect, The Dead Pool, The Good Mother, Husbands and Wives, Shining Through, Leap of Faith, Schindler's List, Nell, Rob Roy, Michael Collins* and *Star Wars: Episode 1*

6. Stephen Rea

Born in Belfast in 1949, Rea's first leading role, as a vengeful saxophone player in Neil Jordan's directorial debut, *Danny Boy* (1982) His breakthrough came ten years later in another Jordan film, *The Crying Game* (1992) where he was cast as an IRA kidnapper who falls for the lover of a man whose death he indirectly caused. He has also enjoyed success on the West End and Broadway stage

7. Maureen O'Hara

Born Maureen FitzSimons on 17 August 1920 in Ranelagh, a suburb of Dublin, O'Hara was the second oldest child of Charles and Marguerite FitzSimons. Discovered by actor Charles Laughton in 1938, she appeared in *Jamaica Inn* before Laughton brought her to America to star with him in *The Hunchback of Notre Dame*. She became John Ford's favourite actress and is most famous for her role in *The Quiet Man.*

8. Richard Harris

Born in Limerick in 1930,. the ruggedly handsome Irish Harris who, after stage experience and several good supporting roles in films, came to prominence in a British film, portraying a rough rugby player in Lindsay Anderson's *This Sporting Life*. His other films include *The Bible* (1966), *Major Dundee* (1965), *Red Desert* (1964), *Camelot* (1967), *A Man Called Horse* (1970), *Cromwell* (1970), *The Cassandra Crossing* (1977), *The Field* (1990) and *Unforgiven* (1992). He was also known for his hit song *MacArthur Park* (1968). He also starred as Professor Dumbledore in the first two Harry Potter films.

9. Cyril Cusack

Born in 1910 in Durban, Natal, South Africa, Cusack made his film debut in *Knockagow* (1917), but did not come into his own as a strong screen character until 1947, with Carol Reed's *Odd Man Out*. Cusack played a cleric in *My Left Foot* (1989) and in *The Spy Who Came in from the Cold* (1965) he played the spy chief. One of the most acclaimed stage actors of his generation, Cusack was famous for his association with Ireland's national theatre, the Abbey; he was at various times also affiliated with the Old Vic and the Royal Shakespeare Company in Britain. Cusack also performed on Broadway. He is the father of actresses Sinéad, Niamh and Sorcha Cusack with whom he co-starred in Dublin's The Gate Theatre's 1990 production of Chekhov's *The Three Sisters.*

10. Peter O'Toole

Born in Connemara in 1932, O'Toole's work with the Royal Shakespeare theatre led to his starring in *Lawrence of Arabia* (1962), *The Lion in Winter* (1968), *Beckett* (1964), *Lord Jim* (1965), *The Last Emperor* (1987), *Zulu Dawn* (1997). He has been nominated for eight Oscars but has never won the award.

11. Colin Farrell

Born in Dublin in 1976, O'Farrell attended the Gaiety School of Drama. Well known to audiences as Danny Byrne in the television series *Ballykissangel.* Following *Ballykissangel*, Farrell landed, among other places, on the London stage, and finally, LA, where he landed his critically-praised role as rebellious Bozz in Joel Schumacher's Vietnam-era drama *Tigerland* (2000). He has also since acted opposite Academy Award winner Kevin Spacey in *Ordinary Decent Criminal* (2000), with Kiefer Sutherland in *Phone Booth* (2002) and Angelina Jolie in *Alexander* (2004) Other films include *The Recruit* (2003), *Daredevil* (2003, *Intermission* (2003), *Miami Vice* (2006) and *Cassandra's Dream* (2007).

12. Daniel Day-Lewis

Although born in London he holds an Irish passport as his father was the Irish-born poet Cecil Day-Lewis, Poet Laureate of England. His mother is Jill Balcon, an English Jewish actress, daughter of Sir Michael Balcon, head of Ealing Studios.

Daniel made his film debut in *Sunday Bloody Sunday* (1971). Notable theatrical performances include *Another Country* (1982-83), *Dracula* (1984), and the *Futurists* (1986). His first major supporting role in a feature film was in *The Bounty* (1984), quickly followed by *My Beautiful Laundrette* (1985) and *A Room with a View* (1985). His brilliant performance as Christy Brown in Jim Sheridan's *My Left Foot* (1989) won him numerous awards, including The Academy Award for best actor.

In 1992 he starred in *The Last of the Mohicans* (1992), a great success at the box office. He worked with American director Martin Scorsese in *The Age of Innocence* (1993). Subsequently, he teamed again with Ireland's Jim Sheridan to star in *In the Name of the Father* (1993). He was nominated again as best actor for his role in *Gangs of New York* (2002).

13. Cillian Murphy

Born in Cork, he is an actor noted for his intense, risky peformances in diverse roles. He first came to international attention in 2003 as the hero in the post-apocalyptic film *28 Days Later*. He went on to have roles in two blockbusters in 2005; *Batman Begins* and *Red Eye*. He also won an Irish Film and Television Award for his role in *Breakfast on Pluto* (2005) and played an Irish revolutionary in *The Wind That Shakes the Barley* (2006).

Twenty Richest People in Ireland (2006)

	Name	Worth	Industry
1.	Hilary Weston	6.912 billion	Retail and groceries (Canada)
2.	Sean Quinn	2.941 billion	Trucks, cement, news and media, insurance, hotels
3.	Tony O'Reilly	2.025 billion	Heinz Foods, Independent Newspapers
4.	John Durant	2.007 billion	Campbells Foods
5.	Dermot Desmond	1.419 billion	Stock broking (IFSC)
6.	Tony Ryan	1.268 billion	Ryanair
7.	Thomas Flatley	1.096 billion	Property
8.	Denis O'Brien	904 million	Telecommunications
9.	John Magnier	871 million	Horseracing/stud
10.	Frank Dunne	746 million	Dunnes Stores
11.	Martin Naughton	721 million	Electric heaters/Dimplex
12.	J.P. MacManus	694 million	Horseracing/Gambling (Sandy Lane Resort)
13.	U2	690 million	Entertainment

14.	**Margaret Heffernan** 603 million	Dunnes Stores
15.	**McMahon Family** 568 million	Dunnes Stores
16.	**Eugene and Bernard Murtagh** 568 million	Insulation/Kingspan Building Materials
17.	**Michael Flatley** 551 million	Entertainment
18.	**Lord Bally Edmond** 515 million	Pharmaceuticals
19.	**Tom and Anne Roche** 482 million	Hotels/toll roads
20.	**Michael O'Leary** 466 million	Ryanair

There are approximately 50,000 millionaires in Ireland.

SPORTS

Eleven Significant Sporting Years in Ireland

1817 – William Sadler makes the first balloon crossing of the Irish sea.

1855 – Ireland play their first ever cricket international, in which they beat England.

1874 – Formation of the Irish Football Union (now IRFU).

1888 – First All-Ireland football final,. Limerick Commercials beat the Dundalk Young Irelanders.

1928 – Dr Pat O'Callagan wins Independent Ireland's first ever Olympic gold medal in the hammer event in Amsterdam.

1956 – Ronnie Delany wins the 1500m at the Melbourne Olympic games.

1978 – John Treacy wins the World Cross Country Championship.

1981 – Irish-bred horse Shergar wins the English derby by the greatest ever margin.

1985 – Barry McGuigan beats Eusebio Pedrosa in London to win the World Featherweight Championship.

1987 – Stephen Roche becomes the first Irishman to win the Tour de France.

1990 – Republic of Ireland plays their first ever match in the finals of the World Cup, drawing with England in Sardinia.

Twenty of the Most Famous Sports Men and Women

1. George Best

George Best (22 May 1946–25 November 2005) was a Northern Irish international footballer who is chiefly remembered for his time playing with Manchester United FC. He played for United between 1963 and 1974, helping them to win the Football League Championship in 1965 and 1967, and the European Cup in 1968; that same year, he was named European Footballer of the Year and Football Writers' Association Player of the Year.

He made 466 appearances for Manchester United in all competitions, scoring 178 goals (including six in one game against Northampton Town). He was capped 37 times for Northern Ireland, scoring nine goals. He played mainly as a winger and was known for his dribbling skills and passing. Diego Maradona has frequently named Best as his all-time favourite player and Pelé once stated that Best was the best player he ever saw play.

While at Manchester United, Best's talent and showmanship made him a crowd and media favourite. He was dubbed 'the fifth Beatle' for his long hair and good looks.

2. John Mary Pius Boland

John Mary Pius Boland (16 September 1870–17 March 1958) was an Irish politician, and the very first Olympic champion in tennis.

Boland visited his friend Thrasyvoalos Manaos in Athens during the 1896 Summer Olympics. Manaos, a member of the organising committee, entered Boland in the tennis tournament. Boland promptly won the singles tournament and entered the doubles event with Traun, the German runner, whom he had defeated in the first round of the singles. Together, they won the doubles event.

Later, Boland was a member of parliament for South Kerry from 1900 to 1918.

3. Ronnie Delany

Ronald Michael Delany (6 March 1935), better known as Ron or Ronnie, is a former Irish athlete, who specialised in the middle distances.

Born in Arklow, Co Wicklow, Delany studied in the United States at Villanova University, where he was coached by the well-known track coach Jumbo Elliott. In 1956, he became the seventh runner to join the club of four-minute milers, but nonetheless struggled to make the Irish team for the 1956 Summer Olympics held in Melbourne.

Delany qualified for the Olympic 1500m final, in which home runner John Landy was the big favourite. Delany kept close to Landy until the final lap, when he started a crushing final sprint, winning the race in a new Olympic Record. Delany thereby became the first Irishman to win an Olympic title in athletics since Bob Tisdall in 1932, and the last one to date.

Delany continued his running career in North America, winning four successive Amateur Athletic Union (AAU) titles in the mile, adding to his total of four Irish national titles, and three National Collegiate Athletic Association (NCAA) titles.

4. Patrick Anthony Jennings

Patrick Anthony Jennings OBE (born 12 June 1945 in Newry, County Down) is a former football player. He played 119 games for his country as a goalkeeper, a figure which at the time was a world record, in an international career which lasted over 22 years. Jennings is considered one of the greatest goalkeepers of all time. During his career Jennings played in over 1,000 top-level games for club and country, he even managed to score a goal in the 1967 Charity Shield match while playing for Tottenham Hotspur.

5. Roy Keane

Roy Maurice Keane (born 10 August 1971) is a soccer player from Cork. He began his career at Cobh Ramblers, then made his name at Nottingham Forest before moving to Manchester United for a British record transfer fee in 1993. He was captain of the Irish national football team for a number of years, representing his country in the 1994 World Cup and playing a major role in their qualification for the 2002 World Cup before walking out at the start of the tournament after an argument with the team's manager. He was also captain for much of his time at Manchester United, when the team won the FA Premier League seven times and the FA Cup four times, and he played a major role in helping the team reach the UEFA Champions League final in 1999.

During his time at United, Keane was widely regarded as one of the finest midfield players of his generation, known for his inspirational leadership, excellent tackling and distribution abilities.

Keane's trophy haul with Manchester United includes: seven Premiership titles (1994, 1996, 1997, 1999, 2000, 2001, 2003), four FA Cups (1994, 1996, 1999, 2004), a European Cup (1999 - though Keane missed the final through suspension) and an Intercontinental Cup (1999). On 5 February 2005, Keane scored his fiftieth goal for Manchester United in a league game against Birmingham City. His appearance in the 2005 FA Cup final (which United lost) was his seventh final. Keane was also picked on the FIFA 100, a list of the greatest living footballers picked by Pelé.

At international level, Keane has represented his country 66 times. Keane was named Ireland's player of the tournament at the 1994 World Cup in the USA. In 2001, with Roy Keane putting in Man of the Match performances, Ireland went undefeated against international soccer heavyweights Portugal and the Netherlands, famously knocking out the Dutch to qualify for the 2002 World Cup in Japan and Korea. He is currently the manager of Sunderland Football Club

6. Sean Kelly

Sean Kelly, or John James Kelly (born 24 May 1956 in Waterford yet raised near Carrick-on-Suir, County Tipperary), is a former professional cyclist and arguably the greatest of his generation.

A natural sprinter, Kelly won numerous Classic cycle races and stages of the Grand Tours. He also won the 1988 Vuelta a España, and was the first rider to win the points classification or *Maillot vert* in the Tour de France four times (1982, 1983, 1985 and 1989).

Sean Kelly was one of the most dominant and successful cyclists of the 1980s and is regarded as one of the finest Classics riders of all time. From the start of his professional career in 1977 until his retirement in 1994, Kelly won nine 'Monuments of Cycling' Classics, and 193 races in total. When *Fédération Internationale de Cyclisme Professionel* (FICP) introduced world cycling rankings in March 1984, Kelly was the first rider to be ranked world number one, a title he held for over six years and which still remains a record. Kelly was known to be one of the hard men of professional cycling and was nicknamed 'The Cannibal' because of his insatiable appetite for victory, acheiving an incredible 33 victories in one season (1984).

7. Willie John McBride

Willie John McBride, MBE is an Irish rugby union player. He was born in Toombridge, County Antrim on 6 June 1940 and was educated at Ballymena Academy. His international rugby union debut was on Saturday 10 February 1962 against England at Twickenham when he was aged 21.

In his international career, which lasted from 1962 until 1975, he played in a record seventeen tests for the Lions. He was capped 63 times (twelve as captain) by Ireland. He won the last 52 of his 63 caps in succession. In the 1960s, when the robust physical play of the All Blacks and Springboks dominated, he was the only forward from the Home Nations who was their match.

Willie John's outstanding leadership qualities led to his appointment as captain of the 1974 Lions tour to South Africa. The test series was won 3-0, with one match drawn.

In 1975 as his international career was ending he played his last home game for Ireland at Lansdowne Road. The game was against France and near the end of the match, he scored his first ever try in an international. It was the crowning moment of a great playing career. His last international game was against Wales on Saturday 15 March 1975.

After retiring from playing the game, Willie John coached the Irish team and was manager of the 1983 Lions tour to New Zealand. He lives in Ballyclare, County Antrim. In 2004 he was named in *Rugby World* magazine as 'Heineken Rugby Personality of the Century'.

8. Barry McGuigan

Barry McGuigan (born 28 February 1961 in Clones, County Monaghan), nicknamed The Clones Cyclone, was a professional boxer who became a world featherweight champion.

McGuigan is a Roman Catholic, and at a time when Roman Catholics and Protestants were in the middle of a deeply rooted conflict in Northern Ireland, McGuigan and his Protestant girlfriend got married. McGuigan gained national hero status, and during the days he was boxing, Irish people had a popular saying: Leave the fighting to Barry.

His record was 32 wins and 3 losses, with 26 wins by knockout. In January 2005, McGuigan was elected into the International Boxing Hall of Fame.

9. Dr Patrick O'Callaghan

Dr Patrick 'Pat' O'Callaghan (15 September 1905-1 December 1991), was an Irish athlete and Olympic gold medallist. O'Callaghan was born in Duhallow near Kanturk in County Cork.

In 1927 he made his hammer-throwing debut in Dublin. The following year at the Olympic Games in Amsterdam he won the hammer-throwing championship. Thus he became the first person to win a gold medal while representing the Irish Free State. He retained his record four years later at the Olympics in Los Angeles where he won Ireland's second gold medal. He was not allowed to compete at the 1936 Olympic Games in Berlin because the International Amateur Athletic Federation refused to recognise the Irish association.

During his career Dr O'Callaghan won six Irish championships: the hammer, shot, discus, 56 lb (25 kg) shot for height and for distance, and high jump. He achieved an unofficial world record for the shot with a throw of 195 feet 5 inches (59.55 m) in 1937 at the Cork county championships, but as the International Association of Athletics Federations (IAAF) still refused to recognise the Irish association, the throw was not accepted. It stood as a record unofficially until 1949.

10. Brian O'Driscoll

Brian Gerald O'Driscoll (born 21 January 1979 in Dublin) is the current captain of the Irish rugby team and was the captain of the British and Irish Lions tour to New Zealand in 2005. He is an outside centre who plays club rugby for Leinster.

Educated at Blackrock College, O'Driscoll made his first appearance for Ireland in 1999, and established himself as one of rugby's most dangerous ball carriers by his ability to cut through defences and create space for his supporting runners.

O'Driscoll also appeared in all three British and Irish Lions tests on the team's 2001 tour of Australia. O'Driscoll also captained the British and Irish Lions team for their 2005 tour of New Zealand. He recently led Ireland to its third Triple Crown trophy in a row in the Six Nations tournament (2005, 2006 and 2007) and he was named player of the tournament in both 2006 and 2007. Included in this was a record-breaking victory over England in the second rugby match ever to be played at Croke Park in Dublin (up until 2007, only Gaelic games had ever been played at this venue).

11. Sonia O'Sullivan
Sonia O'Sullivan (born 28 November 1969) is a runner from Cobh, County Cork.

She was one of the leading female 5000m runners for most of the 1990s and early 2000s. Her crowning achievement was a gold medal at the 1995 World Athletics Championships. She also set a 5000m world record time in 1991, making her the first Irish woman to set a world track record. O'Sullivan entered the 1996 Atlanta Olympics as the favourite but had to withdraw due to a stomach illness. She won a silver medal at the 2000 Olympics, narrowly beaten. She participated in the 2004 Olympics 5000m final but finished in last place in what was possibly her final track and field appearance in the Olympics.

12. Stephen Roche
Stephen Roche (born 28 November 1959 in Dundrum near Dublin, is a retired professional cyclist. In a thirteen-year career, he peaked in 1987, becoming only the second cyclist in history to win the Triple Crown of overall victories in the Tour de France and Giro d'Italia stage races, plus victory in the World Cycling Championship. He was also the first and only Irishman ever to win the Tour de France.

In 1993, Roche retired from professional cycling and subsequently established bicycle training camps on the Spanish island of Majorca.

13. Keith Wood
Keith Wood (born 27 January 1972 in Killaloe, Co Clare) is a former international rugby union footballer who played hooker for Ireland, the Lions, Harlequins and Munster.

He started his career with Garryowen who he helped to All-Ireland titles in 1992 and 1994 before moving to Harlequins. He played 58 times for Ireland and five times for the Lions. Renowned for playing with his heart on his sleeve, Wood always put his body on the line, with trademark charging runs at the defence or bullish tackles. Never the most accurate player in the set piece his real strength was in leadership and open play.

He played on the 1997 and 2001 Lions tours, and was the first winner of the International Rugby Board (IRB) World Player of the Year award in 2001. He played a major part in the Lions' 2-1 series victory over the Springboks in 1997.

Wood also captained Ireland. He was followed as Ireland captain by Brian O'Driscoll. Wood retired from playing after the 2003 Rugby World Cup.

14. Ollie Campbell

Seamus Oliver Campbell was an international rugby player, born in Dublin on 3 March 1954.

He won 22 Ireland caps (eighteen at out-half and four at centre) between 1976 and 1984, and played six Lions Tests (two versus South Africa in 1980 and four versus New Zeland in 1983). His 217 international points was an Irish record until Michael Kiernan surpassed it in 1988.

A brilliant place-kicker, he was a superb all-round player and was the key man in 1982 when Ireland won the Triple Crown after a 33-year gap. He still holds the following Irish scoring records: most points in Five Nation Championships season (52 in four matches, 1982-3); most penalty goals in Five Nations Championship season (fourteen in four matches, 1982-3); most penalty goals in an international (six versus Scotland in Dublin, 1982); most points for Ireland on overseas tour (60, in five matches, Australia, 1979). He was top scorer on both his Lions Tours, with 60 in South Africa in 1980 and 124 in New Zealand in 1983.

15. Christy Ring

Nicholas Christopher 'Christy' Ring (12 December 1920-2 March 1979) was a famous hurler for Cork in the 1940s, 1950s and 1960s. He is universally regarded as the greatest player of all time.

Christy Ring was born in the small village of Cloyne, County Cork in 1920. Ring's first hurling success came when he won a County Junior championship medal with the Cloyne Club in 1939, and later winning a record eleven county senior medals with the Glen Rovers GAA club. He made his senior début with Cork in 1939 and shares with John Doyle of Tipperary the distinction of winning eight All-Ireland medals, from 1941, 1942, 1943, 1944, 1946, 1952, 1953 and 1954.

Throughout his career Ring won a record eighteen Railway Cup medals with Munster between 1942 and 1963, appearing in 22 finals in all. He also won four National Hurling League medals with Cork (1940, 1941, 1948 and 1953) and was top scorer in the game three times (1959, when he became the only player to average over ten points a game, 1961 and 1962, when he shared the honours with Jimmy Doyle of Tipperary)

The Christy Ring Bridge over the River Lee in Cork remembers his achievements. One of Cork city's principle GAA stadia, Páirc Uí Rinn, is named in his honour. Ring was also honoured by the Gaelic Athletic Association in 2000 when he was named on the 'Hurling Team of the Millennium'.

Christy Ring died suddenly at the age of 58 on 2 March 1979. In an interview about his hurling exploits shortly before his death Ring said, 'I always liked to do the impossible'. Ring's graveside oration was delivered by a former teammate and the then Taoiseach, Jack Lynch.

16. Packie Bonner

Patrick Joseph (Packie) Bonner (born 24 May 1960 in Donegal) is a former soccer goalkeeper for the Republic of Ireland, who earned 80 caps after making his debut on his twenty-first birthday.

Many remember Bonner for his famous penalty save from Daniel Timofte of Romania in the 1990 World Cup finals.

In 1978, Jock Stein signed him for Celtic from Leicester City and he went on to play 642 times for them. With Celtic, he won four League Championship badges, three Scottish Cup winners' medals and a League Cup winners' medal. His last appearance for Celtic was winning the 1995 Scottish Cup final under Tommy Burns.

17. Eamonn Coghlan

Eamonn Coghlan (born on 21 November 1952) is a three-time Olympian and retired runner. Coghlan, born in Drimnagh, County Dublin, was nicknamed 'The Chairman of the Boards' because of his success on indoor tracks. He set the world record in the indoor mile run at 3:50.6 in 1981 and again in 1983 at New Jersey's Meadowlands, running 3:49.78. The record stood until 1997 when it was broken by Morocco's Hicham El Guerrouj in a time of 3:48.45. Coghlan's 1983 time remains the fastest mile ever run in the United States, and one of only three sub-3:50 miles run on American soil to date.

He also set the record for the indoor 2000-metre run at 4:54.07 in 1987 which stood until Haile Gebrselassie of Ethiopia ran 4:52.86 in 1998. Coghlan won the world famous Wanamaker Mile at the Millrose games in NYC's Madison Square Garden a record seven times (1977, 1979-81, 1983, 1985, 1987). He won the 5000 metre race at the 1983 World Championships, making up to some degree for his two fourth places in the Olympics. In 1994 became the first man over age 40 to run a sub-four minute mile.

18. Paul McGrath

Paul McGrath (born 4 December 1959 in Ealing, England) is a former international soccer defender and a long-time member of the Republic of Ireland national team.

McGrath worked briefly as an apprentice sheet metal worker in Dublin before becoming a full-time professional footballer. Brought up in a number of orphanages, McGrath was a secondary school student by the time he played his first organised game of soccer. He began playing as a schoolboy with Pearse Rovers and played junior football for Dalkey United. In 1981 he moved to the Football League of Ireland club St Patrick's Athletic. He excelled at St Pat's, earning the nickname 'The Black Pearl of Inchicore' and receiving the Professional Footballers Association of Ireland (PFAI) Young Player of the Year Award in his first and only season.

He moved to Manchester United (1982-89), and later Aston Villa (1989-96), Derby County (1996-97), and Sheffield United (1997-98). While at Villa Park he was nicknamed God, and was named Professional Footballers Association (in England) (PFA) Players' Player of the Year in 1993. He is considered one of the greatest players in Villa's history.

McGrath was capped 83 times for his country, scoring eight goals, and played in the 1990 and 1994 World Cups.

19. D.J. Carey

Denis Joseph Carey was born in November 1970 in Gowran, County Kilkenny. He is a hurling forward for Kilkenny and is regarded as one of the finest hurlers of his generation, or perhaps of all time. Besides having many All-Ireland medals at minor, under-21 and senior level, Carey also has world championship medals in Gaelic handball.

D.J. soon made his way into the Kilkenny minor and under-21 teams. In 1991 he played in his first All-Ireland Senior Hurling Championship against the famous Tipperary team of the late 1980s and early 1990s, and won his first senior All-Ireland medal against Cork the following year. Success continued in 1993 for D.J., now a household name in Ireland, when Kilkenny completed the double, beating Galway in the All-Ireland final. D.J. had been outstanding in the championship, scoring 2-4 against Offaly and 1-5 against

Wexford in the Leinster final replay. D.J.'s performances were widely recognised, and he won All-Star awards in each of these years, as well as Hurler Of The Year in 1993.

20. Steve Collins

Steve Collins was born on 21 July 1964 in Dublin,. His nickname was The Celtic Warrior, and he is a former world boxing champion. He is considered to be one of the toughest boxers of the past century, never having been stopped, in a high profile career. The Irishman was part of a golden age of European supermiddleweight boxing, along with Chris Eubank, Joe Calzaghe and Nigel Benn. He was trained by Freddie Roach throughout his career. Collins started boxing profesionally in 1986. However he was long considered the nearly man of boxing, after losing three world title fights on points. It was not until Collins reached his thirties that he fulfilled his potential, becoming the WBO middleweight champion in 1994 and later the WBO supermiddleweight champion in 1995.

Eighteen GAA Stars in the GAA Hall of Fame

1. Tony Scullion
Club: Ballinascreen
County: Derry
Honours: One All-Ireland Senior, six consecutive Railway Cups, two Ulster Senior, four All-Stars, three National League, one Ulster under-21.

2. Jarlath Burns
Club: Silverbridge Harps
County: Armagh
Honours: One Railway Cup, one Ulster Senior, one Sigerson Cup, one Armagh minor championship.

3. Greg Blaney
Club: Carryduff (football), Ballycran (hurling)
County: Down
Honours: Football – two All-Ireland Senior, one All-Ireland under-21, five Railway Cup, three Ulster Senior, three All-Stars, one National League, one Ulster Minor, one Sigerson Cup. Hurling – one Ulster Senior, one Ulster under-21 and one All-Ireland special minor.

4. Terence 'Sambo' McNaughton
Club: Cushendall Ruairí Óg
County: Antrim
Honours: One All-Star, eight Antrim Senior championships, eighteen Ulster medals (club and county), one All-Australian championship, one All-American championship.

5. Tony Doran
Club: Buffers Alley

County: Wexford

Honours: One All-Ireland Senior Hurling; four Leinster Senior Hurling; one All-Ireland Club; Texaco Hurler of the Year 1976; one All-Ireland Minor; one Leinster Minor; one All-Ireland Under-21; three Leinster Under-21; eleven County Senior Titles.

6. Seanie O'Leary

Club: Youghal

County: Cork

Honours: Four All-Ireland Senior Hurling; nine Munster Senior Hurling; one County Intermediate Hurling.

7. Michael (Babs) Keating

County: Tipperary

Hurling Club: Ballybacon Grange

Football Club: Ardfinnan

Honours Hurling – Three All-Ireland Senior; four Railway Cup medals; All-Ireland under-21; Intermediate All-Ireland. Footbal – Railway Cup; five Tipperary County Senior Medals.

8. Ger Cunningham

Club: St Finbarrs

County: Cork

Honours: Three All-Ireland Senior Hurling medals; seven Munster Senior Hurling medals; three National League medals; four Railway Cup medals ; four All-Stars; six County Senior Hurling medals; Hurler of the Year 1986.

9. Billy Hennessy

Club: Tullaroan

County: Kilkenny

Honours won: Two All-Ireland Senior medals (1992 and 1993); three Leinster Senior medals; two National Leagues; one County title.

10. Gary Kirby

Club: Patrickswell
County: Limerick
Honours: All-Ireland Minor and Under-21 Hurling; two Munster Senior Hurling; two National Leagues; four All-Stars; thirteen County Titles.

11. Seanie Walsh

County: Kerry
Club: Kerrins O'Rahillys (Tralee)
Honours: Seven All-Ireland Senior Football; 11 Munster Senior Football; Two National Football Leagues; Three Railway Cups; Two All-Stars; All-Ireland Minor Football (1975); Three All-Ireland Under-21 Football.

12. Anton O'Toole

Club: Synge Street
County: Dublin
Honours: Four All-Ireland Senior Football Medals; eight Leinster Medals.

13. Gay O'Driscoll

County: Dublin
Club: St Vincents
Honours: Three All-Ireland Senior Football; six Leinster Senior Football; two Leinster Club Football; one All-Ireland Club Football; two All-Stars; one Leinster Under-21 Hurling.

14. Mick Lyons

Club: Summerhill
County: Meath
Honours: All Ireland winner 1987, 1988

15. Tom Spillane
Club: Templenoe
County: Kerry
Honours: Four All-Ireland Senior Medals; five Munster Senior Medals; one Kerry County Title (with Kenmare District); three All-Stars.

16. Larry Tompkins
Clubs: Castlehaven (Cork) and Eadestown (Kildare)
Counties: Cork and Kildare
Honours: Two Cork County Football Championships; two All-Ireland Senior titles; eight Munster titles; one National League; one All-Ireland Under-21 (with Kildare).

17. Bernard Flynn
Clubs: St Colmcille's, Meath. Mullingar Shamrock's, Westmeath
Counties: Meath
Honours: 2 All Ireland titles, 3 National League titles

18. Eamon (Junior) McManus
Club: Clann na Gael
County: Roscommon
Honours: Two Senior Connaught titles; eight Connaught club titles; thirteen County Senior titles.

Eight Facts about the GAA

1. The **Gaelic Athletic Association** (GAA) is an amateur sporting organisation founded by Michael Cusack to preserve and cultivate the national games.

2. When the **GAA** was founded in 1884, it had Davin as its first president. Dr T.W. Croke (Archbishop of Cashel) became the first patron of the Association, and Croke Park in Dublin (the Association Headquarters) is named in his honour.

3. The **Association** was nationalist in outlook and members were banned from playing non-Gaelic games. The Association also banned members of British Crown Forces from membership.

4. The **GAA** is the largest sporting organisation in Ireland, boasting 2,800 clubs, comprising of 182,000 footballers and 97,000 hurlers. Membership of the GAA exceeds 800,000 at home and abroad, ensuring its role as a powerful national movement, with an important social and cultural influence in Irish life.

5. The association's aim is to be 'a national organisation which has as its basic aim the strengthening of the national identity of a 32 county Ireland through the preservation and promotion of Gaelic games and pastimes'.

6. In 1984 the **GAA** celebrated its 100th year in existence. This anniversary was celebrated by the GAA with numerous events throughout the country and the All-Ireland Senior Hurling Championship final was moved to Semple Stadium in Thurles to honour the town in the which the GAA was founded.

7. Croke Park is the biggest **GAA** stadium in the country with a capacity of 82,500 people. After that, the next three biggest stadiums are all in Munster – Semple Stadium in Thurles, County Tipperary (53,000), the Gaelic Grounds in Limerick (50,000) and the Fitzgerald Stadium in Killarney, County Kerry (43,000).

8. On 16 April 2005, the **GAA**'s congress voted to suspend its Rule 42 ban on 'foreign games' to enable the Football Association of Ireland and the Irish Rugby Football Union to play their international fixtures at Croke Park while the Lansdowne stadium was being rebuilt.

Seven Facts about Gaelic Football

1. **Gaelic football** is played by approximately 250,000 men and women, making it the most popular sport in Ireland.

2. The first record of **Gaelic football** is in the Statutes of Galway (1527) which allowed the playing of football but banned hurling. The earliest reported match took place at Slane, County Meath, in 1712 when Meath played their neighbours, Louth.

3. Capacity crowds attend the All-Ireland **Gaelic Football** Final at Croke Park every September (the third Sunday of September). The winners of the Senior Final receive the Sam Maguire Cup.

4. Since the first All-Ireland Senior **Gaelic Football** Final in 1887, Kerry have been the most successful team, winning 30 times. Only Kerry (twice) and Wexford have won in four successive years.

5. The highest attendance ever recorded at an All-Ireland Senior **Gaelic Football** Final was 90,556 at the 1961 Down versus Offaly final. Following the introduction of seating to the Cusack stand in 1966, the largest crowd recorded since has been reduced to 73,588.

6. The highest number of appearances by an individual in the All-Ireland Senior **Gaelic Football** Final is ten. This has been achieved by Paudie O'Shea, Pat Spillane and Denis 'Ogie' Moran. They were each winners on no less than eight occasions.

7. The highest individual score in the modern 70-minute **Gaelic Football** game was recorded by Jimmy Keaveney (Dublin) in the 1977 Final against Armagh where he scored 2-6, and by Mike Sheehy (Kerry) in the 1979 Final against Dublin where he also recorded 2-6.

Nine Facts about Hurling

1. **Hurling** is the oldest Irish sport and dates from pre-Christian times. No standardised rules existed until the GAA was formed in 1884.

2. **Hurling** is the third most popular sport in Ireland and is played by approximately 100,000 Irish people.

3. The women's equivalent of **hurling** is called camogie and is played according to the same basic rules, but with a smaller pitch and smaller sticks. There are 50,000 camogie players in Ireland.

4. **Hurling** is one of the fastest field games in the world, and is played with an ash stick between 30 and 37 inches in length, with a broad end. The stick is used to hit and carry the sliotar which is a small ball weighing about 4oz.

5. Since the first Senior **Hurling** Final in 1887, Cork have won the most times with 27 victories. The provinces of Leinster and Munster dominate the modern game – out of all of Connaught and Ulster, only Galway have managed to win the Hurling championship.

6. The highest individual score in a Senior **Hurling** Final was by Nicky English of Tipperary who scored 18 points 2-12 in the 1989 final against Antrim.

7. The record for most appearances in a Senior **Hurling** Final is held by Christy Ring of Cork (1941-1954) and John Doyle of Tipperary (1949-1965). Each appeared in ten finals, winning eight of them.

8. The record for most All-Ireland **Hurling** Winners medals is held by

Noel Skehan of Kilkenny who won nine medals between 1963 and 1983.

9. The largest attendance at a Senior **Hurling** Final is when Cork beat Wexford in 1954.

THIRTEEN FACTS ABOUT IRELAND AND THE OLYMPICS

1. J.J. Keane, then one of Ireland's leading sports administrators, was elected to the International Olympic Committee (IOC) in 1922. It is now generally accepted that the Irish **Olympic** Council, as it was known at the outset, came into existence in 1922 but due to the loss of the minutes of the early meetings of the Council, the exact date is now not known.

2. Ireland was given formal recognition as an independent nation in the Olympic Movement at the IOC session in Paris in 1924 and it was at the Paris games that Ireland made its first appearance in an **Olympic** Games as an independent nation.

3. No medals in the sporting events were won by Ireland at the Paris games but Jack Yeats was awarded an **Olympic** silver medal for his painting *Swimming* in the Olympic Arts division and Oliver St John Gogarty was awarded a bronze medal for his 'Ode to the Tailteann Games' in the Literature division. (Arts competitions formed part of the Olympic Games during its early years, from 1912 to 1948.)

4. The first Irish-born winner of an **Olympic** gold medal was John Pius Boland, a native of Dublin, who won the Tennis Singles at Athens in 1896 and he was to win a second Olympic gold medal when he partnered Fritz Traun in the doubles.

5. Perhaps the outstanding Irish-born personality of the early years of the **Olympic** games was Tom Kiely, who won the all-round championship, the forerunner of the modern decathlon, at the games in St Louis in 1904.

6. Peter O'Connor and Con Leahy, who won gold medals at the

Olympic games at Athens in 1906, made their own spirited protest on the claims that Ireland was part of the United Kingdom. They did this by raising an Irish Flag to the top of the 200-foot mast which dominated the stadium in Athens.

7. In 1928 Ireland, as an independent nation, had its first **Olympic** gold medal at Amsterdam with Dr Pat O'Callaghan's unexpected victory in the hammer event. At the time he was barely out of the novice class and he had been included in the Irish team mainly to gain experience of top-class competition. Over the years he was to develop into one of the world's greatest hammer throwers and he demonstrated this by winning his second Olympic gold medal at Los Angeles in 1932.

8. By 1952 the Lord Killanin had become president of the **Olympic** Council and had also become the IOC member in Ireland. Significantly one of his first moves was to have the name of the Council changed from the Irish Olympic Council to the Olympic Council of Ireland which, of course, ensured that the name Ireland appeared in the title. He served as President of the International Olympic Committee (IOC) between 1972 and 1980.

9. Ronnie Delany was Ireland's gold medal winner in the 1,500 metres in 1956. After qualifying comfortably in his semi-final he ran an astute race in the final and finished it with a glorious burst of speed which, in addition to the gold medal gave him an **Olympic** record of 3.41.2.

10. A memorable moment for Ireland at the Barcelona Olympics in 1992 was the victory of Michael Carruth of Dublin who became the first Irishman to win an **Olympic** gold medal in boxing.

11. The 1996 Olympic games in Atlanta were a personal triumph for

Michelle Smith de Bruin who became the first Irish woman to win an **Olympic** gold medal and also the first Irish competitor to do so in swimming. In all she won three gold medals and a bronze. She was later disgraced when found to be using performance-enhancing drugs.

12. Ireland's Lord Killanin (1914-1999) became President of the International **Olympic** Committee in 1972, serving until 1980 and he became the Honorary Life President of the IOC in 1980.

13. Cian O'Connor was an Irish equestrian who won a gold show jumping medal at the 2004 **Olympics** with his horse, Waterford Crystal. He became an instant national hero, being the only Irish medallist that year.

However, it emerged that the horse, Waterford Crystal, had tested positive for a prohibited substance. The Federation Equestre International (FEI) ruled that O'Connor must be stripped of his medal and he also received a three-month ban from competition. The Irish Show Jumping Team was also disqualified by the Olympic Board (they had finished in seventh place).

CRIME
AND
TRAGEDY

Eight Criminals' Nicknames

1. The General
Martin Cahill was a prominent Irish criminal from Dublin. In the early 1990s, he gained notoriety in the media, who referred to him as The General. They used the nickname in order to write about Cahill's activities while avoiding legal problems. Cahill was murdered in 1994.

2. Bronco
Christy Dunne led the Dunne family, who were one of Ireland's first family-based firms of armed robbers in the 1970s. They played a major role in ushering in a new era of serious crime in Ireland. He got his nickname from his father (also Christy) who was nicknamed 'Bronco' after the cowboy 'Bronco Bill'.

3. The Psycho
Peter Joseph Judge, or P.J. Judge, was a psychopath who used fear and violence to control a huge drug distribution network. He was from Finglas in Dublin and took pleasure in dispensing pain and death to those who crossed him. He also had the additional nickname of 'The Executioner'. He was shot dead in his car in 1996.

4. The Builder
Paddy Shanahan was from Kildare. He came from a respectable family with no criminal background. He was an auctioneer and owned a tarmacadam business before he turned to crime. He became involved in theft and armed robbery.

He then retired from crime and went back to being a successful businessman. He was, however, assassinated in 1993.

5. The Penguin
George Mitchell was from Ballyfermot in Dublin. The *Sunday World* gave him the nickname when he was first photographed and named by the newspapers in 1995. He was one of the chief gangland bosses in Dublin and was involved in robbing warehouses and paintings. During the daytime, he worked as a lorry driver, delivering biscuits.

6. The Scam Man
Stephen Walsh was one of Dublin's best-known and most elusive gangsters. He was from Pearce Street in Dublin and was involved in armed crime, violence, extortion, intimidation and compensation fraud. He used to organise staged accidents throughout the city and then made fraudulent compensation claims through the courts against the public utilities and insurance companies.

7. The Boxer
Thomas Martin Mullen was at one time the biggest supplier of heroin on the streets of Dublin. He organised his business from a run-down flat in the Lourdes complex off Sean McDermott Street. When he was younger, he was a talented boxer. He represented Ireland as a light-middleweight champion at tournaments around the world.

8. The Monk
Gerry Hutch first appeared in the headlines in 1995, when he was linked to a spectacular robbery worth almost £3 million. This was one of many robberies he was linked to during his career.

His nickname refers to the fact that that he kept to himself, He was not flamboyant and preferred a low-key approach when doing his business, avoiding confrontation. He currently operates a chauffeur business in Dublin.

Nine Facts about the Irish Crown Jewels

1. Insignia
The Insignia of the Knights of St Patrick, commonly known as the Irish Crown Jewels, was a set of jewels worn by the sovereign at the installation of the Knights of the Order of St Patrick, the Irish equivalent of the English Order of the Garter and the Scottish Order of the Thistle. The theft of the 'Irish crown jewels' in Dublin, Ireland in 1907 remains a famous mystery that still is discussed. The Irish crown jewels were never found.

2. Order of St Patrick
King George III instituted the Order of St Patrick in 1783. The Irish crown jewels were the insignia of the Order, and consisted of two items: a star and a badge, each composed of rubies, emeralds and Brazilian diamonds.

3. Dublin Castle
In 1903, the jewels were transferred to a safe, which was to be placed in the newly-constructed strong room in Dublin Castle. The new safe was too large for the doorway to the strong room, and Arthur Vicars, the Officer of Arms of Dublin Castle, instead stored the jewels in his office. Seven latch keys to the door of the Office of Arms were held by Vicars and his staff, and two keys to the safe containing the insignia were both in the custody of Vicars.

4. Jewels Go Missing
The jewels were discovered missing on 6 July 1907, four days before the State Visit of King Edward VII and Queen Alexandra. The theft is reported to have angered the King but the visit went ahead.

5. Sir Arthur Vicars

Vicars refused to resign his position as Officer of Arms, and similarly refused to appear at a Viceregal Commission into the theft (the commission did not possess powers to subpoena witnesses) held from 10 January 1908. Vicars argued for a public royal inquiry in lieu of the commission, and publicly accused his second in command, Francis Shackleton, of the theft, who was suspected of being blackmailed on account of his homosexuality (which was a criminal offence at the time).

6. Shackleton

Shackleton was exonerated in the commission's report, and Vicars was found to have 'not exercise[d] due vigilance or proper care as the custodian of the regalia'. Vicars met a sad end in disgrace: on 14 April 1921 he was shot dead by IRA militia.

7. Never Recovered

It is believed that the Irish crown jewels have never been recovered. It has been rumoured that in 1927 the Irish crown jewels were offered for sale to the Irish Free State for £5000 and that they were bought back on then prime minister W.T. Cosgrave's orders, with the instructions that the fact that the Irish State owned them was not to be revealed, for fear of criticism from republicans and because of the tight budgetary situation in the Irish Free State. However, an extensive search in the Irish National Archives has failed to find any evidence that they were bought or if so, what happened to them subsequently. (The Irish state until the 1940s did have some of the Russian crown jewels which were used as collateral for a loan given to the Russian Republic by the Irish Republic in or around 1920. It is possible the rumour about the state possessing the Irish crown jewels grew because it was known that some crown jewels were stored in government buildings in Dublin, people naturally presuming that they must be the Irish crown jewels.)

8. Last Appointees

The Irish Executive Council under W.T. Cosgrave chose not to keep appointing people to the Order when the Irish Free State left the United Kingdom in 1922. Since then, only two people have been appointed to the Order, both were members of the Royal Family. The then Prince of Wales was appointed with the agreement of W.T. Cosgrave in 1928 while his younger brother, Henry, Duke of Gloucester, was appointed with Eamon de Valéra's agreement in 1934.

9. Death of Last Member

The Duke of Gloucester, at his death, in 1974 was the last surviving member of the Order. It has, however, never actually been abolished and its resurrection has been discussed in Irish government circles on a number of occasions.

Eight Famous Prison Escapes

1. Mountjoy Prison

Gunther Schutz was a German spy who had been sent to Ireland during the Second World War primarily to transmit weather reports to Germany that would assist German assaults on neighbouring Britain. He was also to make contact with the IRA and hire agents in Ireland to report on any military activity there, such as the movement of troops. He was captured shortly after parachuting into Ireland in early 1941 and sent to Mountjoy Prison in Dublin.

In February 1942 he and another German, Van Loon, broke out through the windows of the men's toilets. They had spent the previous months sawing through the steel bars on the windows of the toilets. Van Loon was unable to scale the prison wall and was re-captured, but Schutz made it over (dressed as a woman).

Although he had twisted his ankle coming down from the 20-foot wall, he made his way to a house on Inisfallen Parade where he met by the brother of an IRA inmate. He was then moved to different houses in Drumcondra, Blackrock and Rathmines. He was eventually re-captured trying to leave the country by boat at Ros na Riogh in late April 1942 and ended up back in the more secure prison barracks in Athlone.

2. Derry Prison

In March 1943, 21 IRA internees made their way through an underground tunnel out of Derry Prison. They had spent the previous six months digging the 45-foot tunnel and had broken through to the surface into a house's coal shed on the outside. It was estimated that 15 tonnes of clay had been dispersed around the prison. Paddy Adams was one of the escapees - the uncle of the current Sinn Féin president, Gerry Adams.

Once the prisoners surfaced in the coal shed, they had to make their way through the house of the Logue family to reach a furniture van, which was to be the getaway vehicle. The IRA on the outside had organised the van.

Many of the men were caught again soon afterwards but the Derry escape was a fantastic propoganda coup for the IRA.

3. Crumlin Road Jail
In November 1941, eleven IRA internees had been selected to escape from a Belfast jail. They staged a football match and and during the second half, two rope ladders were thrown over the wall. The 'Crumlin Kangaroos', as they were later known, clambered up the ropes and escaped. Fifteen inmates had been chosen to hold back the wardens.

The men made their way into getaway cars, where civilian clothes were waiting for them and seven of them managed to make their way to Sinn Féin headquarters in Dublin for a press conference, which was another huge propaganda coup for the IRA.

4. HMS *Maidstone*
HMS *Maidstone* was a prison ship moored in Belfast lough. In January 1972, seven IRA internees escaped by sawing through a barred window, climbing down a rope and making a twenty-minute swim to the shore.

They had stored up their margarine rations and black boot polish to smear on their bodies during the swim. Margarine was used to insulate them from the cold and the polish was used to make them less visible to the British army sentries. Their getaway vehicle failed to show so they stole a bus from the nearby Harland and Wolff shipyard. They then drove to the nearest nationalist area, the Markets, where they entered a pub. The nearly naked prisoners were given clothes by the pub's customers and then they were given refuge in safe houses around the city.

Shortly afterwards, the escapees were smuggled across the border and a press conference was held to mark the escape of the 'Magnificent Seven. HMS *Maidstone* was closed three months later and sent to Scotland to be scrapped.

5. Mountjoy Prison
On 31 October 1973, three of the IRA's most senior men (J.B. O'Hagan, Kevin Mallon and Seamus Twomey) were snatched from Dublin's Mountjoy Prison's exercise yard by helicopter. The helicopter had been falsely booked and then hijacked. It was then flown to Baldolye racecourse where a group of volunteers were waiting with transport. The three men were then taken in to Dublin safe houses.

It was a major embarrassment for the government and it resulted in all important political prisoners being moved to the maximum-security prison in Portlaoise. Also, intersecting wires were put over prison yards to prevent similar escapes in the future.

The band, the Wolfe Tones, quickly released their 'Helicopter Song' which was immediately banned. It still managed to become an instant hit, soaring to number one in the charts, having sold over 11,000 copies in a single week.

6. Mountjoy Prison
Kenneth and Keith Littlejohn robbed the Allied Irish Bank on Dublin's Grafton street in 1972. When caught, they were imprisoned in a secure wing of Dublin's Mountjoy Prison. They were kept away from nationalist prisoners as they had links with the British Secret Service.

The brothers managed to get their hands on some hacksaw blades and cut their way through the steel bars on the windows. Kenneth claimed at one stage that he was on hunger strike but actually he was slimming down from 14 stone to 11 stone, to allow him to slip through the bars on the window.

They were having difficulty using their rope to scale the wall but luckily, some labourers working inside the prison had left some planks lying around that the two brothers used to get to the top of the wall. It was a high wall and Keith badly sprained his ankle jumping down and was captured shortly afterwards.

Kenneth made his way through the city and ended up in Corpus Christi Church for a night. He then slept rough on Howth Head for two nights before making his way to Belfast and then onto Amsterdam via Britain.

He was arrested in London almost two years later and returned to Mountjoy Prison.

7. Long Kesh

Long Kesh interment camp was considered to be the most secure prison in western Europe but in 1983, 38 IRA prisoners managed to break out.

Larry Marley had been appointed as the escape officer and realised that there might be an opportunity to escape via the lorry that delivered the prisoner's food each day. Also, Sunday was chosen as the day of escape because the prison ran on a skeleton staff on Sundays due to a huge overtime bill.

Guns were smuggled into the prison and nine wardens were overpowered internally. Some of the prisoners donned the warden's uniforms. They then took the lorry and drove the half a mile to Tally Lodge which was the perimeter of the prison. However, the alarm was raised before they reached the perimeter so all 38 prisoners made a bolt for it through some fencing and out into the countryside. They scattered in different directions and started hijacking cars and making their way to nationalist areas.

Fifteen of the 38 had been re-captured by the end of the day but twenty of the escapees stayed at large for a significant amount of time. Marley, the man who had organised the escape, remained in the prison as ordered by the IRA because he had only a short time left of his sentence to serve.

8. Maze Prison

In September 1973, Fr Gerry Green arrived at the Maze prison to say Mass for the prisoners. During the service, some of the prisoners noticed that he bore a remarkable resemblance to one of the prisoners, John Green. This was due to the fact that they were actually brothers.

Later that day, Fr Green left the prison and told the warden he would be back the following Sunday. He was never seen again. His brother, the real Fr Green, was found bound and gagged inside the prison.

ELEVEN FACTS ABOUT THE *TITANIC*

1. In 1912, the *Titanic*, a steamship in England's White Star Line, set out on its doomed maiden voyage, with 2,227 enthusiastic passengers and crew members on board for the historic trip from Southampton, England, to New York City. Only 705 would survive. On Sunday 14 April 1912, just four days after setting out on its first voyage, the R.M.S. *TITANIC* passenger ship struck an iceberg off the coast of Newfoundland at 11.40pm, and subsequently sank at 2.20am.

2. The *Titanic* was designed to hold 32 lifeboats, though only twenty were on board; White Star management was concerned that too many boats would sully the aesthetic beauty of the ship.

3. Survivors were rescued by the *Carpathia*, which was 58 miles southeast of *Titanic* when it received the distress call.

4. *Titanic* boasted electric elevators, a swimming pool, a squash court, a Turkish Bath and a gymnasium with a mechanical horse and mechanical camel.

5. 3 million rivets were used in *Titanic*'s hull.

6. The wreckage of *Titanic* was located in 1985, 12,500 feet down, about 350 miles (531km) southeast of Newfoundland, Canada.

7. A first class (parlour suite) ticket on *Titanic* cost $4,350, which translates into $50,000 today.

8. *Titanic* was one of the largest movable objects ever built, measuring 883 feet long (1/6 of a mile), 92 feet wide, 104 feet high and

weighing 46.328 tons from keel to bridge.

9. *Titanic* cost an unprecedented $7.5 million to build–which translates into $400 million today.

10. *Titanic* took three years to build.

11. It took *Titanic* approximately 2 hours, 40 minutes to sink.

Ten Provisions on the *Titanic*

1. 75,000lbs of fresh meat

2. 11,000lbs of fresh fish

3. 40,000 fresh eggs

4. 40 tonnes of potatoes

5. 7,000 heads of lettuce

6. 250 barrels of flour

7. 36,000 apples

8. 36,000 oranges

9. 15,000 bottles of ale and stout

10. 8,000 cigars

SIX ITEMS OF CARGO FROM THE *TITANIC* CLAIMED AS LOST

1. One Renault 35hp automobile owned by passenger William Carter

2. 50 cases of toothpaste

3. Eight dozen tennis balls were lost

4. A cask of china headed for Tiffany's

5. Five grand pianos

6. 30 cases of golf clubs and tennis rackets

Ten Kidnappings

1. 1972: Curran Family

Noel Curran was the bank manager of the Royal Bank on Grafton Street, Dublin, which was a subsidiary of Allied Irish Banks. On the morning of 12 October, three armed men rang the doorbell of his family home on Lower Kilmacud Road in Stillorgan.

They proceeded to round up the family members, Curran's wife, his two children and his sister-in-law. Curran was driven in his own car to the bank while his family were held hostage.

The gang took a further 22 bank employees hostage as they arrived for work that morning. The amount taken by the gang was £67,000 which at the time was a record amount stolen in Ireland. All in all, the gang treated their hostages well and there were no physical injuries.

What makes this kidnapping so interesting is that it turned out the men responsible were English brothers, the Littlejohns with their English accomplices.

They were eventually handed over by the British to the Irish government and they served time for their actions. A substantial amount of the money was also recovered.

2. 1973: Thomas Niedmayer

Thomas Niedmayer was the German managing director of the successful Grundig manufacturing plant in Belfast (Grundig produced tapes, tape players / recorders etc).

His kidnapping was an attempt by the IRA to force the British government into releasing two IRA prisoners. The two prisoners were sisters, Dolours and Marian Price. They and six men had been given life sentences for their part in the Old Bailey bombing in London in 1973. The sisters were on hunger strike at the time.

Niedmayer was kidnapped by two men who called at his house.

He had a high profile and had been appointed Northern Ireland Honorary Consul of the Federal Republic of Germany. The role involved promoting Germany's interests in Northern Ireland, developing economic trade links between Germany and the province. The IRA were aware of the economic impact this kidnapping could have on Northern Ireland. The last contact was ten days after the incident when a demand was made for £250,000. Then the trail went cold.

In 1976, the Nuremburg court officially declared Niedmayer dead. This was mainly to ease the death benefits to his family. In 1980, Niedmayer's remains were accidentally found by a man operating a digger in an unofficial dump on the outskirts of Belfast.

In 1981, John Bradley pleaded guilty to Niedmayer's manslaughter. He told the court that on the third day of the kidnapping, Niedmayer confronted his guards and a struggle ensued. Bradley described how they had to hold him down and how he was struck on the back of the head with a pistol. He continued to scream and fight and eventually they had to sit on him and forced his face into the mattress. His body eventually went limp and the man was dead.

3. 1975: Dr Herrema

Dr Herrema was a Dutch industrialist based in Limerick. He worked for the Ferenka corporation.

He was driving his Mercedes car to work on the quiet Monaleen Road when he was stopped by a supposed Garda in a makeshift uniform. Once his identity was confirmed, he was bundled into another car and driven away.

This was masterminded by the nationalist Eddie Gallagher, who at the time was a rogue operative, and Marian Coyle. His lover, Rose Dugdale, was imprisoned for her part in the helicopter bombing of an RUC station. Gallagher now demanded her release along with two other IRA members, Kevin Mallon and James Hyland.

The gang were eventually tracked to a house in Monasterevin. They had no water, no food, no heat and they became dependant on the Gardaí for their basic needs. An eighteen-day siege ensued before Dr Herrera was released in reasonably good condition after his 36-day ordeal. The gang all received lengthy prison sentences.

4. 1978: Fr Hugh Murphy

Fr Murphy was a 59-year-old Catholic priest working in County Antrim. He was kidnapped by two men who turned out to be RUC officers. They were trying to save the life of their colleague who had been shot and kidnapped by the IRA. Their plan was to swap the Catholic priest for their Protestant RUC colleague (one of their other colleagues had already been killed in the initial ambush). Both the kidnappers, McGaughey and Armstrong, were in the RUC Special Patrol Group which was the unit heavily involved in the fight against terrorism. They initially claimed to be representing the Ulster Freedom Fighters (UFF). This was later denied by the UFF who did so using the officially recognised code word.

Fr Murphy was released twelve hours later at night on a country road in his parish. It's thought that the RUC men realised the kidnapping of a priest was not the way to do things.

Unfortuantely, the kidnapped RUC man was not so lucky and his death was confirmed by the IRA the following morning.

NOTE. McGaughy was proved to be acting outside the law on other occasions. He was found guilty for his involvement in the attempted bombing of a Catholic pub, as well as the shooting of a Catholic.

5. 1981: Ben Dunne

Ben Dunne was a well-known Irish multi-millionaire businessman and director of the family business, Dunnes Stores when he was kidnapped in 1981. He was kidnapped as he drove North to the official opening of a new store in Portadown. The incident was reported by a truck driver who witnessed the event and official manhunts were started on both sides of the border. Both the Irish and British governments saw it as an embarrassment that this could happen on one of the most heavily patrolled roads on the island.

The gang made contact and demanded a ransom of £500,000. It appears the Dunne family, against the advice of government and security officials, did make attempts to pay the ransom. It is thought that up to four attempts were made and that one of them was successful as on the sixth/seventh day, Dunne was dropped off at a church in south Armagh.

Dunne was free after his six-day ordeal, but there were strong rumours that a ransom of up to £750,000 was paid.

6. 1983: Shergar

Shergar was a horse bred in Ireland by the Aga Khan. He won the Irish Derby, the King George VI, the Queen Elizabeth Stakes and the Epsom Derby. He was retired to stud and had a stud value of £80,000 a time. He was going to make his owners a lot of money.

Shergar was taken from his loose box at Ballymany Stud in February 1983. Jim Fitzgerald was the stable hand and he was also taken for a short time while the gang made their escape with the famous horse. The IRA were suspected of being involved.

There were some initial phone calls demanding ransom and even some Polaroid pictures of the horse beside the front page of *The Irish Times* on 11 February. But on 12 February, the calls stopped and the trail went cold. The Gardaí had nothing to go on. The story gradually appeared less and less in the newspapers.

The horse was never seen again by its owners and the case was never solved. There were and still are constant rumours as to what happened. The case spawned books and television dramatisations.

One of the most feasible stories of what may have happened came from Seán O'Callaghan, an IRA prisoner, in 1992. He confirmed that the IRA were involved. He said the horse became uncontrollable when he realised he was surrounded by men he did not know. It was the start of the stud season and his blood would have been up. It was the middle of the night and the horse became dis-

tressed. He injured his leg in his panic and he was still uncontrollable. Nothing could be done to calm him so a decision was made
to kill him and bury him in County Leitrim.

7. 1983: The Kirkpatricks/Richard Hill

The Irish National Liberation Army (INLA) was led by Dominick 'Mad
Dog' McGlinchey.

One of his key men, Harry Fitzpatrick, was arrested and had
agreed to turn on the INLA by providing extremely important information to the authorities.

In May 1983, Liz Kirkpatrick (Harry's wife) was kidnapped by the
INLA. The INLA made a statement that the RUC and the British
Attorney General were responsible for her safety. They also requested that the use of super-grasses be stopped. Ultimately, they wanted Harry Kirkpatrick to keep his mouth shut.

This did not stop Harry though and his evidence helped bring
charges against eighteen of his ex-colleagues. It appears a deal was
struck with the Director of Public Prosecutions as he received no min-
imal sentence when at the end of trial for which he was given 5 life
sentences.

A short time later, the INLA kidnapped Harry's thirteen-year-old
sister, Dianne, and her step-father, Richard Hill from a cottage in
County Mayo. They were both rescued a few weeks later from a
house in County Donegal by the Gardaí. It would appear that they
were tipped off.

Two days later, Liz Kirkpatrick was released after thirteen weeks
in captivity. There was some suspicion surrounding her abduction as
she was not long married to Harry and it was felt she was very upset
that he had turned informer.

8. 1983: Don Tidey

Don Tidey was of British origin and was the chief executive of the
Quinnsworth Supermarket chain.

He was abducted from his Daimler car in November 1983. A £5 million ransom was demanded by the Provisional IRA. The government and the security forces were adamant that a ransom should not be paid. Tidey was being held in Derrada Wood in the sparsely populated County Leitrim.

Tidey and the gang had been tracked to Derrada Wood by mid-December. Heavily armed units began their sweeps of the wood. The gang was armed and dangerous and although Tidey was freed, it was at a cost. A young Garda and a soldier were killed by the gang. Another Garda and a civilian were also injured in the cross-fire.

The security forces had found Tidey crawling in the undergrowth and had initially arrested him as a gang member before realising who he was. He had spent 23 days in captivity. The gang escaped.

9. 1986: Jennifer Guinness

Jennifer Guinness was kidnapped from her home in Howth, County Dublin on 8 April 1986. The gang initially wanted to take her fifteen-year-old daughter Gillian but agreed to take Jennifer after she pleaded with them. They then proceeded to take £56,000 in cash from the house and demanded £2 million as ransom for Jennifer's release.

Her husband, John Guinness, was chairman of Guinness Mahon bank. He was not extremely wealthy but he did have access to funds. He was a descendant of Arthur Guinness' brother.

They took Jennifer to a rented bungalow in County Meath. After four days, she was moved to a small flat in Arbour Hill, Dublin. A few days later, she was moved to a more comfortable house in Rathfarnham, County Dublin.

Meanwhile, the Guinness family had called in a specialist negotiating London-based firm, Control Ricks, to negotiate for Jennifer's release. This strained relations with the Gardaí who hadn't turned up any leads. They did call on the Rathfarnham house when a neighbour became suspicious of the activity in and out of the house but the men and the owner of the house convinced the Gardaí that all was in order. The gang became nervous though and moved Jennifer Guinness to a house on Waterloo Road, Ballsbridge, Dublin. This is where they were tracked by the Gardai, who had been tracing the rented car of one of the suspects.

Jennifer Guinness was eventually released unharmed after the Gardaí surrounded the house. All the gang were caught and imprisoned.

10. 1987: John O'Grady

John O'Grady was a successful dentist who was kidnapped in October 1987 by a nationalist terrorist known as the Border Fox, Dessie O'Hare. O'Hare had a vicious reputation and was responsible for murdering dozens of men. He was now desperate for funds.

The original kidnap victim was supposed to be Dr Austin Darragh who had made millions from clinical research and his company was listed on the New York stock exchange.

The kidnapping took place in Dr Darragh's house in Cabinteely, County Dublin, that he had vacated four years earlier. Dr Darragh's name still appeared on the outside of the house but the current occupiers were his daughter and son-in-law, John O'Grady. O'Hare and his gang decided to take O'Grady and demand a ransom of £300,000 for his release. The ransom amount leapt to £1.5 million a few days later after intense media speculation about Dr Darragh's wealth. O'Grady was initially kept in a location on Parkgate Street in Dublin and then moved to a farmer's container in County Cork where conditions were primitive. O'Hare had incredible mood swings, going from very polite and caring to irrational, giving beatings to his prisoner.

The Gardai stumbled across the gang at the Cork location but the gang escaped. The gang made their way back up to Cabra in Dublin.

O'Hare felt his demands were not being taken seriously by the authorities and he flew into a rage, cutting off O'Grady's two little fingers with a hammer and a chisel. He left them in Carlow Cathederal for the authorities as he wanted them to know that this was not a game.

The government decided they would not stand in the way of the family if they wanted to pay a ransom. At the same time, two Gardai tracked the gang to the house in Cabra. There was a fire fight and one of the Gardai was injured. As the gang made their get-away, O'Grady took his opportunity and dived into an overgrown garden, where he was found by two Gardai. O'Grady was brought to hospital for treatment. O'Hare was caught a few days later after a tip-off in Kilkenny. The Gardai were expecting him and had set up a roadblock. He tried to escape but was shot five times. He fell out of the car still wearing O'Grady's gold watch, however, O'Hare survived and was jailed for 40 years.

TWELVE FACTS ABOUT SHERGAR AND HIS KIDNAPPING

1. **Shergar** was bred in Ireland by the Aga Khan and he won six of his eight races. Lester Piggott rode him to a four-length victory in the Irish Derby. The King George VI and Queen Elizabeth Stakes were notched up by the same margin. He won the 1981 Epsom Derby by a record ten lengths.

2. On 8 February 1983 **Shergar** was kidnapped from Ballymany Stud, near the Curragh in County Kildare. An Irish radio station received a ransom demand for £1.5 million. There were suggestions that the IRA were behind the kidnap.

3. When **Sherga**r was retired to stud he was seen as a money-making machine, the syndicate selling his services at £80,000 a time.

4. Voted European horse of the year in 1981, **Shergar** remains the last odds-on favourite to win the Epsom Derby.

5. **Shergar**'s racing prowess is still a barometer for greatness today. His Derby victory earned him a spot in the *Observer*'s 100 Most Memorable Sporting Moments of the Twentieth Century.

6. Nicknamed '**Shergar** the wonder horse', he was at one time valued by Lloyds of London at £10 million at stud and carried an insurance premium of £300,000 at the time of his kidnapping.

7. The disappearance of **Shergar** was even made into a Hollywood film, *Shergar*, in August 1998, starring Sir Ian Holm, Mickey Rourke, David Warner, Gary Cady, Alan Barker, Billy Boyle and Stephen Brennan.

8. The myths surrounding **Shergar**'s disappearance should not disguise the fact that he was one of the most talented flat-race horses in history. His victories earned £436,000 for his owners. His awesome win in the 1981 Epsom Derby was the greatest winning margin in the race's long history.

9. On his first starts as a three-year-old, **Shergar** triumphed in the Classic Trial by ten lengths, the Chester Vase by twelve lengths and the Epsom Derby by ten lengths. He took the Irish Derby and King George VI and Queen Elizabeth Stakes by four lengths each. His victory gave the Aga Khan his first English Classic winner and the horse's stud value a huge boost.

10. When **Shergar** was retired to stud, 34 syndication shares were sold for £250,000 each.

11. In honour of the horse, the **Shergar** Cup was run at Goodwood in 1999. The event, which has now switched to Ascot, is an annual contest between European jockeys and those from the rest of the world – horse racing's version of the Ryder Cup.

12. Colin Turner, racing correspondent of a London radio station, wrote a book arguing that the kidnap had been carried out by the Provisional IRA at the behest of Colonel Ghadafi of Libya, a sworn enemy of the Aga Khan.

The truth may be more mundane. In 1992 Sean O'Callaghan, a leading Provisional-turned-informer and former chief of the Provisional IRA's southern command, claimed knowledge of what really happened. Speaking from inside Maghaberry Prison, County Antrim, he admitted that **Shergar** had indeed been kidnapped by the IRA from Ballymany Stud. According to O'Callaghan, Shergar quickly became distressed. He threshed about inside the horsebox, kicking and stamping. Inevitably, one of his legs was injured. The gang members panicked. A decision was taken to shoot him. Photographs of the horse eating a carrot, his head next to a current edition of *The Irish Times*, were taken just before the unfortunate animal was killed. A pit was dug in the desolate mountains near Ballinamore, County Leitrim. The body was dragged into it and quickly covered over. No markers were left at the grave.

Four Famous Fires

1. The Old Theatre Royal Dublin Fire of 1880

The Old Theatre Royal on Hawkins' Street, Dublin, was about to host a matinée performance of *Ali Baba and the Forty Thieves* on behalf of the Dublin Charities fund. The Duchess of Marlborough was attending as patron.

Evidence suggested a fire began because a plumber had left a gas bracket loose and a gas cloud had formed. An usher, with a lit candle, is thought to have been the catalyst for the gas to ignite and some nearby curtains to catch flame. The fire quickly spread to the rest of the theatre. The theatre manager had tried to fight the fire by himself but alas he got trapped and perished.

The fire spread so quickly that by the time the fire fighters arrived, the theatre was already lost and they then concentrated on saving the adjoining buildings. The fire continued for a number of days and at its height, it put the entire street at risk, before it was eventually brought under control.

2. The Pearse Street Fire of 1936

This fire began at 164 Pearse Street in the centre of Dublin. The building's ground floor was occupied by a battery manufacturing company called Exide Batteries Ltd. A family with five children were living on the first floor of the building.

The fire began on the night of Monday 5 October 1936 so the battery workers were not in the building. The fire brigade at headquarters on Tara street were called to attend the fire. Shortly after they arrived, there was a number of explosions, probably caused by the battery-assembling material, but the family living upstairs managed to escape.

The fire crew experienced problems with the water pressure in the area and it was not long before the neighbouring hotel was fully ablaze. It took some time for the water pressure to be sorted out but once it was, the firemen brought the blaze under control. It is estimated that the time involved was approximately three hours. It was only then that it was realised that three firemen were missing.

A search of the building began and about two hours later at 4am, their bodies were discovered under rubble. They had been killed during one of the large explosions shortly after the crew had first arrived at the scene.

Their bodies lay in state for a number of days afterwards as a tribute to their bravery and they were brought to their burials in Glasnevin cemetery aboard fire trucks.

3. The Cork Opera House Fire of 1955
Tuesday 13 December 1955 was the date that the disastrous fire happened at the Cork Opera House, and left the city without a major theatre for the first time in 250 years. It was the boast of the Opera House that its tradition was continuous. It was during the rehearsals for the forthcoming Christmas pantomime that the fatal fire started. Fortunately, all people were evacuated, but the building, built entirely from wood, did not stand a chance from the merciless fire. What began as an electrical fault blazed into an inferno within minutes. Soon the skyline of the city was lit up as the fire did its worst. The present Opera House was opened by President Eamon de Valéra on 31 October 1965, and was extensively refurbished in 2000.

4. The Stardust Fire of 1981
The Stardust was a nightclub situated on Kilmore Road on the northside of Dublin, about a fifteen-minute drive from the city centre. The night was Friday 13 February 1981 – a Valentine's celebration.

The fire began in a balcony area and was discovered at a reasonably early stage. However, staff were unable to put out the fire and soon it had spread to the ceiling tiles and walls of the nightclub, which resulted in thick black smoke.

People began to panic and have trouble breathing which resulted in a stampede. Some exit doors were locked so people were unable to escape. Others tried to break out through windows but these had iron grilles on them and they were also unable to escape. People were crushed by others panicking behind them.

Forty-eight people died there, with many others suffering from burns and smoke inhalation.

The Stardust nightclub is gone but a memorial park exists in memory of the young people who died and as a reminder to others of what happened that night.

NAMES

65 Irish Boys' Names

1. Aedan, Aodhan, Aidan
A diminutive form of the name *Aed* meaning 'fire' and would imply 'born of fire'. It became a popular name in honour of St Aidan of Iona (*c.* 630 AD) who founded a famous monastery on the island of Lindisfarne.

2. Aengus, Aonghus, Oengus
From *aon* 'excellent' and *gus* 'strength, vigour'. Aengus was the god of love and youth. His words were as sweet as honey, attracting bees and birds.

3. Ardan
From *ardanach* meaning 'high aspiration'. Ardan was one of the sons of Usna who helped Deirdre escape to Scotland so that she would not be forced to marry King Conchobhar MacNessa.

4. Art
In Ireland a seperate name from Arthur, it comes from an ancient word for 'a bear', used in the sense of 'outstanding warrior' or 'champion'. A pagan High King of Ireland, Art's rule was so honest that two angels hovered over him in battle.

5. Bradan, Brendan, Brandan, Brandon
Comes from the word *bradán* meaning 'a salmon'; the *bradán feasa*, the 'Salmon of Knowledge', is central to the tales of Fionn MacCumhail.

6. Brendan
There are at least seventeen saints who bear the name but St Brendan the Navigator is probably the best known. St Brendan is venerated in Ireland as the patron saint of seafarers and travellers.

7. Brian
From *brigh* 'high, noble, strong'. This is one of the most popular Irish names, in honour of the most revered High king of Ireland, Brian Boru, who defeated an army of invading Vikings at the Battle of Clontarf in 1014 but died of wounds he received in the battle.

8. Canice, Coinneach (Kenneth)
Coinneach means 'attractive person', 'pleasant person'. A sixth-century Irish missionary, St Canice founded churches in Ireland, Scotland and Wales. As Coinneach he gave his name to the town of Kilkenny, *Cill Channaigh* 'Canice's Church'.

9. Cathal
Cath means 'battle' and *all* 'mighty' and signifies 'a great warrior'. One of the most common names in Ireland in the Middle Ages, it is popular again now.

10. Cian
From *cian*, meaning 'ancient, enduring'. In legend Cian Mac Mael Muad was the son-in-law of Brian Boru who led the armies from the province of Munster to victory over the invading Vikings at the Battle of Clontarf in 1014, a battle in which both he and Brian were killed.

11. Ciaran
Ciar means 'dark' and the diminutive *-in*, means 'little dark one'. Popular for over 1,500 years, at least 26 saints have borne the name.

12. Cillian, Killian
Cille means 'associated with the church'. One St Cillian left Ireland about 650 AD with eleven companions and carried out his missionary work in the Rhine region of Germany.

13. Colin
From *coll* 'chieftain' and the diminutive -*in*, and would mean 'little chieftan'.

14. Colm, Colum, Colmcille, Columb, Columba
A Gaelic form of the Latin *columba* meaning 'dove'. St Columba of Iona or Colmcille, *colm* + *cille* or 'dove of the church', was a prince of the O'Neill clan, a great poet and scholar.

15. Colman
From the same root as Colm, it means 'little dove' and has developed into a seperate name to Colm. There are said to be 350 saints of the name.

16. Conall, Connall
This name means 'strong as a wolf', a very ancient name, found mainly in Ulster.

17. Conán
Means 'a little hound', as applied to a swift-footed warrior.

18. Conchobar (Conor)
Means 'lover of hounds'. Conchobhar MacNessa was the king of Ulster.

19. Cormac, Cormack, Cormick
From old Irish corbmac 'son of the charioteer'. Cormac Mac Airt was probably the most famous of the ancient kings of Ireland. It was a very popular name in early Ireland and is still used today.

20. Darragh, Daragh, Dara, Daire
Daire means 'fruitful', 'fertile'. At present it is a very popular name in Ireland with all four spellings and it is often used as a girl's name with the spellings Daire and Dara.

21. Dáithí (David)
It is an old Irish name meaning 'swiftness, nimbleness'.

22. Deaglán (Declan)
From *dag* 'good' and *lán* 'full' suggesting 'full of goodness'.

23. Derry
From *doire* 'like an oak'. It is often used as a short version of Derek and Dermot but can be a name in its own right. Derry is also the name of a city in Northern Ireland.

24. Desmond
Meaning 'one from Desmond', Desmond being an area of south Munster, one of the four provinces of Ireland. Popular diminutives are Des and Dessie.

25. Diarmuid (Dermot)
Means 'without enemy'. The name of early kings, legendary heroes and saints, Diarmuid was the lover of Grainne and the most beloved of that warrior band, the Fianna.

26. Donal
Domhan means 'world' and *all* 'mighty' implying 'ruler of the world'.

27. Donncha (Donagh)
Donn 'brown' and *cath* 'battle' meaning 'brown-haired warrior'. Brian Boru's Donncha was a high king of Ireland until his death in 1064.

28. Eamon, Eamonn
Is the Irish form of Old English *ead* 'rich' and *mund* 'guardian', and implies 'guardian of the riches'. Eamon de Valéra was the first Taoiseach in the Republic of Ireland.

29. Earnán, Eirnín
Meaning 'iron'. The name is often linked with Ernest, a Germanic word meaning 'vigour'. The name of sixteen Irish saints, St Earnán is the patron saint of Tory, an island off the coast of County Donegal.

30. Emmet
The name is given to boys as a mark of respect to the great Irish orator and patriot Robert Emmet who was a leader of the unsuccessful 1798 rebellion against the British.

31. Enda
Ean meaning 'bird' and suggests 'birdlike' or 'freedom of spirit'. The name is used for boys and girls.

32. Ennis
Comes from *inis* 'island'. Ennis, a town in County Clare, is situated on an island between two streams of the River Fergus.

33. Eoghan (Owen)
Comes from an old Irish word and means 'born of the yew tree'.

34. Feidhlim
Comes from *Feidhil* 'beauty' or 'ever good'. Three kings of Munster bore the name.

35. Ferdia
Comes from *fear* and *Dia* 'man of God'.

36. Fergal
It seems to come from *fearghal* 'brave, courageous, valorous'. Fergal MacMaolduin was an eighth-century high king renowned for his efforts in battle.

37. Fergus
Derived from *fear* 'man' and *gus* 'strength' and signifies 'a strong warrior, virile'. Fergus was the king of Ulster.

38. Finbar
Meaning 'fair-haired', the name has been popular since the sixth century.

39. Fintan
'Fair-haired' or could mean 'white fire'. There have been 74 saints with this name.

40. Fionn, Finn
Means 'fair-headed'. Fionn MacCumhail, a central character in Irish folklore and mythology, led the warrior band, the Fianna. The name is popular in Ireland with both spellings Fionn and Finn.

41. Gearóid (Garreth Gerald, Gerard)
Means 'brave with a spear' or 'spear carrier'.

42. Hugh
Hugh is a translation of the ancient name Aodh meaning 'fire'. Hugh O'Neill was a famous king in Ireland in the sixteenth century.

43. Jarlath
St Jarlath (born c. 550 AD) was noted for his piety and ability as a teacher. The name is still popular, especially in the west of Ireland.

44. Kevin
Means 'gentle child' or 'well born'. St Kevin founded a great monastery at Glendalough in County Wicklow in the seventh century. The name is still very popular in Ireland.

45. Lee
From *laoi* 'poem' or from the River Lee, the river which runs through County Cork. It is currently popular as a given name for boys.

46. Liam
The Irish form of William, originally a German name will + *helm* 'desire' and 'helmet' and suggests 'strong protector'. It is currently a very fashionable name in Ireland and across the world.

47. Lochlann (Loughlin)
The Vikings plundered Ireland in the ninth and tenth centuries and the native home of the Norwegian invaders was known as Lochlan 'land of the lochs'. But once they settled and intermarried with the Irish, Lochlan became a popular name.

48. Lorcan
Means 'silent' or 'fierce' and was probably used as a nickname for a 'brave warrior'. The name is growing in popularity again in Ireland.

49. Malachi (Malachy)
A name with two sources: St Malachi (1095-1148 AD) was the Bishop of Armagh who adopted the name from the Hebrew prophet 'Malachi' whose name means 'my angel' or 'messenger of God; it is also linked to the High King Maoilseachlainn, 'devotee of St Sechnall', one of St Patrick's first companions.

50. Murtagh
Muir 'sea' and *ceardach* 'skilled' implying 'skilled in the ways of the sea'. The name of three high kings.

51. Niall
The name could come from *nel* 'a cloud'. Niall of the Nine Hostages was a fourth-century king of Tara.

52. Nollaig (Noel)
Nollaig is the Irish word for Christmas and is given to boys or girls born during the Christmas season.

53. Oisín
The son of the legendary warrior Fionn MacCumhaill and the goddess Sive. A very popular name again in Ireland, it means little faun'..

54. Pádraig, Pádraic (Patrick)
From the Latin *patricius* 'nobly born'. Patrick is the patron saint of Ireland. Both Patrick and Pádraig are very popular names in Ireland.

55. Peadar, Peadair (Peter)
Irish form of Peter and thus comes ultimately from Greek *petros* 'the rock'. It is still in common use in Ireland today.

56. Pearse, Pearce, Pierce
Comes from the Norman French name 'Piers' and is still very popular; it was the surname of Padraig Pearse, one of the leaders of the Easter Rising of 1916 when Ireland was fighting for its independence from England.

57. Proinsias (Francis)
The Irish form of Francis, a name originating from the figure of St Francis of Assisi. The name originates from the Latin name Franciscus, meaning 'little French man' and was popularised in Ireland by the Franciscans whose founder was St Francis of Assisi.

58. Ronán
Derived from *rón* 'a seal'. Ronan Keating is a famous Irish entertainer.

59. Ruairí
From *rua* and *rí* meaning 'red king, great king'. Rory O'Connor, the last high king of Ireland, was forced to abdicate the throne in 1175.

60. Séamus
The Irish version of James. Séamus Heaney was the 1995 Nobel Poet Laureate.

61. Seán, Shane
Irish form of John meaning 'God's gracious gift'. Shane is a very popular variant of the name.

62. Tadhg
Irish name meaning 'a poet' or 'a philosopher'. Tadgh Mór (Big Tadhg) O'Kelly fought at the Battle of Clontarf in 1014.

63. Tomás
The Irish form of Thomas, a biblical name meaning 'twin'.

64. Turlach (Terence, Terry)
From an Irish name meaning 'one who aids or assists'. It is usually translated as Terence or Terry.

65. Ultán
Means simply 'an Ulsterman'. There have been eighteen saints named Ultan.

60 Irish Girls' Names

1. Aideen
Formed like Aidan from *aed* 'fire'. Aideen loved her husband Oscar, a grandson of Fionn MacCumhail, so much that when he fell in battle she died of a broken heart.

2. Ailbe
From an old Irish word meaning 'white', the sixth-century St Ailbe was associated with the monastery at Emly in County Tipperary. Ailbe may be used for a boy or a girl.

3. Aileen
Ancient Irish name from *ail* 'noble'.

4. Ailís, Ailish
Irish version of the Norman Alice or Alicia from Elizabeth 'God is my oath'.

5. Aine
Irish version of the Norman Alice or Alicia from Elizabeth 'God is my oath'.

6. Alannah, Alanna, Alana
Adding 'a' to *leanbh*, the word for 'child' in Irish, brings a sense of warmth – 'O child' or 'darling child'. A favoured name in Ireland with all three spellings.

7. Aoibhinn
Aoibhinn 'pleasant, beautiful sheen, of radiant beauty'. Often interpreted as 'little Eve'.

8. Aoife
'Beautiful, radiant, joyful', means 'beauty' from the Gaelic word *aoibh*. Known as the greatest woman warrior in the world.

9. Ashling, Aislin, Aislinn
From *aisling* which means 'a vision' or 'a dream'. A very popular name in Ireland.

10. Bláthnaid, Blanaid
Bláth means 'flower, blossom'; *bláthnaid* means 'little flower'.

11. Bridget, Brigid
The name Brigid has its origins in the Celtic goddess Brigantia. She is equal in esteem, and shares a grave, with St Patrick and St Columcille.

12. Bronagh
Comes from the Irish *brónach* 'sad, sorrowful'.

13. Caireann, Cairenn (Karen)
From the Gaelic *cara* and the diminutive *–in*, meaning 'little friend' or 'little beloved'.

14. Cathleen, Caitlín (Catherine, Kathleen)
Devotion to St Catherine came to Ireland with Christianity. Revered for her courage and purity.

15. Caoilainn, Caoilfhionn
Caol 'slender' and *fionn* 'white, fair, pure'. Several saints were named Caoilainn.

16. Caoimhe (Keeva, Keva)
From *caomhe* 'gentle, beautiful, precious'. The same root as Kevin (from the old Irish word *coemgen* or *coem*, as in 'kind and gentle',

the name has become very popular in Ireland with the original Irish spelling.

17. Cara, Caragh
In Irish *cara* simply means a 'friend'.

18. Cassidy
From *cas* meaning 'curly-haired'.

19. Catriona, Caitriona
An Irish form of Catherine that derives from an older Greek name meaning 'clear, pure'. *(See also Caitlin.)*

20. Ciara
The feminine form of Ciaran, from the Irish *ciar* meaning 'dark' and implies 'dark hair and brown eyes'.

21. Clíona
From *clodhna* meaning 'shapely'. In Irish legend, this was the name of a beautiful goddess.

22. Clodagh
There is a river Clody in County Tipperary and in County Wexford. The word means 'I wash, I clean'.

23. Colleen, Coleen
From the Irish *cailín* meaning 'girl'.

24. Dearbhail, Dearbhal, Deirbhile (Dervla)
From *der* and *fal* 'daughter of Fal'. In ancient times, Ireland was known as 'the plain of Fal'.

25. Deirdre
The meaning is unknown but possibly derived from a Celtic word meaning 'woman'. The most beautiful woman in ancient Ireland, she was bethrothed to the High King Conchobhar Mac Nessa but fell in love with his nephew Naoise.

26. Eibhleann, Eibhlín (Eileen), (Evelyn)
Borrowed from teh Anglo-Norman Aveline.

27. Eithne (Enya)
Eithne means 'kernel of a nut or seed' but it may also be related to Aidan meaning 'little fire'. There are at least nine St Eithnes.

28. Eimear, Emer
Eimear possessed the 'Six Gifts of Womanhood' – 'beauty, a gentle voice, sweet words, wisdom, needlework and chastity!' She was Cú Chulainn's beloved.

29. Enda
Eán means 'bird' and suggests 'birdlike' or 'freedom of spirit'. St Enda was a sixth-century monk associated with the Aran Islands off the west coast of Ireland. The name is used for boys and girls.

30. Etain
It possibly dervived from the old Irish *et* meaning 'jealousy'. Etain surpassed all other women of her time in beauty and gentleness and thus was an object of jealousy herself.

31. Fiona
From *Fionn* meaning 'fair, white, beautiful' Fiona is the feminine form of Fionn.

32. Fionnuala
The name comes from *fionn* and *ghuala* meaning 'fair shouldered'.

33. Grainne, Grania
From *gran* 'grain, corn'. Grainne in ancient Ireland was the patron of the harvest.

34. Íde (Ita)
Meaning 'thirst' as in 'thirst for goodness or knowledge'.

35. Keela
The word *cadhla* means 'beautiful' and implies 'a beauty that only poetry can capture'.

36. Kerry
Ciar means 'dark' and probably implies 'dark hair and brown eyes'. County Kerry means 'the land of the descendant of Ciar' who was the love-child of the high king Fergus Mac Roth and the legendary Queen Maebh.

37. Maebh, Maeve
From an old Irish name *Madb* meaning 'the cause of great joy' or 'she who intoxicates'. It is also the name of the great warrior queen of Connacht and embodiment of sovereignity was Queen Maeve.

38. Máire (Mary)
The name that was used in Ireland for Our Lady was Muire and interestingly, her name was so honoured that it was rarely used as a first name until the end of the fifteenth century. Then Máire became acceptable as a given name but the spelling Muire was reserved from the Blessed Mother.

39. Máiréad
The Irish form of Margaret, it became popular around the fourteenth century.

40. Maol Íosa
Maol and *Íosa* 'follower of Jesus'. A name first used by clerics as early as the tenth century.

41. Muireann, Muirenn
Means 'sea white, sea fair'. The very appropriate name of the sixth-century mermaid caught by a fisherman in Lough Neagh. He brought her to St Comghall who baptised her which transformed her into a woman.

42. Neala, Neila
Meaning 'female champion', it is the feminine form of Niall.

43. Neasa, Nessa
Nessa was the mother of Conchobhar (Conor) Mac Nessa, king of Ulster, a powerful and beautiful woman.

44. Niamh
Meaning 'radiance, lustre, brightness'. The daughter of the sea god Manannan was known as 'Niamh of the Golden Hair', a beautiful princess riding on a white horse.

45. Nola, Noleen
Popular names that are considered to be abbreviated forms of Fionnoula.

46. Nollaig (Noelle)
Used for both male and female, it is the Irish word for Christmas, as in Noel or Noelle.

47. Nora, Norah, Noreen

A classic Irish name, it could be a shortened form of Eleanor meaning 'torch' or could be from the Latin *honora* meaning 'honour, reputation' and became so popular in Ireland in the Middle Ages that many people assumed it was Irish. Noreen is the diminutive of Nora and means 'little honourable one'.

48. Nuala

Nuala is really a shortened version of Fionnuala (see Fionnuala above) and in Ireland it is more widely used than Fionnuala. Meaning 'fair shouldered, exceptionally lovely', the name has been in existence since the thirteenth century.

49. Oonagh, Oona, Una

From the Irish word *uan* 'a lamb' or may come from the Latin *una* meaning 'one', hence it is sometimes translated as 'Unity'. In legend Oonagh was 'queen of the fairies' who had long golden hair which reached the ground and she was also the wife of Fionn MacCumhail.

50. Orlaith, Orlagh

Orlaith means 'golden princess'. The name was shared by both a sister and a daughter of the most famous of the high kings, Brian Boru.

51. Regan

The meaning is unknown but possibly comes from *ri* 'sovereign, king' and the diminutive *-in* and means 'the king's child' or may come from *riogach* 'impulsive, furious'.

52. Ríonach (Ríona)

From *ríonach* meaning 'queenly'. In legend Rionach was the wife of Niall of the Nine Hostages and as such is the maternal ancestor of many of the great Irish family dynasties.

53. Roisín
From the Latin name *Rosa* meaning 'little rose'. Records show that the name has been in use in Ireland since the sixteenth century.

54. Saoirse
From the Irish word *saoirse* meaning 'freedom, liberty'. It has only been used since the 1920s and has strong patriotic overtones.

55. Shauna
The feminine form of Séan, which is the Irish version of the English name, John. It is currently a very popular name in Ireland.

56. Sheenagh
An Irish form of Jane and may be a shortened form of Sinéad.

57. Sile, Sheelagh (Sheila)
The Irish form of the Latin name Cecilia, the patron saint of music and implies 'pure and musical'.

58. Sinéad
Irish form of Jane, which is the English form of 'Jehanne', an old French feminine form of 'Johannes' (John).

59. Siobhán
Siobhán is another Irish form of Jane. A popular name in Ireland, where the anglicised versions are often used.

60. Sorcha
From *sorcha* meaning 'bright, radiant, light'. Popular in the Middle Ages, the name has become popular again in recent years.

100 MOST COMMON IRISH SURNAMES AND THEIR MEANINGS

Rank	Name	Irish Equivalent	Meaning
1.	Murphy	Ó Murchadha	sea-battler
2.	Kelly	Ó Ceallaigh	bright-headed
3.	O'Sullivan	Ó Súilleabháin	dark-eyed
4.	Walsh	Breathnach	Welshman
5.	Smith	Mac Gabhann	son of the smith
6.	O'Brien	Ó Briain	high, noble
7.	Byrne	Ó Broin	a raven
8.	Ryan	Ó Maoilriain	king
9.	O'Connor	Ó Conchobhair	patron of warriors
10.	O'Neill	Ó Néill	from Niall of the Nine Hostages
11.	O'Reilly	Ó Raghallaigh	Unknown
12.	Doyle	Ó Dubhghaill	dark foreigner
13.	McCarthy	Mac Cárthaigh	loving person
14.	Gallagher	Ó Gallchobhair	lover of foreigners
15.	O'Doherty	Ó Dochartaigh	hurtful
16.	Kennedy	Ó Cinnéide	helmet headed
17.	Lynch	Ó Loinsigh	seafarer, exile
18.	Murray	Ó Muireadhaigh	lord, master
19.	Quinn	Ó Cuinn	wisdom, chief
20.	Moore	Ó Mórdha	majestic
21.	McLoughlin	Mac Lochlainn	Viking
22.	O'Carroll	Ó Cearbhaill	valorous in battle
23.	Connolly	Ó Conghaile	fierce as a hound
24.	Daly	Ó Dálaigh	assembles often
25.	O'Connell	Ó Conaill	strong as a wolf
26.	Wilson	Mac Liam	son of William
27.	Dunne	Ó Duinn	brown

Rank	Name	Irish Equivalent	Meaning
28.	Brennan	Ó Braonáin	sorrow
29.	Burke	de Búrca	from Richard de Burgh
30.	Collins	Ó Coileáin	young warrior
31.	Campbell	MacCathmhaoil	crooked mouth
32.	Clarke	Ó Cléirigh	clergyman
33.	Johnston	Mac Seáin	son of John
34.	Hughes	Ó hAodha	fire
35.	O'Farrell	Ó Fearghail	man of valour
36.	Fitzgerald	Mac Gearailt	spear rule
37.	Brown	Mac an Bhreithiún	son of the brehon (judge)
38.	Martin	Mac Giolla Mháirtín	devotee of Saint Martin
39.	Maguire	Mag Uidhir	dun-coloured
40.	Nolan	Ó Nualláin	famous
41.	Flynn	Ó Floinn	bright red
42.	Thompson	Mac Tomáis	son of Thom
43.	O'Callaghan	Ó Ceallacháin	bright headed
44.	O'Donnell	Ó Domhnaill	world mighty
45.	Duffy	Ó Dufaigh	dark, black
46.	O'Mahony	Ó Mathúna	bear calf
47.	Boyle	Ó Baoill	vain pledge
48.	Healy	Ó hÉalaighthe	artistic, scientific
49.	O'Shea	Ó Séaghdha	fine, stately
50.	White	Mac Giolla Bháin	of fair complexion
51.	Sweeney	Mac Suibhne	pleasant
52.	Hayes	Ó hAodha	fire
53.	Kavanagh	Caomhánach	comely, mild
54.	Power	de Paor	the poor man
55.	McGrath	Mac Craith	son of grace
56.	Moran	Ó Móráin	great

Rank	Name	Irish Equivalent	Meaning
57.	Brady	Mac Brádaigh	spirited
58.	Stewart	Stiobhard	one who superintends
59.	Casey	Ó Cathasaigh	vigilant in war, watchful
60.	Foley	Ó Foghladh	a plunderer
61.	Fitzpatrick	Mac Giolla Phádraig	devotee of St Patrick
62.	O'Leary	Ó Laoghaire	calf herd
63.	McDonnell	Mac Domhnaill	world mighty
64.	MacMahon	Mac Mathúna	bear calf
65.	Donnelly	Ó Donnghaile	brown valour
66.	Regan	Ó Riagáin	little king
67.	O'Donovan	Ó Donnabháin	brown, black
68.	Burns	Burns	from Scottish Burness
69.	Flanagan	Ó Flannagáin	red, ruddy
70.	Mullan	Ó Maoláin	bald
71.	Barry	de Barra	Cambro-Norman name
72.	Kane	Ó Catháin	battler
73.	Robinson	None	son of Robert
74.	Cunningham	None	Scottish for 'cunny' (rabbit) and 'hame' (home)
75.	Griffin	Ó Gríofa	Griffin in Welsh means 'crooked nose' or 'hawks beak'
76.	Kenny	Ó Cionaoith	fire sprung
77.	Sheehan	Ó Síodhacháin	peaceful

Rank	Name	Irish Equivalent	Meaning
78.	Ward	Mac an Bháird	son of the bard
79.	Whelan	Ó Faoláin	wolf
80.	Lyons	Ó Laighin	grey
81.	Reid	Ruadh	red haired, ruddy complexion
82.	Graham	None	grey home
83.	Higgins	Ó hUiginn	the son of Hugh
84.	Cullen	Ó Cuilinn	holly
85.	Keane	Mac Catháin	ancient
86.	King	Ó Cionga	from the old English *cyning* meaning 'tribal leader'
87.	Maher	Meagher	fine, majestic
88.	MacKenna	Mac Cionaoith	fire-sprung
89.	Bell	Mac Giolla Mhaoil	from *bel* meaning 'beautiful'
90.	Scott		a Scottish Gael
91.	Hogan	Ó hÓgáin	young
92.	O'Keeffe	Ó Caoimh	gentle
93.	Magee	Mag Aoidh	fire
94.	MacNamara	Mac Conmara	hound of the sea
95.	MacDonald	Mac Dónaill	world mighty
96.	MacDermott	Mac Diarmada	free from jealousy
97.	Molony	Ó Maolomhnaigh	servant of the Church
98.	O'Rourke	Ó Ruairc	from the Norse 'Hrothrekr' as in 'famous ruler'
99.	Buckley	Ó Buachalla	cow herd
100.	O'Dwyer	Ó Duibhir	black

CUSTOMS
AND
SUPERSTITIONS

Thirteen Customs

1. Farmers sometimes tamed a wild horse by whispering the Apostle's Creed into its left ear on a Wednesday and into its right ear on a Friday. The procedure was repeated each week until the animal was controllable.

2. A man who found the iron shoe of a horse or a donkey would bring it home and nail it, heel upwards, on the front door of the house.

3. Meeting a lone magpie was unlucky so it was customary to salute the bird and say '*Lá breag duit, uasail snag breac*' ('Good day to you Mr Magpie') .

4. People used to believe that sneezing could banish the soul from the body, so if a person sneezed it was customary to say '*Dia leat*' or 'God bless you'.

5. Many parents still leave a silver coin under the pillow of a child who has lost a baby tooth. They tell the child that it is a gift from the 'tooth fairy'.

6. An American wake was how a party eased the heartbreak of emigration. The family might never see the emigrant again so neighbours tried to distract them with music and merrymaking.

7. If an infant died during birth, the mourners never nailed the lid of the coffin. Doing so would mean that its mother would never have another child.

8. It was believed that babies born at Whitsuntide would either kill

or be killed. Some families dug a small grave and momentarily laid the infant in it to avert the disaster.

9. People cross themselves passing a church, saying 'In the name of the Father and of the Son and of the Holy Spirit'. This is to honour Jesus in the Tabernacle. (The tabernacle is for the exclusive reservation of the blessed sacrament, the bread and wine, which represents the body and blood of Jesus Christ during the rite of Holy Communion. Thus, the tabernacle represents Jesus Christ.)

10. The Angelus Bell is rung at noon and 6pm. The term 'Angelus Bell' comes from the first word in the Latin version of the prayer that accompanies the ringing, '*Angelus Domini*' ('Angel of the Lord'). There are three sets of chimes, followed by nine chimes. The custom originated when monks in early monasteries called the faithful in the surrounding countryside to pray along with them.

11. It was deemed bad luck to spill salt so this was dealt with by pinching some of the salt and throwing it over one's right shoulder.

12. In the past, Irish people called the day a person dies his third birthday. Natural life began on the first birthday; supernatural life on the second when he received the sacrament of Baptism. The third birthday gave eternal life.

13. Wakes were almost festive occasions, especially if they happened around a holiday or a feast day, and lasted for three days and three nights. A huge gathering at a wake was regarded as a compliment to the departed soul. People regarded it as a farewell to a loved one and, believing in a better after-life, they celebrated.

Seven Irish Fairies

1. The Dullahan

The Dullahan is regarded as one of the most interesting creatures in the Irish fairy world and is to be found in parts of Counties Sligo and Down. It is believed that he appears around midnight on certain Irish festivals or feast days and it appears as a headless horseman wearing a black robe, riding through the countryside.

Although the Dullahan has no head on his shoulders, he carries it either on his saddle-brow or in the air in his right hand. The head is apparently in a state of decay but with a frightening smile on it. The eyes are small and black, and flicker quickly in different directions. The head glows in the light and the Dullahan may use it as a lantern to guide its way along the darkened laneways of the Irish countryside. Wherever the Dullahan stops, a mortal dies; and those who watch from their windows may end up blind in one eye.

The Dullahan usually rides a black horse and uses a human spine as a whip. As the horse thunders through the countryside, sparks and flames come from its nostrils. The Dullahan drives a coach in some parts of the country. The coach is known as the coach-a-bower (from the Irish *coiste bodhar*, meaning 'deaf or silent coach') and is led by six black horses, apparently travelling so fast that it causes sparks and flames to appear, which set fire to the bushes along the side of the road. And no matter how well locked, all gates open up to the Dullahan. No one is safe from this fairy.

2. The Pooka

The Pooka is also known as the Phouka or the Puca, and is the most feared fairy in Ireland. It only appears after nightfall and can appear in a variety of terrible forms. It is generally seen as a powerful, dark horse with glistening yellow eyes and a lenghty wild mane. As a horse, it is known to terrorise the countryside, knocking down fences and gates, ruining crops, chasing the livestock and generally causing havoc wherever it goes.

In some parts of County Down, the Pooka is known to take the form of a little goblin who has facial deformities and insists it is entitled to a share of the farmer's crop at the end of each harvest. This is the reason why some strands are often left behind by the reapers: this is the 'Pooka's share'.

In some areas of County Laois, the Pooka takes the form of a monstrous, hairy bogeyman who terrifies the local areas at night. In Waterford and Wexford, it appears as an eagle with a massive wingspan; and in Roscommon, as a black goat with curling horns.

3. Changelings
Apparently the fairy women of Ireland are renowned for having difficulty when it comes to childbirth and many fairy children die before birth; many of those that do survive at birth are born with deformities. The adult fairies are intolerant of such children and refuse to rear them. Instead, they will try to swap them with healthy children who they steal from the mortal world. The deformed, ill-tempered creature left in place of the human child is generally known as a changeling and had the ability to cause havoc in any household. Any child who is not baptised or who is regarded as a particularly beautiful baby is at risk of being swapped for a changeling.

Babies are generally joyful and pleasant, but the fairy substitute is never happy unless, of course, some misfortune has befallen the house and its family. It spends most of its time screaming and howling. Changelings generally have pasty, yellowish skin, with very dark eyes. They often have physical deformities such as crooked backs or a lame leg. They also have a tendency to grow teeth more quickly than normal babies, with very skinny legs and curved hands, displaying hair.

Any family receiving a changeling will have to endure a life of bad luck and misfortune. The changeling will be responsible for everything bad in their lives.

4. The Grogoch
Grogochs settled in Ireland after travelling from Kintyre in Scotland. They are most common in north Antrim, Rathlin Island and parts of Donegal. They are half-man, half-fairy and take on the form of a very small, elderly man with an even cover of rough red hair or fur. He is almost always naked but wears a variety of leaves and twigs around his body. Grogochs are noted for their personal hygiene problem. There is no record of any female Grogochs.

The Grogach has the ability to make himself invisible and will only allow those people he trusts to observe him. He is a very sociable fairy and sometimes attaches himself to certain individuals and assists them with their planting and harvesting. The Grogoch, like most other fairies, is in fear of the church and will stay away from places where priests frequent. With this in mind, if a Grogoch is visible too often, it is a good idea to ask a priest into the house to drive the creature away.

5. Banshee
The banshee mainly appears in one of two images: a young woman or a weathered old woman. These represent aspects of the Celtic goddess of war and death, namely Badhbh, Macha and Mor-Rioghain. She is known to wear a grey or dark hooded cloak or a burial robe. She is not always seen but it is her mourning call that she is famous for. This is usually heard at night by the person or the family of the person about to die.

The *bean-sidhe* is supposedly linked to certain Irish families. It is thought that she is an ancestral spirit who forewarns members of families of their time of death. Some say that the banshee can only appear for five major Irish families: the O'Neills, the O'Briens, the O'Connors, the O'Gradys and the Kavanaghs. Having said that, intermarriage has apparently extended this original list of five.

The banshee may also appear as a washer woman, and is seen apparently washing the blood-stained clothes of those who are about to die. In this guise she is known as the *bean-nighe* (washing woman).

6. The Leprechaun

It is thought that the word leprechaun may have originated from the word *luacharma'n* (Irish for pygmy). These small, cheeky beings are frequently in a state of drunkenness, having taken too much of their home-brew poteen. The belief that gold is to be found at the bottom of every rainbow can be linked to the leprechaun. They apparently appointed themselves as guardians of ancient treasure, burying it in crocks or pots.

Although the leprechaun has been described as Ireland's national fairy, the term leprechaun was originally only used in the north Leinster area.

7. Merrows

The word merrow or *moruadh* comes from the Irish *muir* (meaning sea) and *oigh* (meaning maid) and refers specifically to the female of the species. Merrows are very beautiful and are known to be promiscuous in their relations with human beings. The Irish merrow are different to female women because of their flatter feet and their webbed fingers. In some parts of the country, people regard them as messengers of doom and death.

Merrow travel through the sea wrapped in sealskin cloaks, taking on the appearance and attributes of seals. In order to come ashore, the merrow abandons her cap or cloak, so any mortal who finds these has power over her, as she cannot return to the sea until they are retrieved. Mermen – the merrows male counterparts – have been rarely seen. They have been described as exceptionally ugly and scaled, with pig-like features and long, pointed teeth.

Ten Irish Folk Cures for Human Conditions

1. Asthma
Chop and press leaves from the bogplant sundew. Mix with honey and fill into bottles. Always keep some in stock and take a table-spoonful when an attack occurs.

2. Flatulence
Boil caraway seeds or put small amounts of ginger in food.

3. Eczema
Mix cabbage juice with unsalted butter and apply to the affected area.

4. Dandruff
Wash head in warm water. Rub in sulpher ointment. Soak any crusts with linseed or almond oil. Repeat daily until the dandruff disap-pears.

5. Common Cold
At the onset of winter, householders should boil carrageen moss, a fine, edible purple seaweed, and allow it to cool. Drinking it helped cure a cold. Some may add nasturtium seeds. Sniffing pine cones also helps relieve nasal blockage.

6. Coughing
Bring knobs of butter, dipped in sugar to the bedside at night. When a bout of coughing occurs, allow a portion to melt in the mouth and trickle down the throat.

7. Sunburn
Soak two tablespoonfuls of quine seed in a teacupful of cold water

for two days. Apply to the affected area.

8. Sore Throat
Drink hot milk and pepper, mixed with a little butter, porter and sugar.

9. Tonsillitis
Crush a garlic clove and mix it with honey. Allow to trickle down the throat.

10. Prostate Gland
For difficulty passing urine, boil four tablespoonfuls of pearl barley in four pints of water and drink each day.

Nine Irish Folk Cures for Animal Conditions

1. Anthrax
Hang the placenta of a cow or mare on a hawthorn bush. Leave there until it disintegrates or is decimated by birds of prey. This protects the livestock from anthrax and other similar diseases.

2. Worms (Tail worm)
The 'Cow doctor' utters incantations before making an incision in the tail close to where it meets the back. He stuffs this with a mixture of turpentine, rue and garlic before binding it with a red cloth.

3. Mange
Mix four ounces of sulpher with one ounce of mercury ointment, one of turpentine and half an ounce of tar spirit. Mix into a pint of linseed oil. Rub on affected parts.

4. Chaffing (Gall)
Dabbing with salted water, human urine or whiskey can prevent or alleviate light chaffing from harnesses. If overgrown flesh forms, cut away and apply a plaster of salted egg yolk. Leave until it falls off, then wash in urine for four days.

5. Itch
Pulverise dock roots, alum, clover and honeysuckle. Boil with lard and honey and then strain. Add sulpher and mix it all into an ointment. Apply to itchy hooves.

6. Sprains
Boil dock leaves in water and strain. Mix leaves in unsalted butter. Heat antiphlogistine and smear on brown paper. Apply to sprained area and bandage.

7. Temper
A regular diet of wild parsley (sometimes called horse parsley) can tame an ill-tempered horse.

8. Liver Fluke
Mix the blooms of any yellow flower (Iris, ragworth, buttercup, dandelion) and feed to the animal.

9. Maggots
Shear the wool away from the affected sore and use it to wipe away the larvae. Then wash the area with salted buttermilk.

FOUR IRISH CURSES

1. May the seven terriers of hell sit on the spool of your breast and bark in at your soulcase.

2. May you be afflicted with the itch and have no nails to scratch with.

3. May the devil take him by the heels and shake him.

4. No butter be on your milk nor on your ducks a web. May your child not walk and your cow be flayed. And may the flame be bigger and wider which will go through your soul than the Connemara mountains if they were on fire.

Nine Facts about Druids and Druidism

1. In the Celtic world in Ireland and much of the western Europe, north of the Alps and in the British Isles, the word **druid** denotes the priestly class.

2. The etymological origins of the word **druid** are varied and it is doubtful that the word is pre-Indo-European. The most widespread view is that 'druid' derives from the Celtic word for an oak tree (*doire* in Gaelic), a word whose root also meant 'wisdom'.

3. **Druidic** practices were part of the culture of all the tribal peoples called Keltoi and Galatai by Greeks, and Celtae and Galli by Romans. These names evolved into the modern English names 'Celtic' and 'Gaulish'.

4. The Irish word for 'magic', *draíocht*, derives from Old Irish *druídecht*.

5. The **druids'** influence was as much social as religious. Druids used not only to take the part that modern priests would but were often the philosophers, scientists, lore-masters, teachers, judges and councillors to the kings.

6. The **druids** linked the Celtic peoples with their numerous gods, the lunar calendar and the sacred natural order. With the arrival of Christianity in each area, all these roles were assumed by the bishop and the abbot, who were never the same individual, however, and might find themselves in direct competition.

7. Our historical knowledge of the **druids** is very limited. Druidic lore consisted of a large number of verses learned by heart, and we are

told that sometimes twenty years were required to complete the course of study.

8. The most important Irish documents relating to **druids** are contained in manuscripts of the twelfth century, but many of the texts themselves go back as far as the eighth. In these texts Druids usually act as advisers to kings and often have the ability to foretell the future.

9. In the lives of saints, martyrs and missionaries, the **druids** are represented as magicians and diviners, opposing the Christian missionaries.

Fourteen Wedding Traditions

1. In the eighteenth and nineteenth centuries, the Irish believed that if the sun shone on the bride, it would bring good luck to the couple.

2. It was also lucky to hear a cuckoo on the wedding morning or to see three magpies.

3. After the wedding ceremony, it was important that a man and not a woman be the first to wish joy to the new bride.

4. It's good luck to have your birthstone in your engagement ring, even if that stone is otherwise thought to be an unlucky gem.

5. The earrings you wear on your wedding day will bring you luck and happiness ever after.

6. It is lucky to tear your wedding dress accidentally on your wedding day.

7. It is good luck if a happily married woman puts the veil on you, but bad luck to put it on yourself.

8. It is lucky to be awakened by birds singing on your wedding morning.

9. Firing rifles and other weaponry into the air as the couple pass to salute the bride is suppposed to bring luck to the couple; of course, over the past centuries this has occasionally been observed with devastating results. Honking the horns of the cars in the procession from the church can be practised instead.

10. The night before the wedding, the bride's family and relatives put the child of Prague statue outside under a bush, to prevent it from raining on the wedding day.

11. It was considered good luck when the married couple were leaving the church if somebody threw an old shoe over the bride's head.

12. Irish brides often returned home by a different path with their new husbands than when entering the church with their fathers. This symbolised her new road in life.

13. In the old days, it was customary for the eldest girl in a family to marry first and her sisters according to age afterwards.

14. In ancient times, it was customary for dowries to be handed over to the groom and his family, from the bride's family. This was to compensate his family for taking on the woman.

TEN FACTS ABOUT ST BRIDGET
– A PATRON SAINT OF IRELAND

1. It is believed that **St Bridget** was born in a small Irish village named Faughart in or around the year 450 AD. St Patrick, with whom she developed a close friendship, baptised her parents.

2. According to legend, **Bridget's** father was an Irish chieftain of Leinster, named Dubhthach, and her mother, Brocca, was a slave at his court.

3. Even as a young girl, **Bridget** showed an inclination to the religious life and as a youth took her first vows from St Macaille at Croghan. She was probably officially professed as a nun by St Mel of Armagh. It is also believed that he conferred on her the authority to establish a religious order and be its abbess.

4. **Bridget** settled with seven other nuns at the foot of Croghan Hill, and, about 468 AD, followed St Mel to the city of Meath.

5. About 470 AD, **Bridget** founded both a monastery and convent and was abbess of the convent, the first of its kind in Ireland. She built her cell under a large oak tree, and thus derives the name of her convent: Cill-Dara [Kildare – cell of the oak]. The convent developed into a centre of learning and spirituality, while around the convent developed the cathedral town of Kildare.

6. **Bridget** founded a school of art at Kildare and its illuminated manuscripts became famous, notably the 'Book of Kildare'. This book, which was praised as one of the finest of all illuminated Irish manuscripts, disappeared three centuries ago, when England invad-

ed Ireland and killed thousands of Irish Catholics, and destroying many Irish treasures and buildings.

7. Bridget died at Kildare on 1 February 525 A.D. This is also the traditional date of her feast day. Called 'Mary of the Gael', she is buried at Downpatrick.

8. **Bridget** shares the title 'Patron of Ireland' with St Patrick.

9. Some biographies of St **Bridget** tell us that as she sat beside her dying father, she was meditating and began weaving a cross, made from the river 'rushes'. Rushes was the common floor material that covered an Irish home. Her father saw the cross and asked her to explain its meaning. After Bridget explained the cross' significance, her father wanted to join the Church and was baptised by St Patrick before he died. Today, people place a 'St Bridget Cross' in their homes and farm buildings believing that, with their faith, it protects them and their animals from evil and deprivation.

10. In Ireland, the festival of St Bridget is still celebrated on 1 February around the country with local fairs and festivals.

NINE IRISH SAINTS

1. St Aidan (died AD 651)
According to the historian Bede, Aidan was an Irish monk living on the island of Iona before he was sent to preach the gospel in Northumbria after a period of pagan resurgence. Aidan established his headquarters on the island of Lindisfarne, where he founded a monastery to train English boys to become missionaries to their own people. He himself went about on foot, preaching and setting up missionary centres, which had the support of the king, Oswald of Northumbria.

Eventually, Lindisfarne became a great centre of Celtic Christianity and a storehouse of European learning during the Dark Ages. It is where the Lindisfarne Gospels, an illuminated Latin manuscript of the gospels, were composed about 700.

2. St Ita (AD 480?–AD 570?)
Also known as St Ide and Brigid of Munster, Ita was born in County Waterford. She later settled in County Limerick, at a place that came to be known as Killeedy, or 'church of Ita'. In addition to founding a community of nuns there, she also seems to have run a school for boys, who were taught faith in God, simplicity of life, and generosity with love. St Brendan the Voyager was one of several Irish saints who were her pupils.

St Ita was known especially for her rigorous fasting and austere personal habits. According to one story, when a rich man pressed a gold piece into her hand, she immediately sent for water to wash her hand. She is said to have written an Irish lullaby, which she sang to the baby Jesus when he appeared to her.

3. St Brendan (AD 486?–AD 578?)
Also known as St Brendan the Voyager, St Brendan the Navigator,

and St Brandon, he was born near Tralee in County Kerry. Brendan spent his childhood in the care of St Ita at Killeedy and continued his studies under a number of other Irish saints before being ordained a priest in 512. From an early age Brendan was a great traveller, establishing a number of monasteries in Ireland, of which the most famous was Clonfert, founded about 560. Brendan also reputedly journeyed to Scotland, Wales and Brittany, furthering the spread of Christianity to these areas.

But Brendan's fame as a traveller really rests on his voyage, a tale popularised during the Middle Ages. According to this account, Brendan and a company of monks set sail on a fantastic journey in search of a fabled paradise. Along the way they visited a number of islands in the Atlantic - one of which turned out to be the back of a whale – and possibly even reached the Americas. Although there is no historical proof of this journey, an expedition organised in the mid-1970s demonstrated that it was possible for the monks to have sailed a boat made of wood and leather that far. Whether or not the monks reached the New World centuries before Columbus will probably never be known.

4. St Kevin (AD 498?–AD 618)

Also known as Coemgen and Kevin of the Angels, Kevin, like St Columba, was born of noble parents and studied for the priesthood from an early age. Unlike his saintly colleague, however, Kevin took to the hills after his ordination rather than the road, becoming a hermit in a cave at Glendalough, or 'valley of the two lakes', in County Wicklow. There he wore skins, ate nettles and berries, and prayed. As word of his holiness spread, others came to join him, and Kevin eventually founded a monastery at Glendalough, where he served as abbot until his death at the age of 120.

Not surprising for a hermit, St Kevin had a special love for animals, which is illustrated in numerous stories about the saint. For example, once, when Kevin had stretched out his arm in prayer, a blackbird laid an egg in his hand. He remained in that position until the baby bird hatched. Another story relates how a cow, given to licking Kevin's clothes while he was praying, gave as much milk as 50 other cows.

5. St Kieran (AD 516?–AD 549?)
Also known as St Ciaran, he was born in Roscommon and left his boyhood home to study at the famous monastery at Clonard in Meath. From there he went to Aranmore in Galway Bay, where, like most contemporary saints, he communed with the holy abbot, Enda. One night, the two men had a shared vision of a great tree, heavy with fruit, by a stream in the middle of Ireland. Enda interpreted this to mean that Kieran should go and search for such a place and found a church there.

Obeying the vision, Kieran eventually settled at Clonmacnoise on the Shannon River and established (in 548) one of the greatest Irish monasteries, which attracted scholars from all over Europe. Kieran did not direct the monastery for long, however, as he died of a plague in early middle life. Despite Viking raids and a dozen major fires, the monastery survived for 1,000 years, until it was destroyed by the English in the sixteenth century.

6. St Columba (AD 521–AD 597)
Also known as St Columcille, he is the patron of bookbinders, Ireland, poets, and Scotland.

Columba's family were Irish nobility, and from his youth he studied with the best teachers of his time in preparation for the priesthood. After ordination Columba spent some fifteen years wandering throughout Ireland, working as an itinerant preacher and founding numerous monasteries, including those at Derry and Durrow. Then, at the age of 42, he left his country for the island of Iona, where he and twelve followers founded a monastery. Columba and his monks spent the next decades converting the Picts of northern Britain, who were greatly impressed by the miracles he performed. One of these miracles involved driving away a monster from the Ness River with the sign of the cross.

Columba is the Latin form of the Irish name Colum, which means 'dove'. Columcille means 'dove of the church'.

7. St Malachy (AD 1094?– AD 1148)

St Malachy is known principally as a reformer of the Irish clergy, enforcing the rule of celibacy and other disciplines. By the age of 30 he had been appointed abbot of Bangor in Down and bishop of Connor. By 35 he was archbishop of Armagh. However, it was some time before Malachy gained control of his see, as his appointment was violently opposed by supporters of the family that had been in control of the monastery and church of Armagh for generations. Despite being in danger of his life, Malachy cleaned up the diocese and restored it to peace.

In 1137 Malachy journeyed to Rome, where Pope Innocent II appointed him papal legate for Ireland. On his travels back and forth, he visited St Bernard at Clairvaux, who aided him in establishing (in 1142) the first Cistercian house in Ireland, the abbey of Mellifont in Louth. It was on one such visit to Clairvaux that Malachy was taken ill and died in St Bernard's arms. St Bernard later wrote Malachy's biography, saying of him: 'his first and greatest miracle was himself. His inward beauty, strength and purity are proved by his life; there was nothing in his behaviour that could offend anyone.'

Legend says that Malachy had the gift of prophecy and while in Rome had a vision of all the popes from his day forward. According to Malachy's written description of the vision, which was lost until 1590, there were to be only two popes after John Paul II. Today, however, most people believe the manuscript to be a fake.

8. St Columban (AD 540?–AD 615)

Also known as St Columbanus, Columban had been a monk at the abbey of Bangor when at the age of 45 he was granted leave to go to Europe. He set forth with a dozen companions and together they founded three monastic centers, including Luxeuil, in the Vosges Mountains of eastern France. But Columban's strict rule and rigid adherence to Irish church customs drew criticism, and he was forced to defend himself in letters to Pope Gregory the Great. In 610, after an impolitic run-in with the local nobility, the Irish-born monks were ordered to return home.

The monks, however, moved south, making their way through Switzerland and over the Alps into Lombardy. Although now at least 70 years old, Columban was again embroiled in an ecclesiastical controversy that also involved Pope Boniface IV. Nevertheless, the monks were given land to establish the great abbey of Bobbio in 614. St Columban died there the following year.

One of the twelve monks who accompanied St Columban on his mission was another Irishman, St Gall (died c. 630), after whom a famous monastery was named in Switzerland.

9. St Oliver Plunket (AD 1629–AD 1681)

Born in County Meath, Oliver Plunket went to Rome to be educated by the Jesuits at the newly-established Irish College. Ordained in 1654, he remained in Rome teaching theology until he was appointed archbishop of Armagh and primate of all Ireland in 1669. He established the Jesuits in Drogheda, where they conducted a school for boys and a theological college. He also sought to extend his ministry to the Gaelic-speaking Catholics of Scotland.

Then in 1678 an English conspirator, Titus Oates, implicated Plunket in what he claimed was a Jesuit plot to assassinate Charles II. As a result, Plunket was arrested and tried before a kangaroo court in London. Found guilty of treason, Oliver Plunket was hanged at Tyburn, mercifully dying before he could be drawn and quartered. His head was removed and is now enshrined at St Peter's in Drogheda. The rest of his remains are at Downside Abbey in England.

ANIMALS

Ten Animals of Ireland

1. Irish Wolfhound

The Irish Wolfhound is the world's largest breed of dog. The name is a recent one. The name the dog was given in ancient Ireland was 'Cu' (variously translated as hound, Irish hound, war dog, wolf dog, etc.) and it is mentioned in Irish laws, which predate Christianity, and in Irish literature which dates from the fifth century or, in the case of the Sagas, from the Old Irish period AD 600-900. The great Irish hound was only permitted to be owned by kings and the nobility but there were plenty of them as there were 150 kingdoms in ancient Ireland. The hounds were used as war dogs to haul men off horseback and out of chariots and there are many tales in Irish mythology of their ferocity and bravery in battle. They were also used as guards of property and herds and for hunting Irish elk as well as deer, boar and wolves, and they were held in such high esteem that battles were fought over them.

2. Hare

The Irish hare is related to the Arctic hare more so than the brown hare of Britain and as a result, represents a descendant of an animal that existed 10,000 years ago in the Ice Age. These hares can run as speeds of up to 40 mph and are extremely difficult to catch when at full flight. Their eyesight is helped with the positioning of their eyes on the side of their head which gives them wider vision. They also rely on their strong sense of smell and hearing to warn against their predators.

Around the mating season, which is in early spring, the male hares become involved is unusual pre-mating behaviour. They start to chase each other and then confront one other in what can best be described as boxing matches. Dozens together can be seen at this. The young are known as leverets and are born together in litters.

3. Irish Setter

This red dog is recognised throughout the world for his silky crimson coat and outgoing personality. The red setter was originally a red and white dog, and it was only in the early ninteenth century that the solid red dog caught the eyes of the Irish breeders.

The Irish Setter is a popular gun dog not only in his native Ireland, but in England and America as well. A spaniel-pointer-English and Gordon setter combination is commonly thought to be the correct mix in the Irish Setter's ancestry. The Setter is also called *an madra rua*, Irish for 'red dog'.

The Irish Setter once trained, will stay trained for life. Highly intelligent, with a friendly personality, they make great and loyal companions.

4. Red deer

Formerly a creature of the forests, the red deer has adapted to life above the tree line and the last herds are found in the mountain moorlands of Donegal and Kerry. It is thought that the only truly native Red deer remaining are found in Kerry; those found elsewhere have been affected by introduction and hybridisation with Sika deer.

Red deer are herbivores, relishing rough grasses, mosses and other mountain herbs. These are supplemented by woodland understorey plants in winter when the deer come down to the shelter of the trees. Access to the best grazing is dependent on the hierarchical system of the herd. The dominant male and his harem gain this privilege, thus ensuring the continued strength of the strain. Intense sparring during the rutting season is characteristic of Red deer. Deep gutteral roaring heralds the start of the rut and acts as a warning to potential rivals.

5. Irish Water Spaniel

The Irish Water Spaniel is a dog of ancient lineage and, although there are a number of theories about the exact origin of the breed, it is generally accepted that it shares a common ancestry with the poodle and other ancient breeds of water dogs. To fanciers, the Irish Water Spaniel is recognisable by his coat of puce, liver-coloured curls, his smooth face with topknot falling over inquisitive eyes, and his distinctive rat tail.

The development of the modern Irish Water Spaniel is credited to Justin McCarthy in the mid-1800s. His dog 'Boatswain' (1834-1852) is accepted as the foundation Irish Water Spaniel we know today. It is also generally accepted that Boatswain descended from the Southern Irish Water Spaniel whose ancestors existed in Ireland for over 1,000 years. These dogs are still bred for their original purposes – for hunting and as a companion dogs.

6. Dexter Cattle

The native home of the Dexter is in the southern part of Ireland where they were bred by small holders and roamed about the shelterless mountainous districts in an almost wild state of nature.

The origin of the Dexter is quite obscure. The common assumption has been that this breed is a cross between the Kerry and, perhaps, the Devon. It has also been claimed that a 'Mr Dexter', who was agent to Lord Hawarden, is responsible for this Irish breed.

In recent years there has been a worldwide surge of interest in Dexter cattle. These gentle, hardy and easy to handle animals are one of the world's smallest bovines. They require less pasture and feed than other breeds. They thrive in hot as well as cold climates and do well outdoors all year round, needing only a windbreak, shelter and fresh water. Fertility is high and calves are dropped in the field without difficulty. They are dual purpose, being raised for both milk and meat. There are two varieties of Dexters, short legged and long legged (also known as the Kerry type).

7. Irish Moiled Cattle

The Irish Moiled is a rare cattle breed. It is a traditional Irish breed of ancient lineage with a long history as a dual purpose, hardy animal, producing both high quality beef and milk. It is an economical producer being a resourceful forager, easily maintained on less acreage and less concentrate than most other cattle breeds.

The name moiled means polled or hornless. It is red in colour, marked by a white line or 'finching' on the back and under parts, but can vary from white with red ears to nearly all red.

8. Connemara Pony

Over the centuries in the ruggedness of their western Irish environment, the Connemara Pony has developed its prized qualities of hardiness, agility and extraordinary jumping ability.

The Connemara Pony's origins go back some 2,500 years to the time when Celtic warriors brought their dun-coloured ponies and used them to draw war chariots and carts along the beaches and river plains of their new-found home. The history is obscure, yet the Connemara Pony is considered Ireland's only native breed. Like the Irish people, the Connemara has been exported all over the world. Adapting to extremes of climate, they have made useful working partners with those who own them.

The Connemara 'Stands on short legs and moves freely, with little knee action, in surprisingly large strides for its height'. On this strong, sturdy body is set a handsome pony head. The most common colours are grey and dun, but there are blacks, bays, browns, chestnuts and palominos. Full maturity is at five years of age, sometimes older, and they can live well into their thirties.

9. Irish Draught Horse

The Irish Draught's history lies as much in battle as it does in agriculture. Written in 1BC, the 'Cúchulainn Saga' describes mighty chariot horses of Irish Draught type. In the twelfth century came the arrival in Ireland of the Anglo-Normans with their strong war horses. Later, in the sixteenth century, trade between southern Ireland and Spain brought a strong mix of Spanish blood to the native horses.

The Irish Draught has been exported in huge numbers into the armies of Europe since the Middle Ages. As recently as the First World War the Irish Draught served on the front lines in the thousands.

Over a century of selection produced a very sound, sensible animal with good bone and substance, great stamina and an uncanny jumping ability. It is these qualities that, when crossed with the thoroughbred, produced the world renowned Irish Hunter. This cross is now known as the Irish Sport Horse, and representatives are winning gold medals and grand prix all over the world.

10. Galway Sheep

The Galway originates in the west of Ireland as a result of the importation of English Longwools from the late seventeenthth century onwards and the majority of pedigree flocks are found in Galway and County Clare. The Galway is hornless, with a clean white face. It is a large sheep, classified as a Longwool. The Galway is docile, easily managed and is very durable.

Five Irish Animals and
What They Represent in Celtic Belief

1. Salmon
The salmon has always been a symbol of great wisdom in the minds of the Celts. In Irish folklore the salmon is considered to be guardian spirits of wells, pools and streams.

2. Seal
Seals were believed to be fallen angels; this is the Christianised version of much older folk beliefs concerning the selkies, the seal people. Many folk stories recount how seals have transformed into humans.

3. Horse
One of the Celtic totem animals that is inextricably linked with goddess worship in ancient times is the horse. This fine, majestic beast has been an important totem throughout Europe for many centuries. The same symbolism mentioned with the Gaelic goddess Etain. Her full title is Etain Echraidhe (*echraide* means horse riding).

4. Hound
Dogs have been faithful guardians, workers and companions for humankind since ancient times. It comes as no surprise, then, to find the dog as an important totem animal in the Celtic tradition.

5. Boar / Pig
The strong, wild boar was one of the most important animals to the Gaelic Celts. Many bronze statues of boars have been discovered and there are numerous references to be found in the legends that bear testimony to the importance of this fierce, untamed beast.

Six Birds of Prey in Ireland

Birds of prey are still relatively uncommon in Ireland and are only now beginning to recover from even lower levels that resulted from human activity. It is fair to comment that the countryside can sustain more birds of prey than currently occupy it.

1. Peregrine Falcon

The peregrine is a large, powerful falcon, found throughout Ireland. Coastal cliffs, mountain crags and open moorland are its preferred hunting grounds, although they are increasingly found in cities. Its black hood distinguishes the peregrine from other, similar-sized falcons. Adult birds have slate coloured upperparts with grey barring below. The preferred method of hunting used by the peregrine is to circle high overhead and then descend onto its prey in an action referred to as the 'stoop'. Peregrine numbers in Ireland are on the increase, particularly in Northern Ireland where in excess of 100 pairs of birds have been recorded.

2. Sparrowhawk

Despite its name, the sparrowhawk's prey extends to well over 100 bird species. This is in addition to a number of small mammals. It is not uncommon for several sparrowhawks to hunt over the same piece of ground. As a species they are on the increase throughout Ireland, they are now the most common bird of prey on the island. The sparrowhawk's colouring is bluish black for the male and a brownish colour for the female. Both sexes have the barred underparts that is common to many birds of prey. They hunt primarily along hedgerows where they are exponents of flying fast and low, threading their way between saplings and hedgerow shrubs. Here it is the small songbirds they search for, although garden bird tables are also a popular location for this bird.

3. Goshawk

Once quite common, the goshawk was persecuted to the stage of extinction by the late nineteenth century. The goshawk's appearance is very similar to the sparrowhawk and, indeed, their method of hunting is not dissimilar. These are woodland hunters and their prey are the larger woodland birds. Hence the reasons for their persecution by gamekeepers of the Victorian period. Whilst not established in the majority of areas where they once roamed freely, the goshawk has been re-introduced to Ireand. Falconers are credited with the re-introduction of the species during the 1950s and 1960s. It is unlikely, however, that these birds of prey will ever recover from the damage caused to their numbers in this country.

4. Merlin

The adult, male merlin is not a big bird and at a distance they can be confused with a kestrel. Merlins are more compact than the kestrel, with a shorter tail and they have deep brown upper parts as opposed to the reddish brown of the kestrel. Merlins are quite aggressive, especially when around other birds of prey and are often seen in encounters with larger raptors. They are usually solitary hunters but there are many reports of pairs working as a team, diving alternatively at song birds. Happily their numbers in Ireland are on the increase where they breed on our moorland or sea cliffs.

5. Buzzard

In Ireland, buzzards are found principally in the north-eastern part of the country and are easily distinguished from other hawks and falcons because of their size alone. Their wingspans can range from 48-60 inches, with their body length often exceeding 20 inches. The 'mewing' sound of a buzzard as it soars in the sky is unmistakable as is its slow, gliding flight. Rabbits are its main diet, although carrion of all sorts is picked up by the buzzard. Preferring the tallest of trees as a perch and for nesting, a mere lift of its wings sets it skywards where it is an exponent of the updrafts and air currents. This bird is a slow flier and depends upon its bulk and talons when it sweeps down on an unsuspecting prey.

6. Golden Eagle

In Ireland there have always been golden eagles in the more rugged parts of the country, although their numbers have suffered during the twentieth century. A recent scheme in Donegal on Ireland's north-west coast saw the re-introduction of several breeding pair into the wild.

Eight Irish Bird Superstitions

1. Hedgewarbler / Irish Nightingale
This bird appears to be happy enough during the day, out-singing the other birds. However, if it sings at night, particularly around the hour of midnight, its soft notes are supposed to represent the voices of young children temporarily returning from the spirit land to soothe their heartbroken mothers for their loss.

2. Starling
The starling always follow grazing cattle so when they fail to do so, it is believed that the cattle have been cursed.

3. Magpie
The magpie, as with the ancient Greeks, is regarded as being of the soul of an evil-minded and gossiping woman.

4. Raven
For as long as people can remember, the raven has been linked with death, plague and misfortune and its harsh croaking always considered to be evil. When a raven is spotted near herds of cattle or sheep, it is believed a blight has been set upon those animals and they are about to start dying.

5. Cuckoo
If you happen to be lucky enough to hear the cuckoo sing her first notes of spring, look under your right foot for a white hair. Pick it up and keep it with you. After this, the first name you hear will be the name of your future husband or wife.

6. Linnet
The linnet has a particularly melancholy reputations, and it is

thought to represent some tortured soul in the spirit land.

7. Yellow Bunting
This bird is linked to a specific belief. It begins its singing at 3pm each afternoon and it is believed that its songs are directed towards those souls stuck in purgatory, as a reminder for the living souls to pray for those still in purgatory.

8. Swan
The expression 'swan song' is based on the idea that swans always sing before their death. It was quite common a belief that souls departed in the form of a bird, and as swans, were never heard to sing during their life. It was thought that they must, therefore, reserve a sweet song for their last moments.

Eleven Fish Commonly Found in Irish Waters

Irish waters have a huge variety of fish. Here is a list of the more common.

1. Tope
Tope is a medium-sized shallow water shark, fairly common on all coasts of Ireland during summer. Greyish in colour with short, triangular pectorals and a deeply notched tail fin, it is a very popular sport fish, particularly with inshore boat anglers.

2. Mackerel
Very common on all coasts in summer when they can be taken by both boat and shore anglers in very large numbers at times. They are easily identified by dark, wavy stripes of green upper body and silver undersides.

3. Monkfish
Large, ugly, squat cartilaginous fish which resemble a cross between a shark and a skate. Dark brown in colour, they are localised in distribution but common at one time in several bays on the west coast of Ireland.

4. Pollack
Pollack are very popular sport fish. They can be taken from both boat and shore on most coasts and are common over areas of rough ground, reefs and sunken wrecks. Easily identified by from its near relation, the coalfish, by the protruding lower jaw and by the shape of the lateral line which is bent over the pectoral fin, its tail is forked. The pollack is usually brown or bronze on back and flanks and grows to over 20lbs.

5. Cod

Common on most Irish coasts and unlikely to be mistaken for any other species, even though the colour of adults varies. Cod are caught over a wide range of seabed from reefs and wrecks to areas of shingle and sand, and in many of the larger estuaries. They grow to over 50lbs.

6. Skate

Three species of Skate have been recorded by anglers in Irish waters: They are White Skate (*Raja alba*); Long Nose Skate (*Raja oxyrinchs);* and the Common Skate (*Raja batis*). In the interests of conservation, the Irish Specimen Fish Committee removed the Common Skate from its list of acceptable species in 1976. Since then, all Common Skate taken by anglers have been returned alive to the water. In recent years, fish to almost 200lbs have again reappeared at a number of west coast venues.

7. Conger Eel

Conger eels have smooth skin without scales, large pectoral fins and dorsal fins. They do not have any pelvic fin. they have strong muscular bodies, large mouths and very strong jaws. They can grow to over 100lbs .

8. Flounder

The flounder is a flatfish that inhabits the waters of Ireland. Both their eyes are situated on one side of their head. They are dark brown to greenish-grey in colour, sometimes with vague orange spots thought their blind side is opaque white. They can grow to about 5lbs.

9. Bass

This blue backed, silver cousin of the American striped bass is one of Ireland's most sought after sport fish. It is equally at home in the turmoil of the Atlantic surf beach or in the quietness of an estuarine back water; it is most common below a line drawn from Galway to Dublin but localised populations exist beyond this area. The bass grows to about 20lbs.

10. Shark
There are five species of Shark which anglers may contact in Irish waters: the Mako (*Isurus oxyrinchus*); Thresher (*Alopias vulpinus*); six gilled (*Hexanchus griseus*); Porbeagle (*Lamna nasus*); and the Blue (*Prionace glauca*).

11. Ray
Normally found in shallow water during the summer months, there are eight species of ray recorded by anglers in Irish waters.

Six Other Mammals Found In
or Around Ireland

1. Badger
Although its closest relations are other carnivores like the otter and the marten. They are known to grow to a metre in length but never more than 50cm tall..

2. Dolphins
Many people are unaware of the fact that dolphins are found in Irish inshore waters as wild animals as distinct from those found in marinas and aquaria.

3. Grey Squirrel
The Grey Squirrel was introduced into County Longford in the early years of the twentieth century and have since spread to other counties in the midlands and north.

4. Killer Whale
The killer whale is arguably the most spectacular animal to be found in or around Ireland. The biggest concentration of them are over the continental shelf and around the offshore islands on the west coast of Ireland.

5. Irish Seals
This seal is known also as the Atlantic seal as its range corresponds roughly with the north-western seaboard of the Atlantic. Seals are warm-blooded creatures and are torpedo shaped to allow ease of movement in the water.

6. Viviparous lizard

This, Ireland's only lizard, is found in all sorts of dry habitats but favours sandy or rocky places, particularly near the sea. They are usually between 4 and 6 inches long. They have long bodies, short legs and a long, tapering tail. They can be a variety of colours but mainly greys and browns.

HUMOUR

Twelve Humorous Quotes

1. The idea is well and good in theory, but tell me this, who is going to feed them?

> *Wicklow Councillor objects to a proposal to boost tourism by putting gondolas on Blessington Lake*

2. Stephen Roche, the only British or Irish cyclist to win the Tour De France. *ITV commentator*

3. Clap your feet! *Bernie of the Nolan Sisters*

4. *Larry Gogan*: With what town in Britain is Shakespeare associated?
Contestant: Hamlet.

5. *Larry Gogan*: What was Jeeves' occupation?
Contestant: He was a carpenter.

6. When I said they'd scored two goals, of course I meant they'd scored one. *RTÉ commentator George Hamilton*

7. What we are doing is in the interest of everybody, bar possibly the consumer. *Aer Lingus spokesman*

8. Deep down, I'm a very shallow person. *Charles Haughey*

9. I'm always suspicious of games where you're the only ones that play it. *Jack Charlton on hurling*

10. Mrs Windsor can come and go as she wants.

> *Gerry Adams on a visit by the queen to Northern Ireland*

11. Ludicrous. Ridiculous.

1989 edition of Collins Concise Dictionary *defines the word 'Irish"*

12. Get married again.

*Charles Haughey, to women asking for an increase
in the widows' pension*

Twelve Quotes on the GAA from Michael Ó Muirheartaigh

1. ... and Brian Dooher is down injured. And while he is, I'll tell ye a little story. I was in Times' Square in New York last week, and I was missing the championship back home. So I approached a newsstand and I said, 'I suppose ye wouldn't have the *Kerryman* would ye?' To which, the Egyptian behind the counter turned to me and he said 'do you want the north Kerry edition or the south Kerry edition?' He had both ... so I bought both. And Dooher is back on his feet ...

2. Anthony Lynch, the Cork corner back, will be the last person to let you down ... his people are undertakers.

3. I saw a few Sligo people at Mass in Gardiner Street this morning and the omens seem to be good for them; the priest was wearing the same colours as the Sligo jersey. Forty yards out on the Hogan Stand side of the field, Dublin's Ciaran Whelan goes on a rampage, it's a goal! So much for religion.

4. Colin Corkery on the 45 lets go with the right boot. It's over the bar. This man shouldn't be playing football. He's made an almost Lazarus-like recovery from a heart condition. Lazarus was a great man but he couldn't kick points like Colin Corkery.

5. 1-5 to 0-8 ... well, from Lapland to the Antarctic, that's level scores in any man's language.

6. Pat Fox has it on his hurl and is motoring well now ... but here comes Joe Rabbitte hot on his tail ... I've seen it all now, a Rabbitte chasing a Fox around Croke Park!

7. I see John O'Donnell dispensing water on the sideline. Tipperary sponsored by a water company. Cork sponsored by a tae company. I wonder will they meet later for afternoon tae.

8. Teddy looks at the ball ... the ball looks at Teddy.

9. He grabs the sliotar, he's on the 50 ... he's on the 40 ... he's on the 30 ... he's on the ground.

10. Pat Fox out to the 40 and grabs the sliothar; I bought a dog from his father last week. Fox turns and sprints for goal. The dog ran a great race last Tuesday in Limerick. Fox to the 21, fires a shot; it goes to the left and wide ... and the dog lost as well.

11. Sean Óg O Hailpín ... his father's from Fermanagh, his mother's from Fiji, neither a hurling stronghold.

12. Teddy McCarthy to John McCarthy, no relation. John McCarthy back to Teddy McCarthy, still no relation.

Eleven Other GAA Quotes

1. The first half was even, the second half was even worse.

Pat Spillane

2. Is the ref going to finally blow his whistle? ... No, he's going to blow his shaggin' nose!

Radio Kilkenny, Kilkenny v Wexford National League match

3. He'll regret this to his dying day, if he lives that long.

Dublin fan after Charlie Redmond missed a penalty in the 1994 All-Ireland final

4. Now listen lads, I'm not happy with our tackling. We're hurting them but they keep getting up.

John B. Keane ventures into coaching

5. Meath are like Dracula. They're never dead till there's a stake through their heart.
Martin Carney

6. Meath players like to get their retaliation in first.

Cork fan in 1988

7. Meath make football a colourful game – you get all black and blue.
Another Cork fan

8. The rules of Meath football are basically simple: if it moves, kick it; if it doesn't move, kick it until it does.

Tyrone fan after a controversial All-Ireland semi-final

9. I love Cork so much that if I caught one of their hurlers in bed with my missus, I'd tiptoe downstairs and make him a cup of tea.

Joe Lynch, actor

10. The main thing is, they'd eat grass to win. That's what I want. I'm not interested in lads ringing me up saying that they can't train because they need a babysitter, or their mother is not well, or there's someone after passing away.

Larry Tompkins reveals the calibre of player best suited to his laid-back style of management

11. I'm not giving away any secrets like that to Tipp. If I had my way, I wouldn't even tell them the time of the throw-in.

Ger Loughnane on his controversial selection policy

Eleven Irish drinking jokes

1. An Irish man walks into a pub. The bartender asks him, 'what'll you have?'

The man says, 'Give me three pints of Guinness please.'

So the bartender brings him three pints and the man proceeds to alternately sip one, then the other, then the third until they're gone. He then orders three more.

The bartender says, 'Sir, I know you like them cold. You don't have to order three at a time. I can keep an eye on it and when you get low I'll bring you a fresh cold one.'

The man says, 'You don't understand. I have two brothers, one in Australia and one in the States. We made a vow to each other that every Saturday night we'd still drink together. So right now, my brothers have three Guinness Stouts too, and we're drinking together.

The bartender thought that was a wonderful tradition.

Every week the man came in and ordered three beers. Then one week he came in and ordered only two. He drank them and then ordered two more.

The bartender said to him, 'I know what your tradition is, and I'd just like to say that I'm sorry that one of your brothers died.'

The man said, 'Oh, me brothers are fine ... I just quit drinking.'

2. McQuillan walked into a bar and ordered martini after martini, each time removing the olives and placing them in a jar. When the jar was filled with olives and all the drinks consumed, the Irishman started to leave. 'S'cuse me,' said a customer, who was puzzled over what McQuillan had done. 'What was that all about?' 'Nothing,' said the Irishman, 'my wife just sent me out for a jar of olives.'

3. A man stumbles up to the only other patron in a bar and asks if he could buy him a drink.

'Why, of course,' comes the reply.

The first man then asks: 'Where are you from?'

'I'm from Ireland,' replies the second man.

The first man responds: 'You don't say, I'm from Ireland too! Let's have another round to Ireland.'

'Of course,' replies the second man. Curious, the first man then asks: 'Where in Ireland are you from?'

'Dublin,' comes the reply.

'I can't believe it,' says the first man. 'I'm from Dublin too! Let's have another drink to Dublin.'

'Of course,' replies the second man. Curiosity again strikes and the first man asks: 'What school did you go to?'

'St Mary's,' replies the second man. 'I graduated in '62.'

'This is unbelievable!' the first man says. 'I went to St Mary's and I graduated in '62, too!'

About that time in comes one of the regulars and sits down at the bar.

'What's been going on?' he asks the bartender.

'Nothing much,' replies the bartender. 'The O'Malley twins are drunk again.'

4. Padraic Flaherty came home drunk every evening towards ten. Now, the missus was never too happy about it. So one night she hides in the cemetery and figures to scare the beejeezus out of him. As poor Pat wanders by, up from behind a tombstone she jumps in a red devil costume screaming, 'Padraic Sean Flaherty, sure and ya' don't give up you're drinkin' and it's to Hell I'll take ye.'

Pat, undaunted, staggered back and demanded, 'Who the hell ARE you?'

To that the missus replied, 'I'm the Devil ya' damned old fool.'

To which Flaherty remarked, 'Damned glad to meet you sir, I'm married to yer sister.'

5. Paddy was an inveterate drunkard. The priest met him one day and gave him a strong lecture about drink. He said, 'If you continue drinking as you do, you'll gradually get smaller and smaller, and eventually you'll turn into a mouse.' This frightened the life out of Paddy. He went home that night, and said to his wife, 'Bridget ... if you should notice me getting smaller and smaller, will ye kill that blasted cat?'

6. After the British Beer Festival, in London, all the brewery presidents decided to go out for a beer.

The guy from Corona sits down and says, 'Hey Senor, I would like the world's best beer, a Corona.' The bartender dusts off a bottle from the shelf and gives it to him.

The guy from Budweiser says, 'I'd like the best beer in the world, give me "The King Of Beers", a Budweiser.' The bartender gives him one.

The guy from Coors says, 'I'd like the only beer made with Rocky Mountain spring water, give me a Coors.' He gets it.

The guy from Guinness sits down and says, 'Give me a Coke'. The bartender is a little taken aback but gives him what he ordered. The other brewery presidents look over at him and ask, 'Why aren't you drinking a Guinness?' and the Guinness president replies, 'Well, I figured if you guys aren't drinking beer, neither would I.'

7. For a holiday, Mulvaney decided to go to Switzerland to fulfil a lifelong dream and climb the Matterhorn. He hired a guide and just as they neared the top, the men were caught in a snow slide.

Three hours later, a St Bernard plowed through to them, a keg of brandy tied under his chin.

'Hooray!' shouted the guide. 'Here comes man's best friend!'

'Yeah', said Mulvaney. 'An' look at the size of the dog that's bringin' it!'

8. An Irish priest is driving down to New York and gets stopped for speeding in Connecticut. The state trooper smells alcohol on the priest's breath and then sees an empty wine bottle on the floor of the car. He says, 'Sir, have you been drinking?' 'Just water," says the priest. The trooper says, 'Then why do I smell wine?' The priest looks at the bottle and says, 'Good Lord! He's done it again!'

9. Well now, you see it's like this ...

A herd of buffalo can only move as fast as the slowest buffalo. And when the herd is hunted, it is the slowest and weakest ones at the rear that are killed. This natural selection is good for the herd as a whole because only the fittest survive, thus improving the general health and speed of the entire herd.

In much the same way the human brain only operates as quickly as the slowest of its brain cells. Excessive intake of alcohol kills brain cells, as we all know, and naturally the alcohol attacks the slowest/weakest cells first ...

So it is as plain as the nose on your face that regular consumption of Guinness will eliminate the weaker, slower brain cells thus leaving the remaining cells the best in the brain.

The end result, of course, is a faster, more efficient brain.

If you doubt this at all, tell me, isn't it true that we always feel a bit smarter after a few pints?

10. An American walks into an Irish pub and says, 'I'll give anyone $100 if they can drink ten pints of Guinness in ten minutes.' Most people just ignore the absurd bet and go back to their conversations. One guy even leaves the bar. A little while later that guy comes back and asks the American, 'Is that bet still on?'

'Sure.' So the bartender lines ten pints of Guinness up on the bar and the Irishman drinks them all in less than ten minutes. As the American hands over the money he asks, 'Where did you go when you just left?' The Irishman answers, 'I went next door to the other pub to see if I could do it.'

11. Seamus was walking along the coast of Galway early one morning with a bit of a sore head when he tripped over something in the sand. Reaching down, he picked up a lamp and starting rubbing it. There was a huge crack of thunder, an awesome amount of smoke, and lo and behold, a genie appeared.

'Mornin' boyo,' said the genie. 'For releasing me from two thousand years of bondage, I'll be grantin' ya three wishes.'

'Isn't this grand,' said Seamus. 'Can I have a pint of Guinness?'

'Sure of course ye can,' said the genie. And poof! A pint appeared in Seamus' hand. Seamus starting sipping away at the pint. 'For the love o' Jaysus, this has to be the best pint I've ever been tasting.'

'Of course it is,' said the genie. 'I'm an Irish genie, after all, and I do know a bit about pints. Now, let's get on with business. You've got two more wishes left, and I haven't got all day!'

'Now just be bidin' yer time,' said Seamus. 'I want to enjoy me pint.'

'Ah,' said the genie. 'That's a magic pint.'

'And what do ye be meanin' by that?' asked Seamus.

'Well,' said the genie, 'as soon as it's done, it'll fill right back up again just as good as the first.'

'Is that so," said Seamus, finishing off the pint. Sure enough, back up it came, and when he tasted it, it really was every bit as good.

'Now,' said the genie, 'about those other two wishes?'

'Ah,' said Seamus, 'I'll have two more o' these!'

Six Fun Facts about Ireland

1. Petroglyphs of ogham writings have been found in West Virginia and New Mexico. The translations of this ancient mode of writing reveal a fervour in spreading Christ's word. St Brendan's account of his voyage in *Navagatio Brendani* of the seventh century seems to have been an account based on reality making him the first to discover America. (Read *America B.C.* by Barry Fell).

2. The largest dog in the world, known as the gentle giant, is the Irish Wolfhound.

3. Dracula's creator, Bram Stoker, was Irish.

4. The symbol of the Union Jack represents three crosses: 1.) St Andrew's for Scotland; 2.) St George's for England; and 3.) St Patrick's for Ireland. The Welsh flag, by implication, is represented by England's St George's Cross.

5. A series of carvings on a rock at Knowth has been identified as the most ancient moon map yet discovered. It is estimated to have been carved around 5,000 years ago.

6. Wellington, Britain's hero, was Irish born. He was descended from an ancient Irish family named Cooley. A massive mural of their hero is prominently displayed in the House of Lords along with the four country standard, a mural representing the UK member countries of England, Wales, Scotland and Ireland.